CRITICAL INSIGHTS

Dystopia

CRITICAL
INSIGHTS

Dystopia

Editor
M. Keith Booker
University of Arkansas

SALEM PRESS
A Division of EBSCO Publishing
Ipswich, Massachusetts

Library of Congress Cataloging-in-Publication Data
Dystopia / editor M. Keith Booker.
    p. cm. -- (Critical insights)
  Includes bibliographical references and index.
  ISBN 978-1-4298-3733-0 (hardcover) -- ISBN 978-1-4298-3781-1 (ebook) 1. Dystopias in literature. 2. Utopias in literature. 3. Fiction--20th century--History and criticism. 4. Fiction--21st century--History and criticism. 5. Science fiction--History and criticism. 6. Science fiction films--History and criticism. 7. Literature and society. I. Booker, M. Keith.
  PN56.D94D97 2013
  809'.93372--dc23
                              2012019666

PRINTED IN THE UNITED STATES OF AMERICA

Contents

Resources

About This Volume

M. Keith Booker

Critical Insights: Dystopia offers a diverse selection of critical essays on dystopian fiction and film, one of the most telling and distinctive phenomena of contemporary Western culture. Coming on the heels of a wave of utopian fiction in the late nineteenth century, this new genre, based on dire predictions of a dark future, rose to prominence in the twentieth century, reflecting a growing skepticism toward the Enlightenment faith in progress that had dominated Western thought in the previous two centuries. Spurred by events such as two world wars, the Nazi Holocaust, the failed attempt to build socialism in the Soviet Union, and the growing control of consumer capitalism over the lives of ordinary individuals in the West, the dystopian genre expressed a widespread social anxiety. That dystopia as an idea, and as a literary genre, should then experience an additional explosive growth in popularity in the first years of the twenty-first century evinces an increasing lack of confidence that governments can deal with our mounting social, economic, and environmental problems, or that heartless corporations can be prevented from colonizing every aspect of daily life in the new century. At the same time, even the darkest dystopian fiction contains certain utopian energies, if only because the very motivation behind dystopian fiction is so often an attempt to provide satirical, cautionary warnings that might help us to prevent the undesirable events depicted in the fictions.

This volume is divided into two sections. The first section helps to provide critical contexts for the discussion and consideration of dystopian fiction. It begins with Derek Thiess's survey of the critical reception of dystopian fiction, in which he outlines some of the most important critical discussions of the genre over the past few decades, including attempts to theorize it within its historical context. As Thiess notes, dystopia has not only attracted a number of important writers (and their readers) but also proved particularly interesting to critics and theorists. Thiess points out that dystopian theorizing goes back at least to the ancient Greeks, and that modern dystopian criticism can be seen as beginning with the efforts of Karl Marx and Friedrich Engels to analyze the flaws in nineteenth-century capitalism. As a whole, Thiess concludes, the body of available dystopian criticism, including the contemporary criticism of scholars such as Tom Moylan, Raffaella Baccolini, Krishan Kumar, Lyman Tower Sargent, and myself, is particularly interesting because its project is very often quite similar to that of the fiction itself.

In the next essay, Raffaella Baccolini looks at the work of the important science-fiction and fantasy author Ursula K. Le Guin through the lens of the *critical dystopia*, a concept pioneered by Tom Moylan and Baccolini herself. In so doing, Baccolini highlights the ways in which works such as Le Guin's *The Left Hand of Darkness* (1969), *The Dispossessed* (1974), *The Word for World Is Forest* (1976), and *The Telling* (2000) are generically "impure" works that contain both dystopian and utopian impulses, thus allowing for the possibility of change. Next, Thomas Horan explores the cultural and historical context of the dystopian genre, focusing in particular on the rise of the "totalitarian technocracy" in the twentieth century. Noting how utopian thinkers of the early twentieth century, such as H. G. Wells, often believed that scientists and engineers were the ones best suited to provide leadership in the modern technological world, Horan observes that the authors of dystopian fiction have often been motivated by a desire to argue against this sort of technocratic rule in favor of humanism.

I close the first section of this volume by comparing and contrasting Ray Bradbury's *Fahrenheit 451* (1953) with M. T. Anderson's *Feed* (2002) in order to highlight some of the crucial issues of concern to dystopian fiction. In the essay, I note that both books focus on the role of the media in maintaining and promoting consumer capitalism while setting their consumerist dystopias against a background of coming apocalypse. In Bradbury's case, that apocalypse involves nuclear war and is treated as an almost welcome event that clears the way for a renewal of society; Anderson's apocalypse, involving environmental decay, is more gradual and less welcome. The two books involve different communication technologies, indicating the technological changes that occurred in the half century between them. However, both books, as I note, detail very similar phenomena involving the crucial role of the media in the growing commodification of every aspect of American life, which only became more intense in the time between the writing of the two books.

The second section of this volume is devoted to critical readings of specific works of dystopian fiction, beginning with Tony Burns's discussion of the role played by science in the political culture of George Orwell's *Nineteen Eighty-Four* (1949), perhaps the best known of all dystopian fictions. Burns concludes that Orwell identifies conventional science, based on an objective notion of truth about physical reality, as standing in opposition to the philosophical basis of most oppressive political regimes (including that of *Nineteen Eighty-Four*), which rely on more relativist notions of truth. In this sense, according to Burns, Orwell differs from many recent postmodern and poststructuralist thinkers, who have figured objectivist science, and even the very notion of objective truth, as aligned with political oppression.

In the next essay, Andrew Milner looks at classic dystopian fictions such as Karel Čapek's *R.U.R.* (1920), Yevgeny Zamyatin's *We* (1924), Aldous Huxley's *Brave New World* (1932), and George Orwell's *Nineteen Eighty-Four*, noting that the endings of such fictions quite often, if in subtle ways, stand in opposition to the generally pessimistic texture of the bulk of narrative that came before. Milner concludes that this opposition opens up a space in which these fictions can be regarded as more hopeful than they have generally been seen to be. Thus, while many have read these works as anti-utopias that dismiss the entire notion that humans are capable of creating better societies, they are in fact critical dystopias that leave room for meditation on the possibility of a better future.

Rafeeq McGiveron follows with an essay that ponders the significance of the fact that many classic dystopian fictions, including *Nineteen Eighty-Four*, *Brave New World*, and *Fahrenheit 451*, feature key supporters of the dystopian regime who are themselves largely sympathetic characters. For McGiveron, these characters and their seemingly reasonable arguments in favor of the status quo stand in for the numerous seductive aspects of our modern world that seem to promise a better life but can ultimately bring about enslavement.

Next, Brian Ireland offers a critical analysis of Harry Harrison's 1966 novel *Make Room! Make Room!,* which was the inspiration for the film *Soylent Green* (1973). The novel offers a particularly vivid picture of a future New York in which corporations have become multinational conglomerates and have replaced governments as the major decision makers. This society, a product of present-day overconsumption and overpopulation, suffers from acute food and housing shortages, disease, and crime. Food and water are rationed and supplied by the government, food riots are commonplace, and a demoralized and corrupt police force functions to protect the property of the city's elite rather than prevent or solve crime. A sense of chaos prevails in this society that, on closer examination, bears more similarity to our own than we might like to admit.

Peter Stillman's essay focuses on Yevgeny Zamyatin's *We*, one of the founding texts of the modern genre of dystopian fiction. Noting that Zamyatin's novel transforms a relatively simple science-fiction adventure story into "serious utopian political theory," Stillman focuses on the way in which *We* engages with a number of important issues of ongoing relevance to the modern world. He concludes that the novel is ultimately about the ways in which the quest for efficiency in technological societies can lead to a squelching of freedom and the human imagination, and that it points toward the ways in which the humanist tradition can open up the imagination, presenting us with new ways of looking at the world and leading to new human possibilities.

Aaron Weinacht next looks at Ayn Rand's dystopian novel *Anthem* (1938), a radically individualist work based on the notion that any political system that requires the individual person to be subordinate to the group is a dystopian one. In Rand's dystopian future, individualism has been virtually eradicated and humans exist among the ruins of modern technology, symbolizing the creative potential that must remain dormant as long as humans are barred from thinking of themselves as individuals. Rand's novel was written particularly in opposition to the collectivist tendencies of the Soviet Union, though Weinacht notes that her own individualist views are extreme enough that, if carried to their logical conclusions, they could be at least as inhumane as Joseph Stalin's rule.

In the next essay, Enrica Picarelli discusses Frederik Pohl and Cyril M. Kornbluth's classic science-fiction novel *The Space Merchants* (1953) within the context of dystopian fiction. Here, Pohl and Kornbluth imagine a future consumerist dystopia in which advertising agencies dominate a world marked by shortages, overcrowding, and environmental decay. Picarelli notes how the novel's vision of colonizing the planet Venus as a solution to these woes resonates with the frontier tradition in American history, as well as illustrating disenchantment with contemporary capitalist society.

Moving into more contemporary fiction, Alexander Charles Oliver Hall discusses John Twelve Hawks's recent Fourth Realm trilogy (2005–9) as a successor to *Nineteen Eighty-Four*. This trilogy takes place in a future world in which powerful forces use advanced communication technologies to keep the general population under heavy surveillance. As Hall notes, the dystopian conditions of this world reflect a sort of update of Orwell's *Nineteen Eighty-Four*, filtered through the contemporary reality of Bush-administration America.

Sandy Rankin notes how the conditions depicted in the works of the acclaimed contemporary British science-fiction and fantasy writer China Miéville often resonate with those depicted in classic dystopian fictions, though Miéville's work is distinctive in the way it employs specific images and uses language itself in specific ways to enhance the dystopian atmosphere. On the other hand, Miéville's writing is infused with a sense of energy and vitality that helps it to convey an atmosphere of utopian hope, no matter how dystopian its images, language, and situations might at first appear to be.

Susan Stewart's essay compares Cory Doctorow's *Little Brother* (2008) with Orwell's *Nineteen Eighty-Four*, a comparison that Doctorow's book invites in a number of obvious ways. Stewart argues that while Doctorow's novel addresses a number of crucial problems of concern to contemporary readers, its tendency to employ binary logic limits its ability to provide useful solutions to these problems. This essay also calls attention to the fact that one of the most important trends in recent dystopian fiction has involved the popularity of dystopian works within what is generally described as young-adult fiction.

Finally, Sean Redmond ends the collection with a survey of dystopian films, one of the most important tendencies within science-fiction film in recent years. Importantly, Redmond notes many of the ways in which, beyond thematic representation, the audiovisual aspects of film have been used to reinforce the emotional impact of dystopia on the viewer. That these resources of film as a medium are so well suited to this task might partly explain why dystopian films have been so popular in recent years.

Together, these essays explore the significance of dystopian fiction over the past century, focusing in particular on the reasons why dystopian works have reached such unpecedented heights of popularity in recent years. These works clearly resonate with the air of crisis and anxiety that pervades our contemporary world, while at the same time hinting that we might still have the resources to deal effectively with the daunting problems that face us in this new millennium.

On Dystopia

M. Keith Booker

A review of the film *Never Let Me Go* (2010) by *USA Today* writer Maria Puente is tellingly titled "According to Sci-Fi Movies, the Future Isn't Looking So Good." Though the film at the center of the article is not actually set in the future, Puente notes that it resembles many recent films that are set in the future in the way it envisions a world informed by social practices that seem horrifyingly grim—in this case, the production and raising of human clones specifically so that they can be used as organ donors, their organs harvested one by one until they die. For Puente, this film is thus a typical one, illustrating the tendency of recent science-fiction films to present "a near or far-off future that is dystopian—the failed utopia in which ideals have been replaced by repression, violence and rampant inhumanity."

If nothing else, this invocation of the notion of dystopia in a discussion of popular culture within the pages of a popular newspaper for general readers indicates the way in which this notion, once used mostly by critics and scholars within the academy, has since gained much broader currency. And it is certainly true that the addition of the word *dystopia* to our common, everyday vocabulary is indicative of both a dark turn taken by our popular culture and a broader pessimistic turn in the general mood. Partly, no doubt, this development is due to the imitative nature of our popular culture; thus, the earlier success of dark cinematic visions of the future, from *Blade Runner* (1982) to the *Terminator* sequence (1984–2009) to the *Matrix* trilogy (1999–2003), breeds a tendency for audiences to expect such visions and for filmmakers to gravitate toward producing them. Moreover, the prevalence of dystopian visions of the future can no doubt be attributed to the fact that such visions probably open up more interesting visual and narrative possibilities than do more utopian ones.

On the other hand, the dark turn taken by the American popular mood and the dystopian turn taken by American literature and popular culture in the early twenty-first century are also responses to real, specific events in recent history, such as the September 11, 2001, bombings that essentially ushered in the new century, not to mention the fact that the US economy has been in sad shape pretty much throughout the century's first decade and beyond. It would be a mistake, however, to overemphasize these events alone as background to the trend toward dystopian visions of the future in Western culture. A certain turn toward pessimism in modern culture really starts not at the beginning of the twenty-first century but at the end of the nineteenth, when an even deeper economic depression had bedeviled the capitalist economies of western Europe for some time and colonial misadventures such as the Boer War had contributed to an overall sense of crisis, perhaps most clearly embodied in the turn-of-the-century notion of *degeneration*: the theory that, far from moving inexorably forward in its social and biological evolution, the human race could quite possibly move backward toward savagery. As R. B. Kershner notes, much popular discourse at the time was informed by a quite far-ranging fascination with this notion. Such fears seemed all but confirmed a few years later when World War I, an event without any clear, logical purpose or cause, became the most deadly and destructive occurrence in human history.

In the realm of literature and the arts, this early twentieth-century sense of crisis was embodied in the phenomenon of modernism, in which writers and artists sought new forms and techniques out of a sense that the world was changing so rapidly that earlier approaches to art and literature were becoming obsolete and irrelevant. Such artists quite often envisioned even bigger changes on the horizon, as is perhaps most vividly captured in the poet W. B. Yeats's image of a "rough beast" of uncertain nature slouching apocalyptically toward Bethlehem to be born, along with an entire new era of human history.

Meanwhile, much of the thought that transformed Western civilization in the first decades of the twentieth century was fraught with anxiety and warnings that the changes taking place would not necessarily be for the good. The three great thinkers who together created the intellectual background to modernism—Karl Marx, Friedrich Nietzsche, and Sigmund Freud—all in their own ways introduced exciting ideas that could be used to envision brave new worlds of the future, while at the same time providing warnings that the future might in fact be dark indeed. For example, Nietzsche's vision of the potential rise of a new form of superior human who could throw off the shackles of a repressive past might have been cast in emancipatory overtones, but for some it provided philosophical support for the ruthless treatment of the weak by the strong. However inappropriately, Nietzsche's vision was thus conscripted by the German Nazis as intellectual justification for some of the most horrific atrocities in human history. Meanwhile, Freud's attempts to help humanity break free of other forms of repression took a dark turn even within his own career, as he himself came to conclude, in the late work *Civilization and Its Discontents* (1930), that the social contract binding human societies together was repressive and that civilization itself was inimical to human happiness. And Marx's own critiques of capitalism contained the warning that what he saw as the inevitable collapse of capitalism would not necessarily lead to a more enlightened socialist world, but might instead lead to an even more barbaric social system.

As the twentieth century proceeded, events such as World War I, the Great Depression, the Holocaust, World War II, and the Cold War arms race seemed to add support to the notion that the darker sides of the visions of thinkers such as Marx, Nietzsche, and Freud were more likely glosses on human history than the brighter ones. Even in post–World War II America, when the United States was emerging as the most affluent and powerful society on the planet, individuals came more and more to suspect that they were becoming little more than faceless cogs in a huge and impersonal corporate mechanism. Little wonder, then, that literature would respond with the dark visions that we have come to know as dystopian. As Tom Moylan puts it, clearly identifying the real-world roots of dystopian fiction, "Dystopian narrative is largely the product of the terrors of the twentieth century . . .

[such as] exploitation, repression, state violence, war, genocide, disease . . . and the steady depletion of humanity through the buying and selling of everyday life" (xi).

This pervasive modern sense of crisis underlies any number of modern cultural forms, linking such phenomena as modernism, dystopian fiction, and film noir and identifying all of them as part of a widespread anxiety in reaction to the tribulations of modernity. Further, and especially in relation to dystopian fiction, it is important to recognize that this modern sense of crisis was made all the more intense by the extent to which it was a reaction to frustration at the outcome of centuries of utopian dreams related to the coming of the Enlightenment in the West. Informed by a new faith in the capabilities of individual human beings and in the ability of humans to comprehend their world through the application of reason and rationality, the Enlightenment also involved an early confidence that human beings would be able to use this new understanding of the world to modify and improve it, eventually building better or even ideal societies.

It is no accident, for example, that one of the earliest texts heralding the coming of the modern era was Thomas More's *Utopia* (1516), which gave its name to a new genre of fiction devoted to imagining the possibilities of better human societies in which the social, political, and economic problems of the real present have been solved (or at least in which effective mechanisms for the solutions to these problems are in place). Just over a hundred years later, Francis Bacon's *New Atlantis* (1627) marked the growing importance of science as the key to utopian progress. And by the late nineteenth century, Edward Bellamy's *Looking Backward* (1888), one of a flurry of contemporary utopian fictions, responded directly to the recent Industrial Revolution to provide still greater details concerning the possibilities of building a better world through science. By this time, however, the concerns and events noted above were beginning to create increasing concern that Enlightenment modernity was leading not to utopian dreams but to dystopian nightmares.

Types of Dystopia

As novels and films widely regarded as dystopian have become more and more common, it has become increasingly obvious that the general term *dystopia* can be (and has been) applied in a number of different ways. It should be emphasized, however, that the mere fact that a novel or film features a grim future does not make the work dystopian. To be dystopian, a work needs to foreground the oppressive society in which it is set, using that setting as an opportunity to comment in a critical way on some other society, typically that of the author or the audience. In other worlds, the bleak dystopian world should encourage the reader or viewer to think critically about it, then transfer this critical thinking to his or her own world. Thus, dystopian fiction closely resembles Darko Suvin's influential characterization of science fiction as the literature of "cognitive estrangement," placing readers in a world different from our own so as to stimulate thought about the nature of those differences and cause us to view our own world from a fresh perspective. Indeed, for our purposes here, dystopian fiction can be defined as the subgenre of science fiction that uses its negative portrayal of an alternative society to stimulate new critical insights into real-world societies.

In contrast, one might compare dystopian fiction with the related category of postapocalyptic fiction, which deals with human attempts to survive in the aftermath of some sort of widespread disaster (such as a nuclear war, a devastating plague, or a large-scale environmental catastrophe) so destructive as to bring about the collapse of civilization as we know it. Postapocalyptic fictions can lead to the rise of dystopian regimes, and they can certainly serve as cautionary tales, as when they warn of the potential consequences of continued nuclear-arms development or environmental irresponsibility. But postapocalyptic texts do not generally focus on the details of the imaginary societies they portray so much as on the collapse of the preexisting society and are not therefore properly dystopian.

One of the most widely cited attempts to establish a coherent terminology for utopian and dystopian fiction is that proposed by the eminent scholar of utopianism Lyman Tower Sargent, who has suggested the following scheme:

Utopia—a non-existent society described in considerable detail and normally located in time and space.

Eutopia or positive utopia—a non-existent society described in considerable detail and normally located in time and space that the author intended a contemporaneous reader to view as considerably better than the society in which that reader lived.

Dystopia or negative utopia—a non-existent society described in considerable detail and normally located in time and space that the author intended a contemporaneous reader to view as considerably worse than the society in which that reader lived. . . .

Anti-utopia—a non-existent society described in considerable detail and normally located in time and space that the author intended a contemporaneous reader to view as a criticism of utopianism or of some particular eutopia. (9)

However, Sargent's distinction between utopia and eutopia is seldom observed. In this volume, for example, the term *utopia* will generally be used to mean an imagined better society, in place of his eutopia. Further, this volume will use the term *dystopia* for both the negative utopia and the anti-utopia.

Sargent's categories do, however, provide a way of distinguishing between two basic types of dystopia. The first type, what he calls the negative utopia, is generally an "if this goes on" cautionary tale, warning of the dire consequences that might occur should certain trends already under way in some contemporary real-world society, usually the author's own, be allowed to continue. For example, Margaret Atwood's *The Handmaid's Tale* (1985) responds directly to then-recent developments in American politics, such as the defeat of the Equal Rights Amendment and the growing political power of the religious right, to imagine the sort of society that might be established should right-wing religious groups be allowed to enact their antifeminist political agenda as official policy. The second type of dystopia, what Sargent calls the anti-utopia, warns against the potential negative consequences of seemingly utopian projects, as when Yevgeny Zamyatin's *We* (1924) warns (presciently, as it turns out) about a possible dark side to the utopian dreams of the then-new Soviet Union and of rationalist modernity as a whole. In its extreme form, the anti-utopia is skeptical not just of any particular utopian program but of utopianism in general. Finally, though, it should be noted that these two categories of dystopia are generally a matter more of emphasis than of distinct difference. Thus, the Christian conservatism featured in *The Handmaid's Tale* might be seen by many of its proponents as utopian, but Atwood's central concern is to critique it as a current trend in American politics. Similarly, *We* makes indirect reference to real-world tendencies in the postrevolutionary Soviet Union, but Zamyatin is primarily concerned with dangers involved in the overly rigid pursuit of the rationalist utopianism that informed the Soviet project.

Alternatively, one could categorize dystopias in terms of their fundamental relationship with utopian thought. In this scheme, one might see the *classic* dystopia as one that focuses on critique of whatever social or political practices are examined in the text. The *critical* dystopia, on the other hand, is more nuanced; while critiquing certain negative practices or institutions, this type of dystopia retains a strong utopian dimension, emphasizing that there are alternatives to the dystopian conditions being portrayed.

Brief Survey of Dystopian Fiction

Bellamy's *Looking Backward* was the classic late nineteenth-century vision of a utopia based on scientific and technological progress. Yet it was followed two years later by William Morris's *News from Nowhere* (1890), an equally compelling utopian text that challenged Bellamy's premise and imagined instead a peaceful, pastoral utopia in which technology has largely been abandoned in favor of living in harmony with nature. This fundamental opposition among classic utopian texts made clear the notion that one person's utopia might be another person's dystopia. Soon afterward, H. G. Wells became the father of modern science fiction with a series of works in the 1890s, many of which contained strong dystopian impulses, though Wells would become known as a crucial utopian writer as well. In 1907, the American Jack London published *The Iron Heel*, which is sometimes considered the first true dystopian novel, though it has utopian components as well and looks back on its dystopia as a thing of the past. Soon afterward, E. M. Forster's short story "The Machine Stops" (1909) was another one of the first purely dystopian works, and one that already illustrated the common ground between dystopian fiction and literary modernism.

Zamyatin's *We* can be considered the first novel-length true dystopian text; it would be followed by Aldous Huxley's *Brave New World* (1932) and George Orwell's *Nineteen Eighty-Four* (1949), which joined *We* in defining the terms of the modern genre as a response to the anxieties of the modern world. For example, if *We* warns most specifically against potential abuses of the postrevolutionary system in the Soviet Union, *Brave New World* looks in the other direction, projecting nightmarish extensions of the current system of Western consumer capitalism, which had recently emerged and was already in a state of collapse. *Nineteen Eighty-Four* is suspicious of both capitalism and socialism, suggesting that either, as it exists in Orwell's 1940s world, has the potential to develop into an oppressive totalitarian system devoted primarily to its own preservation rather than to enriching the lives of the human beings who must live in that system. The plots of all three of these novels center on the (failed) attempts of individual heroes—Zamyatin's D-503, Huxley's Bernard Marx, and Orwell's Winston Smith—to overcome the suppression of individualism by their dystopian states. In this and other ways, they set the tone for many of the dystopian texts that followed them.

All of these three founding texts are primarily of the anti-utopia type, and the same might be said of Ayn Rand's *Anthem* (1938), one of the earliest American dystopias. Though Rand's novel clearly targets the Soviet Union, it is first and foremost a radically individualist work that expresses skepticism of the communalism that has been common to utopian visions from More's onward. However, if-this-goes-on cautionary tales began to appear early on as well. In *To Tell the Truth . . .* (1933), for example, Amabel Williams-Ellis follows Huxley in warning of the dystopian potential of capitalism, but she specifically imagines a Britain in which the worst tendencies of the early 1930s have continued to develop, producing a grim, authoritarian, and impoverished (though in many ways technologically advanced) society. In the United States, Sinclair Lewis's *It Can't Happen Here* (1935) warns that contemporary fear of communism might push America toward fascism. Such antifascist cautionary tales were particularly prominent in Great Britain in the 1930s, including Storm Jameson's *In the Second Year* (1936), Katharine Burdekin's *Swastika Night* (1937), and Ruthven Todd's *Over the Mountain* (1939).

This tradition, especially Burdekin's text, helped to set the stage for Orwell's *Nineteen Eighty-Four*, which has been important background to virtually every dystopian text since, including the work of Anthony Burgess, who, in works such as *A Clockwork Orange* (1962) and *The Wanting Seed* (1962), was clearly influenced by Orwell. Particularly important in British dystopian fiction is the series of novels written by John Brunner, beginning with *Stand on Zanzibar* (1968) and extending through *The Jagged Orbit* (1969), *The Sheep Look Up* (1972), and *The Shockwave Rider* (1975). Of these, *The Jagged Orbit* focuses on racism and the criminalistic tendencies of the military-industrial complex, while *The Shockwave Rider* focuses on the impact of a worldwide communications explosion, in many ways anticipating the later phenomenon of cyberpunk science fiction, a movement that has itself shown considerable dystopian leanings.

In the United States, Kurt Vonnegut's *Player Piano* (1952) responded to certain specific American anxieties of the early 1950s, especially the fear that automation was beginning to make human labor obsolete, while at the same time turning people into machinelike automatons living thoroughly scripted, regulated lives. Ray Bradbury followed soon after with *Fahrenheit 451* (1953), wherein an oppressive state employs teams of "firemen" whose job it is to seek out and burn books, which are strictly forbidden in this society. Harry Harrison's *Make Room! Make Room!* (1966), meanwhile, resembles *The Wanting Seed* and *Stand on Zanzibar* in focusing on the social and political problems that might arise from overpopulation. Harrison's novel, however, is probably most important as the basis for a 1973 film adaptation, *Soylent Green*; this film was typical of the dystopian turn taken by American science-fiction film in the early 1970s, with such films as Stanley Kubrick's adaptation of *A Clockwork Orange* (1971), George Lucas's *THX-1138* (1971), Douglas Trumbull's *Silent Running* (1972), Norman Jewison's *Rollerball* (1975), and Michael Anderson's *Logan's Run* (1976) all exploring dystopian themes. Films such as *Blade Runner* (1982), *Total Recall* (1990), *The Matrix* (1999), *Minority Report* (2002), *Equilibrium* (2002), *V for Vendetta* (2006), *Children of Men* (2006), and *Never Let Me Go* (2010) have extended the genre of dystopian film into the twenty-first century.

The 1970s have been widely recognized as a time of resurgence in utopian fiction, especially by women, but the decade also saw a notable surge in the production of women's dystopian fiction. For example, Ursula K. Le Guin's *The Dispossessed* (1974), perhaps the most important of the women's utopian novels of the decade, contrasted its anarchist utopia with a capitalist dystopia within the same text. Joanna Russ's *The Female Man* (1975) also presented both utopian and dystopian visions, as did Marge Piercy's *Woman on the Edge of Time* (1976). These novels, along with works such as Suzy McKee Charnas's *Walk to the End of the World* (1974), started a trend that culminated in Atwood's *The Handmaid's Tale*, undoubtedly the most prominent dystopian text to date to focus on issues of gender and patriarchy. Other works, including Octavia Butler's *Parable of the Sower* (1993), have focused on similar issues as part of a generally dystopian vision.

New Trends in Dystopian Fiction

The increasing popularity of dystopian fiction and film in the early twenty-first century raises the possibility that dystopian visions are increasingly becoming mere spectacles of misery that, if anything, simply encourage audiences to feel better about the present, therefore losing the critical power that is key to the genre. In addition, it could be argued that the increasing familiarity of dystopian visions threatens to strip even the most powerful dystopian fictions of their critical power; no longer shocking or even surprising, the images presented in these works may make it harder for the fictions to produce the kind of cognitive estrangement that is crucial to their impact as works of social and political critique. At the same time, there are new trends that may potentially reenergize the genre for new generations of readers and viewers.

The first of these trends is a growing tendency to situate the repressive power normally associated with dystopian societies not in governments but in private corporations. This phenomenon dates back at least to Frederik Pohl and Cyril M. Kornbluth's classic work *The Space Merchants* (1953), in which corporations dominate a grim, dystopian future and US congressmen represent specific corporations rather than constituencies of voters. And sinister corporations, such as the Weyland-Yutani Corporation of the *Alien* films (1979–97), have been prominent in science fiction ever since. But this tendency, fueled by the growing power of corporations that marked the Reagan-Bush years (1981–92) in the United States, began to accelerate with works such as Jack Womack's *Ambient* (1987), which turned out to be the first in a sequence of six novels in which the huge Dryco Corporation becomes the dominant force in American society, culminating in the 2000 novel *Going, Going, Gone*. In the meantime, Neal Stephenson's *Snow Crash* (1992), in which rampant privatization has rendered governments almost irrelevant, also joined this tendency. More recent works exploring the dystopian aspects of corporate capitalism include Max Barry's *Jennifer Government* (2003) and *Company* (2007), Richard K. Morgan's *Market Forces* (2005), Thomas Nevins's *The Age of Conglomerates* (2008), and Dani and Eytan Kollin's *The Unincorporated Man* (2010).

Another important new trend in recent dystopian fiction is the growing importance of the genre in young-adult fiction. Again, this trend goes back several decades, at least to such works as Andre Norton's *Outside* (1974) and Monica Hughes's *The Tomorrow City* (1978). A major impetus in the growth of young-adult dystopian fiction came with the publication of Lois Lowry's *The Giver* (1993), which became a popular teaching text in American schools, though it was controversial and was frequently banned from school curricula and libraries. As Carrie Hintz notes in her discussion of young-adult dystopias, the popularity of this book "sensitized readers to the important subgenre of utopian and dystopian writing for children and young adults" (254). It then became not only the first volume in a trilogy, and the basis of a planned 2012 film adaptation, but also a forerunner of numerous other young adult dystopias.

For example, in Philip Reeve's *Mortal Engines* (2001), an example of the postapocalyptic dystopia, the world known to young readers at the beginning of the twenty-first century has collapsed. The social world has fragmented into a dog-eat-dog (actually, city-eat-city) world in which much of the planet has degenerated into independent city-states, many of which (including London, with which the book is centrally concerned) travel about on wheels, driven by gigantic engines, raiding smaller cities for technology and raw materials. This book was hugely successful in Great Britain, where it triggered a resurgence in young-adult science fiction in general. It also gained a following in the

United States, where a number of other young-adult dystopias have appeared recently, including Jeanne DuPrau's *The City of Ember* (2003), which later became the first volume in a quadrilogy as well as the basis of a 2008 film adaptation. Other recent young-adult dystopias include M. T. Anderson's *Feed* (2002), Caragh M. O'Brien's *Birthmarked* (2010), Maria V. Snyder's *Inside Out* (2010), Ann Aguirre's *Enclave* (2011), and Veronica Roth's *Divergent* (2011).

Particularly indicative of the dark turn taken by young-adult science fiction in recent years are Cory Doctorow's *Little Brother* (2008) and Suzanne Collins's *The Hunger Games* (2008), both of which present dark, dystopian pictures of the American future, though in very different modes. Doctorow's book, written in a vaguely cyberpunk mode, presents a very-near-future account of an oppressive American political climate that is extrapolated only slightly from the present-day realities of PATRIOT Act America. Here, the "War on Terror" morphs easily into a war on American civil liberties, accepted passively by most adults but battled heroically by a group of high-school computer hackers. Meanwhile, the title's reference to Orwell's *Nineteen Eighty-Four* makes it clear that the book is to be read within the tradition of dystopian fiction. On the other hand, Collins's book, the first volume in a trilogy, looks into a more distant future in which more extreme changes have occurred. Collins gives few details, merely mentioning in passing "the disasters, the droughts, the storms, the fires, the encroaching seas that swallowed up so much of the land, the brutal war for what little sustenance remained" (18). In short, mostly natural and environmental disasters have created a crisis that is made even more severe by the human response to the crisis, leading to the collapse of the United States and the rise of Panem, described as a "shining Capitol" (18) somewhere in the Rockies, surrounded by thirteen subordinate districts, though one of these districts has been obliterated in an uprising against the Capitol that was brutally put down.

Ultimately, Collins's teenage protagonist helps to lead a successful revolution against the Capitol; it is not clear that the new regime is all that much better than the old, though at least the Hunger Games will presumably be terminated. Doctorow's teenage protagonist uses his computer skills (and the help of several allies) to score a temporary victory over the forces of oppression, which in that text are largely composed of the US Department of Homeland Security. Neither of these texts has an unequivocally happy ending, though their protagonists are more successful than are those of most adult dystopias. Other recent young-adult dystopias have had even more positive conclusions, raising the question of their effectiveness as cautionary tales, as does the fact that they often focus more on plot and character than on exploring the characteristics of their dystopian societies. Nevertheless, the growing popularity of young-adult dystopian fiction and its subsequent spillover into film suggests that the form will remain vital for the foreseeable future.

Critical Resources

Dystopian fiction and film have received considerable critical attention, and significant resources are available to provide better critical understanding of the genre. In addition to many published essays on individual works or groups of works, a number of book-length studies have attempted to describe the phenomenon of dystopia in a larger critical context. For example, Mark Hillegas's *The Future as Nightmare: H. G. Wells and the Anti-utopians* (1967) remains useful, if limited in its focus, for its discussion of the work of H. G. Wells as a starting point for modern dystopian fiction. More recently, Gary Saul Morson's *The Boundaries of Genre: Dostoevsky's* Diary of a Writer *and the Traditions of Literary Utopia* (1981) explores the phenomena of utopia and dystopia within the framework of genre theory, while Krishan Kumar's *Utopia and Anti-utopia in Modern Times* (1987) provides helpful historical backgrounds to a number of specific works. *No Place Else: Explorations in Utopian and Dystopian Fiction* (1983), a collection edited by Eric Rabkin, Martin Greenberg, and Joseph Olander, is one of the most useful of several edited collections on utopian and dystopian fiction.

My own *Dystopian Literature: A Theory and Research Guide* (1994) provides brief discussions of dozens of dystopian novels, as well as a number of dystopian plays and films; it also includes discussions of some of the most important utopian works and some of the most relevant theoretical backgrounds to modern dystopian fiction. This reference work accompanies my critical study *The Dystopian Impulse in Modern Literature: Fiction as Social Criticism* (1994), which focuses on the dual modern traditions of anti-Soviet and anticapitalist dystopias, among other things. The most important recent work on dystopian fiction has been that of Tom Moylan, beginning with *Demand the Impossible: Science Fiction and the Utopian Imagination* (1986), which focuses on the resurgence of utopian fiction in the 1970s but also contains substantial commentary on dystopian fiction. Moylan's *Scraps of the Untainted Sky: Science Fiction, Utopia, Dystopia* (2000) is a more sustained study of dystopian fiction with a special emphasis on the critical dystopia. Finally, the essay collection *Dark Horizons: Science Fiction and the Dystopian Imagination* (2003), edited by Moylan and Raffaella Baccolini, contains a number of discussions of various dystopian works and the phenomenon of dystopian thought as a whole.

Works Cited

Collins, Suzanne. *The Hunger Games*. New York: Scholastic, 2009.

Freud, Sigmund. *Civilization and Its Discontents*. Trans. James Strachey. New York: Norton, 1961.

Hintz, Carrie. "Monica Hughes, Lois Lowry, and Young Adult Dystopias." *Lion and the Unicorn* 26.2 (2002): 254–64.

Kershner, R. B., Jr. "Degeneration: The Explanatory Nightmare." *Georgia Review* 40.2 (1986): 416–44.

Moylan, Tom. *Scraps of the Untainted Sky: Science Fiction, Utopia, Dystopia*. Boulder, CO: Westview, 2000.

Puente, Maria. "According to Sci-Fi Movies, the Future Isn't Looking So Good." *USA Today*. USA Today, 20 Sept. 2010. Web. 11 Apr. 2012.

Sargent, Lyman Tower. "The Three Faces of Utopianism Revisited." *Utopian Studies* 5.1 (1994): 1–37.

Suvin, Darko. *Metamorphoses of Science Fiction: On the Poetics and History of a Literary Genre*. New Haven, CT: Yale UP, 1979.

CRITICAL CONTEXTS

Critical Reception _____

Derek Thiess

Introduction

The body of critical contexts for dystopia is large, and therefore it is important to keep in mind several distinctions. Perhaps most important is the subtle distinction between what we mean by dystopian literature and dystopian criticism. It would be easy to think that dystopian literature is fiction (novels, poems, et cetera) and that criticism is nonfiction. However, some dystopian literature may be nonfiction but not necessarily critical; likewise, a work may be fictional but also contribute greatly to the realm of dystopian criticism. But how? And what, one might ask, do we mean by *dystopia* in this context anyway? This brief introduction will try to answer these questions, and the rest of this chapter will highlight some of the greatest contributors to dystopian criticism.

So what is dystopia? As the rest of the chapters in this volume indicate, there are many different answers to that question. This is because each author has his or her own vision of dystopia, just as each critic has his or her own definition. Some writers even use different terms, such as *cacotopia* or *anti-utopia*. Some writers and scholars use the various terms interchangeably, while others create important distinctions between them. What each of these words, and each of these authors, has in common is that they all comment on a society that is less than ideal. Throughout most if not all of dystopian criticism, dystopia is a negative response to utopia, which is, roughly speaking, a "good place." One might, then, think of dystopia as a "bad place," but it is not so simple. Sometimes a dystopia looks a great deal like a utopia, only falling short by a bit—especially after a dystopian critic gets done with it.

All we may safely say, therefore, is that dystopia is not utopia or is a flawed utopia, and that each author or critic defines it in his or her own way. In one sense, it is impossible to speak of a criticism of dystopia prior to that term's entering the English language, which most likely did not happen until John Stuart Mill's speech before the House of Commons in 1868. However, simply because the term dystopia was not in use does not mean that the concept itself was not discussed before 1868. As we shall soon see, several authors and critics responded to what they saw as flawed utopias long before Mill applied the term to his contemporary Great Britain. Also, we would probably not get a very complete picture of dystopian criticism if we confined ourselves to texts written only in English. Thus we shall discuss several critics, some of whose work did not first appear in English, though for the most part they come from what we often call the Western tradition.

I shall let the other authors in this volume further discuss the nuances of what is or is not a dystopia. But what is dystopian criticism? An easy answer might be that it is a work that discusses the nuances of what is or is not a utopia (thus some of the other chapters in this volume are critical contexts). As mentioned before, however, this formula is not always easy to recognize. For example, Thomas More's *Utopia* (1516) contains many nonfictional elements, but we generally recognize that the text is not meant as criticism. On the other hand, a dystopian critic might interpret More's utopia in a way that paints his imagined society as falling short of utopia—as a dystopia, in fact. That act of interpretation, of explaining why a place is or is not a dystopia, is criticism as we mean it here.

Yet, as I mentioned before, sometimes a fictional text can also work in a critical way. We shall see this fictional criticism firsthand in the precursors section of this chapter, but the reason that fiction is able to function as criticism is that even fiction authors sometimes respond to their contemporary society in critical ways, *criticize* in this case meaning to analyze or explain rather than to judge. Dystopias from the science-fiction genre are especially known for commenting on our contemporary society in a critical manner, and one can find excellent dystopian criticism in the works of contemporary authors such as Ursula K. Le Guin and Iain M. Banks. Though it may at first be difficult to recognize, dystopian criticism can be found in many different and surprising places. While this chapter cannot provide a comprehensive list, the contemporary works listed toward the end of the chapter have extensive bibliographies that point to many more examples.

Precursors

Whatever term one uses, the history of dystopian writing is as old as that of utopian writing. One does not seem to find one without the other. For instance, one critic cites the ancient Greek writer Hesiod, who in his seventh-century BCE text *Works and Days* envisions a succession of ages or epochs, each worse than the one that came before it (Kumar 100). The Golden Age would give way to the Silver Age, then to the Bronze Age, the Heroic Age, and finally the Iron Age, the latter of which would be a time of great sorrow and pain. If we consider the English literary tradition, it appears that there, too, dystopia was present from the very beginning. *Beowulf,* one of the earliest texts in the English tradition, dating to the oral tradition of eighth-century England, is well known for its epic battle between Beowulf and the monster Grendel, and several critics have suggested that the story is the poet's vision of a society trapped in a cycle of violence in which families and clans vow unending vengeance for the deaths of their respective kinsmen. The dystopian elements of such texts are unmistakable, and the fact that these elements appear so early in our Western literary traditions points to a widespread tendency toward dystopian thought.

In this section, then, we shall look at some of the more well-known early instances of dystopian criticism from time periods prior to Mill's coining of the term dystopia. In these early texts, we find several of the elements that will emerge later in modern dystopias. However, we shall here consider them as precursors to the modern dystopian work of criticism, often vitally important to the development of modern dystopia.

Aristophanes: Greek Satirist

Many scholars consider *The Republic* (ca. 360 BCE), by the Greek philosopher Plato, to be one of the first utopian texts. What is perhaps not well known is that a contemporary of Plato's responded to his utopia with what one might interpret as dystopian criticism. The Greek playwright Aristophanes's texts, while certainly fictional, respond in a rather powerful way to critical utopias like Plato's *Republic*. As such, we must take his plays as seriously as scholars tend to take the utopian writings to which he responds. If we focus, for example, on Aristophanes's play *Clouds* (423 BCE), we find a scathing critique of what the writer evidently viewed as Plato's teacher Socrates's overemphasis on philosophy and rationalism.

As mentioned above, dystopian criticism is typically a response to utopia, whether a specific utopia or the general idea. Socrates and Plato certainly imagined utopia at times, and nowhere more clearly than in *The Republic*, in which Plato imagines a "just" society ruled over by philosopher-kings. While *Clouds* is obviously not a direct reaction to Plato, as it was written much earlier, it is a direct reaction to the philosophy of Socrates. In the satirical (and rather bawdy) method of the classical Greek comedians, Aristophanes attacks the philosophy of Socrates through the story of Pheidippides, whose father sends him to Socrates to learn how to argue his way out of debt. Socrates teaches him, but the boy uses his new cleverness to first beat his father and then argue his way out of it. The play ends with the beaten father destroying Socrates's school because Socrates was "so insolent with gods in what [he] studied and when [he] explored the moon's abode" (lines 1916–18).

Clouds, therefore, responds to the kind of dreaming of the philosophers who imagined a perfect society with themselves at the head. Aristophanes claims that such a society would be dystopian because of the absurdity of the philosophers' logic that may corrupt one's sons, and because "the gods hold no currency with [philosophers]" (line 301). Anyone who doubts that Aristophanes's play works as a critical dystopia need look no further than the trial of Socrates, recorded in Plato's *Apology* (ca. 360 BCE), in which the philosopher defends himself against this very play; he is ultimately put to death for impiety and corrupting the youth.

Augustine and the Early Christian Apologists

Just as Aristophanes responded to the rational and natural philosophic utopias of the ancient Greeks, so did the early Christian apologists such as Augustine of Hippo mean to respond to both Roman and Greek natural philosophy. Especially in his *De civitate dei*, or *The City of God* (ca. 410 CE), Augustine displays both utopian and dystopian elements (also compare to Tertullian's *De corona militis*). In what he sees as a contemporary struggle between the city of God and the city of man—in other words, the spiritual and the political—Augustine envisions a future utopia in which Christianity, which at the time had only recently become the state religion of the Roman Empire, is triumphant over a lingering paganism.

This utopia, however, is not the subject of the majority of this work. Rather, Augustine spends the bulk of the volume writing an apology in the old sense of the term, meaning a defense of one's position through an attack on the opposition. In the process, *The City of God* highlights the flaws of Roman society and becomes something of a spiritual dystopian critique. Thus Augustine challenges the Romans in their attempt to create their own perfect society, or utopia, saying, "What you desire in the restoration of a peaceful and secure state, is not the tranquility of the commonwealth, but the impunity of your own vicious luxury" (45). He makes these statements partially in response to philosophers who "apply the term 'goods' to external and bodily advantages" (356) rather than to God. Augustine claims that the city of man, in which philosophers find sovereign good, is inherently flawed and dystopian, as this "good" is only earthly vices.

Many later dystopian critics would draw on the work of Augustine, especially Oswald Spengler, whose emphasis is on the city as a site of dystopian decline. Contemporary critic Krishan Kumar, whom we shall discuss in a moment, also claims that all Western dystopias owe much to Augustine. *The City of God* therefore has a long legacy in dystopian criticism.

Early Modern Dystopia: The Scientific Revolution

As demonstrated by the other two precursors listed in this section, critical dystopias are especially popular during historical moments of great advancement, whether political, philosophical, or technological. If we consider again that this dystopian impulse is typically a response to utopianism, defined by one critic as simply "social dreaming" (Sargent 3), then we may see why dystopian thought arises at moments when great advancements in philosophy or science and technology inspire such great social dreams. It perhaps makes sense, then, to make a historical leap over the so-called Dark Ages, a time of feudalism in the West popularly thought of as an era of philosophical and scientific nonproductivity, directly into the early modern period (roughly speaking, the early sixteenth to the early nineteenth century).

Indeed, the kind of utopian thought that the scientific revolution in Europe gave rise to was a fitting target for dystopian responses. The work of Nicolas Copernicus, Galileo Galilei, and Johannes Kepler in using new developments in technology and mathematics to theorize that the sun was the center of the universe inspired the Western world to dream of the possibilities of science as they never had before. Francis Bacon even imagined a new utopian society ruled by science and reason in his text *The Great Instauration* (1620). While this optimism for science and technology would continue for years to come and inspire much utopian thinking, it also inspired several to respond with dystopian criticism. One of the most well-known responses to this optimism is Jonathan Swift's *Gulliver's Travels* (1726). Among other contemporary institutions, Swift, an Anglican priest, targets an overemphasis on science and reason as deeply flawed. One sees this particular dystopian element in Gulliver's time at the Grand Academy of Lagado in the third part of the text.

Another example of dystopian criticism from later in this time period is Edmund Burke's *Reflections on the Revolution in France* (1790). Burke is often considered one of the first modern conservative thinkers for his critique of the rationalist and utopian principles underlying the French Revolution. In such prophetic statements as "when the old feudal and chivalrous spirit of fealty . . . shall be extinct in the minds of men, plots and assassinations will be anticipated by preventive murder and preventive confiscation" (88), one might see clearly the flawed utopia, even dystopia, to which he saw the French Revolution leading. Furthermore, the Reign of Terror that followed the Revolution seems to have given birth to the very dystopia that people such as Burke imagined, and many consider the Terror to be the end of the early modern period. And Burke's is only one of the many examples, too numerous to list, of dystopian thinking from this time.

Modern Dystopian Criticism

While modern (and in this case I mean the modern period, stretching roughly from the mid-nineteenth to the late twentieth century) dystopian fiction features a number of crucial texts, modern dystopian criticism is spread throughout several other arenas of scholarship. From philosophy and psychology to history and classical literary studies, modern dystopian criticism works with much the same principles as that which came before it; the main difference may be simply that modern authors are much more critically aware of the flaws of utopia than any authors since Thomas More's famous work brought the concept into the intellectual mainstream. Works from the modern period maintain a strong interest in the philosophy and politics of dystopia, with an even greater emphasis on the failings of contemporary political and economic systems. Meanwhile, as the Industrial Revolution blossomed, the time was again ripe for continued technophobia.

Karl Marx and Friedrich Engels are perhaps best known for their text *Das Kapital* (1867), a long critique of capitalism that shows the progression from feudalism to capitalism and posits the eventual evolution of capitalism into socialism. This critique centers on what they regarded as the alienation of the labor force. In other words, the less workers have to do with the products of their labor, the less interest they have in those products, the more alienated they become, and the more they are exploited by the upper class. For instance, a factory worker may get paid in cash money, which he or she uses to buy the very goods he or she produces for the employer, thus producing both factory goods and cash for the upper-class employer (and not for himself or herself, thus creating alienation). Marx and Engels saw this exploitation as inevitable as the upper classes acquired an ever-greater majority of capital. In a society in which the common man is exploited and alienated, one might already see the dystopian nature of their thought.

However, there are differences between the dystopian thinking of these two authors and that of most who came before them. For one, they viewed their dystopia, capitalism, as destined to end. Comparing their progression to that of Hesiod's, there is a hint of utopianism here in the fact that socialism is expected to eventually overcome the dystopian capitalist state. Perhaps an even starker difference, though, lies in the scientific manner in which they saw this progression happening. Much like their contemporary Charles Darwin, whose work most of the world would see as dystopian rather than utopian, Marx and Engels saw the progression from capitalism to socialism as entirely natural. This emphasis is especially apparent in Engels's later work *The Development of Socialism from Utopia to Science* (1892). Few if any dystopian critics had previously put as much hope in science or technology as did Marx and Engels, and few have since. While theirs may not be the best example of dystopian criticism due to the hope they place in science, they are significant for their emphasis on political economy. In this regard, they left a legacy on which many contemporary and later scholars would draw.

Friedrich Nietzsche

Like Marx and Engels, Friedrich Nietzsche had some hope for science as an answer to what he saw as a dystopian world. Yet there are two major differences in Nietzsche's writings: what he means by science is anything but what we would think of, and he is far less hopeful about this "gay science," as he calls it, solving the world's problems. In his first work, *The Birth of Tragedy* (1872), Nietzsche, a trained scholar of classical philology, paints a picture of ancient Greek drama—indeed, of our world in general—as a struggle between the Apollonian and the Dionysian. These two categories represent the ordered, refined elements of society and the darker and chaotic elements, respectively. Nietzsche viewed life and society as an irreconcilable struggle between these two extremes. Furthermore, as he points to clear societal institutions, such as science and Christianity, and our inability to escape them, his work acquires an overtly dystopian character.

However, we said that Nietzsche held some hope for science, but that this science is different. We may perhaps find the same dystopian impulse in his attitude toward typical scientific progress as it relates to religion: "In every teacher and preacher of what is *new* we encounter the same 'wickedness' that makes conquerors notorious" (79; italics in orig.). In his work *The Gay Science* (1887), science, like religion, conquers; it makes mankind its servant. To the classical philosopher, however—like Nietzsche, who famously declares that "the old god is dead"—"the sea, *our* sea, lies open again" (Nietzsche 280; italics in orig.). In other words, the philosopher may find a way to strike that precarious balance between Apollonian and Dionysian. Yet even Nietzsche does not see how this balance might actually be accomplished, and this text, too, ends with philosophy frustrated and falling back into tragedy. Nietzsche is both Plato and Aristophanes at once.

The philosophical legacy that Nietzsche left behind is as important for modern dystopian critics as is Marx and Engels's political and economic legacy. And Nietzsche's thoughts are not so far from Marx's: humans are trapped in a dystopian system through which they must hopelessly struggle; there is joy, but there is also pain, and thus any utopia will be inevitably flawed.

Sigmund Freud

Freud is another very well-known thinker, albeit one whose use of dystopia is probably not immediately apparent. However, it is not so different from Nietzsche's. In Freud's dystopia, people are in a constant state of struggle between their conscious waking lives and their unconscious and libidinal (especially sexual) desires, and frustration is inevitable. More specifically, a person's consciousness can be divided into the ego (conscious), id (unconscious), and superego. The id, to Freud, represents our unconscious urges and desires, which the ego and superego attempt to make conscious in realistic (ego) and moral (superego) ways. Our psychological lives—and Freud, of course, relates these to society in general—are a constant battle between these three components. In other words, Freud does with psychoanalysis what Marx and Engels and Nietzsche do with economics and philosophy, respectively: he paints a rather bleak dystopia.

Certainly his thought is most dystopian when he relates it to society at large, as he does in several of his texts, including *Group Psychology and the Analysis of the Ego* (1921) and *The Future of an Illusion* (1927), both of which treat religion as an especially problematic social institution. However, Freud is perhaps most clearly dystopian in his *Civilization and Its Discontents* (1930). In this text, he engages not just religion but all of civilization, telling us, "Unhappiness is much less difficult to experience. We are threatened with suffering from three directions: from our own body, . . . from the external world, . . . and finally from our relations to other men. The suffering which comes from this last source is perhaps more painful to us than any other" (24). Civilization, in classical Freudian style, might be inherently dystopian in part in its "tendency . . . to restrict sexual life" (51). Thus he concludes that "the price we pay for our advance in civilization is a loss of happiness" (81). In Freud's view, civilization is inherently dystopian because, like our own consciousnesses, it represses our sexuality and takes away our happiness. Although his approach to dystopia is certainly unique, that he belongs in this history of critical dystopias is undeniable.

Theodor Adorno and Max Horkheimer

Adorno and Horkheimer's 1947 text *Dialectic of Enlightenment*, first published in 1944 as *Philosophische Fragmente*, is easily one of the most influential philosophical treatises of the twentieth century. In this collection of fragmentary essays, the two authors combine the dystopian elements of the greatest nineteenth-century thinkers, including the philosophy of those like Nietzsche, Freudian psychology, and especially Marxist political and economic thought. The result is a work that shows a dystopian world entirely dominated by what Adorno and Horkheimer call "the culture industry," which sells the world on the progress that science and technology give rise to while simultaneously causing people to lose sight of the "barbaric," often-damaging nature of science (much as researchers suggest that violent video games cause us to be less sympathetic to other people). This confusing coincidence gives rise to the text's title: *dialectic*, or the coexistence of two seemingly contradictory truths, of *Enlightenment*, or the time period (roughly the eighteenth century) that saw an increased optimism about science and reason, also called the Age of Reason.

It is not surprising that in 1944, toward the end of World War II, Adorno and Horkheimer returned science and technology to the foreground of their dystopian world. Thus they tell us that "the hygienic shop-floor and everything that goes with it, the Volkswagen or the sportsdrome, leads to an insensitive liquidation of metaphysics" and that "in the social whole they themselves become a metaphysics, an ideological curtain behind which the real evil is concentrated" (xv).

These technological signs of progress only hide evil as they themselves become a force of domination, much like capital does for Marx. For Adorno and Horkheimer, the surest sign of this evil is the Nazi, whom they saw as embodying the ideals of the Enlightenment and extending them into a social arena, obviously in a horrifying way. As they also tell us, "The horde which so assuredly appears in the organization of the Hitler Youth is not a return to barbarism but the triumph of repressive equality" (13). Under the Nazis, even equality would be taken to extremes that would lead to repression.

Certainly the world looked bleak to these German authors, both of whom spent the years of World War II in the United States as exiles, and to many others. *Dialectic of Enlightenment* itself serves as one of the more powerful critical dystopias ever written. No one may doubt the importance of these two authors to dystopian criticism, as their work coincides with what many consider to be the end of the modernist period. Some have even suggested that they ushered in the postmodern period with their statement that after Auschwitz, there can be no more art.

Contemporary Dystopian Scholarship

Utopian Studies Societies and Journals

However many historical examples of critical dystopia exist, there is perhaps an even greater number of contemporary scholars working with some aspect of dystopia. A good way to start is to look into the scholarly societies and journals that exist with the primary interest of promoting study of utopias and dystopias. These include the Society for Utopian Studies, a North American–based society that publishes the peer-reviewed *Utopian Studies* journal, and its European counterpart, the Utopian Studies Society. Their members are scholars and independent researchers with an interest in some aspect of utopia, including dystopia, and they hold annual conferences where many scholars meet to share their work. *Utopian Studies* also frequently features articles on the topic of dystopia, including several by some of the contemporary critics mentioned below.

Krishan Kumar

In 1987, Krishan Kumar published a lengthy work titled *Utopia and Anti-utopia in Modern Times*. As we may immediately note in the title, Kumar uses the term anti-utopia in place of dystopia, and his reasons for doing so are complicated. However, we may for the purposes of this chapter use the two terms nearly interchangeably (below, Lyman Tower Sargent will help us to distinguish them a bit), because Kumar's definition of anti-utopia is so remarkably similar to other critics' definitions of dystopia: "Anti-utopia draws its material from utopia and reassembles it in a manner that denies the affirmation of utopia. It is the mirror-image of utopia—but a distorted image, seen in a cracked mirror" (100). Insofar as Kumar's definition simply describes a flawed utopia, his contribution to dystopian studies is significant as he compares the dystopian worlds of such texts as Aldous Huxley's *Brave New World* (1932) and George Orwell's *Nineteen Eighty-Four* (1949).

However, where Kumar differs from other critics is equally interesting. As mentioned before, the anti-utopian to Kumar is inherently Augustinian. In other words, the anti-utopian temperament "underlies Christian objections to perfectibility, conservative opposition to radical reforms, and cynical reflections on human incapacity" (103). Thus the anti-utopian in this text is primarily a Christian and conservative response to the utopian, which is very often scientific. As we have already seen, this argument has some merit and should not be dismissed easily. Later critics have differed with him, however, especially as Kumar uses this argument to suggest that utopia and its opposite are inherently Western concepts. Still, his book lays a solid framework, which later critics have further refined.

We shall only touch briefly on Sargent's work here, as his is the only article-length text mentioned in this section, but his contribution to dystopian studies should not be underestimated. A founding member of the Society for Utopian Studies, Sargent presented this article to the inaugural meeting of that society in 1993, and it was later published in *Utopian Studies*. Titled "The Three Faces of Utopianism Revisited," this piece lays out a taxonomy, or system of classification, of the different terms used around the concepts of utopia and dystopia. Thus, Sargent's major contribution to dystopian criticism in this work is the distinctions that he begins to make between, for example, dystopia and anti-utopia.

For this contribution in particular, dystopian critics still frequently find Sargent's taxonomy useful. Very briefly, he tells us that a dystopia is "a non-existent society described in considerable detail and normally located in time and space that the author intended a contemporaneous reader to view as considerably worse than the society in which that reader lived." The anti-utopia, on the other hand, the reader is meant "to view as a criticism of utopianism or of some particular eutopia" (9). The main difference, then, is that the dystopia comments on one's own society, while the anti-utopia is a response specifically to utopia, fictional or supposedly real. Although few subsequent critics have been as careful as Sargent in their definitions, his work began to refine dystopian criticism (and utopian, for that matter) into a formal arena of academic study.

M. Keith Booker

At nearly the same time as Sargent published his work, Keith Booker published his book *The Dystopian Impulse in Modern Literature: Fiction as Social Criticism* (1994). If Sargent's work (along with that of many others not mentioned here, such as Ruth Levitas) helped to establish utopian and dystopian studies as an academic pursuit, Booker's text brought dystopian studies firmly into conversation with the field of literary studies. He uses dystopia as "a general term encompassing any imaginative view of a society that is oriented toward highlighting in a critical way negative or problematic features of that society's vision of the ideal." In other words, for Booker, dystopia encompasses all the terms that other critics had "quibble[d] over" previously (22). Moreover, the similarity of the wide range of terminology is evident in Booker's analyses of, once again, Huxley's *Brave New World* and Orwell's *Nineteen Eighty-Four*. As he also considers Yevgeny Zamyatin's novel *We* (1924) in this context, he begins to establish something of a canon, or list of standard texts, in dystopian studies, as later critics will frequently reference these same texts as classics of dystopian fiction.

And this canon is only one of Booker's contributions. One of his text's most poignant contributions to dystopian studies is the clear connection he makes between dystopian literature and society at large. As he tells us, "Dystopian fictions provide fresh perspectives on problematic social and political practices that might otherwise be taken for granted or considered natural" (19). And again, the imaginative nature of dystopian fiction is important in this process. As he ties together various strands of dystopian thought, from the literary to the political and the philosophical, Booker ably shows how dystopian literature "serves as a locus for valuable dialogues among literature, popular culture, and social criticism" (174). This emphasis on the external, nonliterary world is exceedingly important and is sometimes forgotten in dystopian criticism. Booker also provides useful surveys of a wide number of dystopian texts in a companion reference volume, *Dystopian Literature: A Theory and Research Guide* (1994).

Raffaella Baccolini and Tom Moylan

Extending his earlier work on utopian literature, Tom Moylan became an important figure in dystopian criticism with the publication of *Scraps of the Untainted Sky: Science Fiction, Utopia, Dystopia* in 2000. Here, Moylan discusses both utopian and dystopian fiction, especially the way both intersect with science fiction. This volume also brought the notion of the critical dystopia into widespread use. Moylan then focused even more on dystopian fiction in the essay collection *Dark Horizons: Science Fiction and the Dystopian Imagination* (2003), which he coedited with Raffaella Baccolini. This volume again emphasizes the real-world implications of dystopian criticism, presenting a very comprehensive view of practical dystopia. In their introduction, Baccolini and Moylan briefly trace the development of critical dystopias from simply "places worse than the ones we live in" (1) to "new dystopias [that] not only critique the present triumphal system but also explore ways to transform it that go beyond compromised left-centrist solutions" (8). In other words, they want to consider not just what dystopia is but also what solutions might have a chance of working in the present political climate.

One may also see their focus on practicality in their choice of essays in this collection, especially in their focus on the present, postmodern world. With essays on topics such as critical feminism, cyberpunk science fiction, and posthumanism, Baccolini and Moylan's collection is very timely for the twenty-first-century student of dystopia. In the essay by David Seed, for example, the author discusses the cyberpunk novels of Pat Cadigan and her emphasis on networks. In our current academic climate, networks or systems have become popular interpretive tools—in studies of climate change, for example—and Seed suggests that Cadigan's fiction is "packed with tropes of connectedness that foreground the problematic nature of such connections" (70). As he enables the contemporary critic to interpret such fiction as a direct response to situations such as climate change, he allows us to respond to our contemporary world in a practical way. And Seed's work is just one example of the able responses to postmodern (contemporary) dystopias that *Dark Horizons* contains.

Fredric Jameson

Since the previous section mentioned postmodernism, the work of Fredric Jameson also deserves mention here. Especially in his texts

Postmodernism; or, The Cultural Logic of Late Capitalism (1991) and *Archaeologies of the Future: The Desire Called Utopia and Other Science Fictions* (2005), Jameson responds to the postmodern dystopias of such philosophers as Michel Foucault using classical philosophic methods and Marxist criticism. Having long been a leading theorist of utopian thought, Jameson tends to be quite critical of dystopias, but he also emphasizes that even dystopias have utopian elements. While Jameson's texts do not lend themselves easily to brief citations, his work, especially *Archaeologies of the Future*, is vitally important to contemporary dystopian criticism for its history of, and response to, postmodern dystopia.

Concluding Thoughts

As this chapter has demonstrated, perspectives on dystopia are numerous and extremely varied, and the history of these perspectives can be daunting. We must realize that dystopian study is an ongoing field continually producing more scholarship. Not only do journals such as *Utopian Studies* continue to feature cutting-edge scholarship, but there are always new collections being published, and the output of criticism will not stop anytime soon. For somebody interested in pursuing dystopian studies, that means potentially narrowing one's focus. On the topic of religion and utopia, Kumar may be a great place to start; for a more philosophic focus, Booker and even Nietzsche may be more fitting. The work of Moylan might be particularly helpful for reading dystopia within the context of science fiction. One thing that is certain is that interested scholars will not run out of problems or issues to discuss in the varied, exciting, and contentious world of dystopian studies.

Works Cited

Aristophanes. *Clouds*. Trans. Ian Johnston. *Johnstonia*. Ian Johnston, n.d. Web. 11 Apr. 2012.

Augustine of Hippo. *The City of God*. Ed. and trans. Marcus Dods. Edinburgh: Clark, 1888.

Baccolini, Raffaella, and Tom Moylan, eds. *Dark Horizons: Science Fiction and the Dystopian Imagination*. London: Routledge, 2003.

Booker, M. Keith. *The Dystopian Impulse in Modern Literature: Fiction as Social Criticism*. Westport, CT: Greenwood, 1994.

_____. *Dystopian Literature: A Theory and Research Guide*. Westport, CT: Greenwood, 1994.

Burke, Edmund. *Reflections on the Revolution in France*. New York: Lib. of Liberal Arts, 1955.

Freud, Sigmund. *Civilization and Its Discontents*. Trans. James Strachey. New York: Norton, 1962.

Horkheimer, Max, and Theodor W. Adorno. *Dialectic of Enlightenment*. Trans. John Cumming. New York: Continuum, 1972.

Jameson, Fredric. *Archaeologies of the Future: The Desire Called Utopia and Other Science Fictions*. London: Verso, 2005.

_____. *Postmodernism; or, The Cultural Logic of Late Capitalism*. Durham, NC: Duke UP, 1991.

Kumar, Krishan. *Utopia and Anti-utopia in Modern Times*. Oxford: Blackwell, 1987.

Moylan, Tom. *Scraps of the Untainted Sky: Science Fiction, Utopia, Dystopia*. Boulder, CO: Westview, 2000.

Nietzsche, Friedrich. *The Gay Science: With a Prelude in Rhymes and an Appendix of Songs*. Trans. Walter Kaufmann. New York: Vintage, 1974.

Sargent, Lyman Tower. "The Three Faces of Utopianism Revisited." *Utopian Studies* 5.1 (1994): 1–37.

Seed, David. "Cyberpunk and Dystopia: Pat Cadigan's Networks." Baccolini and Moylan 69–89.

Ursula K. Le Guin's Critical Dystopias_____

Raffaella Baccolini

It is by now commonly accepted that the utopian imagination today finds its strongest expression in science fiction (SF) and, perhaps paradoxically, in what a number of critics have called the *critical dystopia* (see Baccolini, "Gender and Genre"; Moylan, *Scraps*; Baccolini and Moylan). After the important renewal of utopian thought and literature through the critical utopias of the 1960s and 1970s (see Moylan, *Demand*), a number of social and historical conditions have steered utopian writing toward dystopia. In fact, utopian writing, be it eutopia or dystopia (see Sargent, "Three Faces," for definitions), is always occasioned by and related to the historical, political, and cultural atmosphere in which a writer is living and working. Early in the twentieth century, for example, the 1917 Russian Revolution, the rise of Fascism and Nazism, and the disillusionment that ensued about the experience of real "utopias" brought about a decline in utopian writing and an increase in classical dystopias such as Yevgeny Zamyatin's *We* (1924), Aldous Huxley's *Brave New World* (1932), and George Orwell's *Nineteen Eighty-Four* (1949). And while the oppositional political culture of the late 1960s and 1970s occasioned the revival of eutopian writings (with works, for instance, by Ursula K. Le Guin, Samuel R. Delany, Joanna Russ, Ernst Callenbach, and Marge Piercy), the turn to right-wing politics, the rise of different fundamentalisms and nationalisms, and the escalation of commodification in the last two decades of the twentieth century resonate throughout the dystopian writing of those years, including Margaret Atwood's *The Handmaid's Tale* (1985), Octavia E. Butler's *Kindred* (1979) and *Parable of the Sower* (1993), Piercy's *He, She and It* (1991), and Le Guin's *The Telling* (2000). Similarly, the traumatic event of the September 11, 2001, terrorist attacks on New York and Washington, DC, and what followed seem to have influenced contemporary SF writing, and especially cinema, toward the representation of postapocalyptic dystopias centered on characters involved in quests for self-survival or to rescue loved ones; see, for example, Cormac McCarthy's novel *The Road* (2006) or Atwood's *Oryx and Crake* (2003).

If the different kinds of utopian writings share the fact that they are products of history and of the times in which they have been created, they are different in other respects. Although they are all located in time and space, utopia demands, by its own definition (*ou-/eu-topos* = no/good place), a suspension of real time and space. Dystopia, on the other hand, by its very function—that is, to warn readers about the possible outcomes of our present society—is very much rooted in history. Unlike utopias, dystopias often do away with the convention of the voyage and frequently revolve around the character of the misfit, a citizen who feels or learns to feel out of place and at odds with the generally accepted norms and values of the dystopian society. By contrast, the eutopian visitor may end up at odds with his or her own society only *after* an encounter with the utopian world. A dialogue between the visitor and a guide characterizes almost all eutopias, whereas the presence of a hegemonic narrative (the constructed, controlled social order) and a counter-narrative of resistance that the rebellious protagonist develops as he or she moves from apparent contentment into displacement, alienation, and struggle seems to compose one of the textual strategies of the dystopian text (see Baccolini, "It's Not"). This formal structure frequently occurs through the use and control of language. The notions of coercion and consent, as developed by the Italian political philosopher Antonio Gramsci (see Boothman), in fact lie at the basis of the hegemonic order of most dystopias:

Language is a key weapon for the reigning dystopian power structure. Therefore, the dystopian protagonist's resistance often begins with a verbal confrontation and the reappropriation of language, since s/he is generally prohibited from using language, and, when s/he does, it means nothing but empty propaganda. From Kuno's conversations in [E. M. Forster's] "The Machine Stops" to Sutty's in *The Telling*, from D-503's diary in *We* to Lauren's journal in *Parable of the Sower*, from the book people in [Ray Bradbury's] *Fahrenheit 451* to Jim's history in [Kim Stanley Robinson's] *Gold Coast*, the process of taking control over the means of language, representation, memory, and interpellation is a crucial weapon and strategy in moving dystopian resistance from an initial consciousness to an action that leads to a climactic event that attempts to change the society. As opposed to the eutopian plot of dislocation, education, and return of an informed visitor, the dystopia therefore generates its own didactic account in the critical encounter that ensues when the citizen confronts, or is confronted by, the contradictions of the society that is present on the very first page. (Baccolini and Moylan 5–6)

Language and its reappropriation, memory, and a critical knowledge of history are all necessary ingredients to stimulate resistance in dystopias—resistance that is nevertheless always crushed at the end of the novel. Classical dystopias, in fact, invariably end with the victory of the totalitarian state over the individual, and if hope is maintained at some level in these works, it is only possible outside the story: "It is only if we consider dystopia as a warning, that we as readers can hope to escape such a pessimistic future" (Baccolini, "Gender and Genre" 18). Such an option is not granted, for example, to the protagonists of Orwell's or Huxley's dystopias, for whom there is neither learning nor escape.

One other recurring feature of these dystopias is the passivity and silence of the female characters. Women seem generally indifferent to, and at times even content with, the restrictions the regime has imposed on individual freedom, and if they rebel against such limits, they do so irrationally, as Winston Smith's (in)famous remark about Julia suggests in Orwell's *Nineteen Eighty-Four*: she is "a rebel from the waist downwards" (129) who falls asleep every time he tries to instruct her about the past.

The condition and role of women is particularly relevant because it is one of the features that characterize the first critical dystopias—works predominantly by women writers that, with a few exceptions, started to appear with a certain regularity in the late 1970s and early 1980s. With regard to one of the first such works, *The Handmaid's Tale*, author Margaret Atwood has emphasized that it was precisely her desire to do something different from the otherwise influential classical dystopias:

> The majority of dystopias—Orwell's included—have been written by men, and the point of view has been male. When women have appeared in them, they have been either sexless automatons or rebels who have defied the sex rules of the regime. They have acted as the temptresses of the male protagonists, however welcome this temptation may be to the men themselves.
>
> Thus Julia; thus the cami-knicker-wearing, orgy-porgy seducer of the Savage in *Brave New World*; thus the subversive femme fatale of Yevgeny Zamyatin's 1924 seminal classic, *We*. I wanted to try a dystopia from the female point of view—the world according to Julia, as it were.

In their formal revisions of the conventions of dystopia, Atwood and other women writers also fashioned what I, Tom Moylan, and others have called "critical or open-ended dystopias," that is, "texts that maintain a utopian core at their center, a locus of hope that contributes to deconstructing tradition and reconstructing alternatives" (Baccolini, "Gender and Genre" 13; see also Moylan, *Scraps*; Cavalcanti; Baccolini and Moylan). Unlike the classical dystopian texts, the ambiguous, open endings of these novels "maintain the utopian impulse *within* the work. In fact, by rejecting the traditional subjugation of the individual at the end of the novel, the critical dystopia opens a space of contestation and opposition for those groups . . . for whom subjectivity has yet to be attained" (Baccolini, "Gender and Genre" 18; italics in orig.).

Another element that characterizes these texts as both critical and feminist, and thus makes them sites of resistance and opposition, is the practice of genre blurring. By drawing on the feminist critique of universalist assumptions and borrowing specific conventions from other genres, such as the epistolary novel, the diary, the slave narrative, and the historical novel, the critical dystopias resist the discourse of genre purity: "It is the very notion of an *impure* science fiction genre, with permeable borders that allow contamination from other genres, that represents resistance to hegemonic ideology and renovates the resisting nature of science fiction and makes the new science fiction genre also *multi*-oppositional" (Baccolini, "Gender and Genre" 18; italics in orig.). Thus, despite the dreary events and societies these texts describe, the critical dystopia retains the potential for change and political renewal.

Among the writers who have most creatively experimented with and thus blurred the utopian genre, Ursula K. Le Guin certainly represents one of the most significant and critical voices (on Le Guin, see Bernardo and Murphy). Le Guin was one of the first to point out the limits of utopia and blur the genre itself by juxtaposing eutopian and dystopian elements in the same novel. In her famous Hainish cycle—a series of novels and short stories that include such classics as *The Left Hand of Darkness* (1969), *The Dispossessed* (1974), "The Day Before the Revolution" (1974), *The Word for World Is Forest* (1976), "A Fisherman of the Inland Sea" (1994), and *The Telling*—she often explores the difficult concurrence of and reconciliation between diverse or opposite cultures. Communication, understanding, and acceptance of differences are central concerns of Le Guin's Hainish series, where the utopian idea of the Ekumen, an interplanetary "League of All Worlds" working to maintain a peaceful coexistence among all planets of the universe, allows her to explore intercultural potentialities and imagine possibilities as regards gender, politics, religion, and so on. The very notion of the Ekumen embodies the critical notion of utopia that is central to Le Guin's work. In *The Left Hand of Darkness*, Genly Ai, an emissary from the Ekumen on a visit to the planet Gethen in order to convince its people to join the League, attempts to explain the complex, hybrid nature of the organization:

But the Ekumen is not essentially a government at all. It is an attempt to reunify the mystical with the political, and as such is of course mostly a failure; but its failure has done more good for humanity so far than the successes of its predecessors. It is a society and it has, at least potentially, a culture. It is a form of education; in one aspect, it's a sort of very large school—very large indeed. The motives of communication and cooperation are of its essence, and therefore in another aspect it's a league or union of worlds, possessing some degree of centralized conventional organization. . . . The Ekumen as a political entity functions through coordination, not by rule. It does not enforce laws; decisions are reached by council and consent, not by consensus or command. As an economic entity it is immensely active, looking after interworld communication, keeping the balance of trade among the Eighty Worlds. (119)

Failure, imperfection, and limits underscore Genly Ai's description of the Ekumen, and yet these are the necessary ingredients for the survival of the utopian project. These same features characterize the very notion of utopia that emerged in the 1960s and 1970s. As Tom Moylan has observed, the texts by Le Guin and others "reject utopia as blueprint while preserving it as dream" (*Demand* 10). By focusing on the presence of difference and imperfection within the utopian world, the critical utopia counters "static ideals, preserves radical action, and creates a neutral space in which opposition can be articulated and received" (51). Such a transformation in the notion of utopia has brought critics and writers alike to focus on utopia not as the space to be ultimately reached but, rather, as the process that must be undertaken. In light of this, *The Left Hand of Darkness* can be read as a text that explores themes of cultural diversity and the possibility of pacific coexistence. At the same time, the educational journey embarked on by the two protagonists, the Ekumen envoy Genly Ai and Gethen's prime minister Estraven, and the use of androgyny to characterize Gethenian sexuality allow Le Guin to radically transform the genre. (The inhabitants of Gethen maintain an androgynous state most of the time until they reach the peak of their sexual cycle, called "kemmer," when they develop either male or female genitals.) On the one hand, Le Guin emphasizes the function of utopia that "reverts from that of goal and catalyst of change to one of criticism and the education of desire" (Levitas 226); "utopia does not express desire, but enables people to work towards an understanding of what is necessary for human fulfilment, a broadening, deepening and raising of aspirations in terms quite different from those of their everyday life" (141). On the other, her use of androgyny becomes a critique of the social construction of gender and its implications for society, as well as a way to open up possibilities by deconstructing heteronormativity (on *Left Hand* as a queer critical dystopia, see Thibodeau).

The work of Le Guin that best exemplifies the copresence of utopia and dystopia is *The Dispossessed*. Situated at the beginning of the internal chronology of Le Guin's Hainish cycle, the action takes place before the Ekumen comes into being; in fact, it is the book's protagonist, the scientist Shevek, who invents the "ansible," an instrument of instantaneous communication that will aid in the foundation of the Ekumen. The novel's setting, theme, and structure all contribute to this copresence. The novel is in fact set on two planets, Urras and Anarres—respectively, an opulent capitalist society and one that is anarchist-pacifist— which are constantly in conflict, and it alternates chapters on each one. The theme of the journey from reality to utopia is here reversed: Shevek leaves his planet, an imperfect utopia, to go to Urras, which, after an initial positive impression, nevertheless turns out to be a dystopia; as a result, he will be an outsider in both worlds. By employing the utopian strategy of juxtaposing different realities as seen through the traveler's eye, Le Guin criticizes our society while offering critical models of possible social change. On this journey, Shevek, the utopian traveler, returns to the problematic world of his ancestors—which is none other than a dystopian representation of Western societies, with their military hierarchies, capitalist economics, and patriarchies. The juxtaposition of worlds conveys Le Guin's idea of democracy as a dynamic process that must negotiate between oppositions without erasing differences.

The themes of ambiguity and utopia-as-process are also maintained at the level of narrative structure. While the alternating scenes between the planets displace the overall traditional linear narrative, the narrative line on Anarres unfolds in sequential time, following Shevek from childhood until his departure for Urras (and thus ending where the story began). The structure of the novel is circular, thus reinforcing the Anarresti principle that "true journey is return" (Le Guin, *Dispossessed* 386), provided that it is also clear that you "*can* go home again . . . so long as you understand that home is a place where you have never been" (55; italics in orig.). But, like the juxtaposition of different worlds, the alternating chapters describing life on the planets at different times in Shevek's life also serve to emphasize how the future is inevitably linked to the past and is a product of the present. Or, as Shevek says, stressing the importance of agency and memory, "Unless the past and the future were made part of the present by memory and intention, there was, in human terms, no road, nowhere to go" (183–84). Most of all, the novel suggests the importance of maintaining utopia as impulse and not as blueprint. This is made clear by what is now considered to be the subtitle of the novel—"an ambiguous utopia"—as well as by the depiction of Anarres. Shevek's planet is, in fact, defined and delimited by a wall that becomes an apt metaphor for its contradictions and ambiguity; looked at from Shevek's double perspective, the wall protects Anarres from an external attack, but it also makes it a prison, cut off from other worlds. Anarres becomes, then, the representation of an imperfect and flawed utopian society: it is self-sufficient and maintains its integrity only at the cost of detaching itself from other realities. Shevek's journey and experience, therefore, also become metaphors for the importance of retaining utopia as process.

The theme of the contradictions and the cost of eutopia is perhaps best embodied by Le Guin's short story "The Ones Who Walk Away from Omelas" (1973). The existence of the short story's utopian society, Omelas, is dependent on the sacrifice and suffering of one child. Le Guin is therefore raising uncomfortable questions about our behavior and standard of living. What is the cost of our material uto-pia? How many of us would knowingly and responsibly accept such a cost? And how many of us would be willing to lower our standard of living so that people in the so-called third world could raise theirs (see Sargent, "Problem")? But the theme of the cost and contradictions of eutopia is also central to Le Guin's novella *The Word for World Is Forest*. As in "Omelas," exploitation and enslavement combined with the price of protecting one's eutopia make up the themes of *Word*, a space-exploration or space-western story combined with the genre of war literature. *Word* has in fact been considered an explicit condem-nation of colonial exploitation and a thinly veiled metaphor for the Vietnam War experience. It represents a clear indictment of what Greg Grewell calls the "combative"—as opposed to "explorative" or "do-mesticative" (28)—master narrative typical of final-frontier SF stories, in which one civilization "battl[es] it out with another for existence or sometimes for something less immediate such as territorial or trade rights" (29). Set on Athshe, a planet peopled by a nonviolent race of short green individuals, the novella narrates the conflict between the natives of the planet and the humans who have been sent there to gath-er lumber, which has become scarce on their own planet. The Terran protagonists are represented by Davidson and Lyubov, two extremes of our own culture: Davidson is a caricature of the macho who embraces the Western disregard for native populations in the way of progress, while Lyubov is a liberal scientist interested in understanding the other culture. The forest is the central metaphor for the representation of dif-ferent philosophies of and attitudes toward life. The Terrans' arrival upsets and violates the peaceful utopian community, and their contin-ual enslavement and exploitation of the natives force the alien race to resist by embracing violence. The painful decision to resort to violence comes to Selver, the Athshean protagonist, in a "dream," which is the way native men reach a deeper consciousness, while women help them interpret these dreams. By recognizing the need to resort to armed re-sistance, Selver becomes a god-translator for his people. The price of

freedom is a terrible one for a pacifist society that uses ritualized singing to replace physical combat; the loss of many lives is accompanied
by the tragic doubt, almost a recognition, that once violence has entered their culture, it will never leave it:

> "Sometimes a god comes," Selver said. "He brings a new way to do a
> thing, or a new thing to be done. A new kind of singing, or a new kind
> of death. He brings this across the bridge between the dream-time and
> the world-time. When he has done this, it is done. You cannot take things
> that exist in the world and try to drive them back into the dream, to hold
> them inside the dream with walls and pretenses. That is insanity. What is,
> is. There is no use pretending, now, that we do not know how to kill one
> another." (Le Guin, *Word* 188–89)

Called a pessimist utopia (see Baggesen), Le Guin's dystopian novella
investigates the possibility of utopia itself; it is a story about resistance,
the right to and the moral imperative of self-defense, the difficult task
of accepting and reconciling differences as well as that of accepting
responsibilities, but it is also about the contradictions and the price of
utopia.

The Telling is one of Le Guin's few clear forays into the dystopian
genre. Yet when she chooses to experiment with this genre, it is not to
classical dystopia that Le Guin turns but rather to critical dystopia. Like
most of her fiction, it is a story of cultural contact, the type of anthro-
pological SF that is characteristic of her work. The novel also marks Le
Guin's full-length return to the Hainish cycle after more than twenty
years. As in the previous novels here discussed, *The Telling* features a
visitor to an alien planet who must come to terms with the difficulties
arising from the encounter between different cultures and values. The
novel follows the experiences and struggles of Sutty, a young Terran
observer for the Ekumen who is on a mission to planet Aka to study
its language and culture, both of which have been destroyed during

---

her journey. Unlike novels such as *The Dispossessed* or *The Word for World Is Forest* that posit two contrasting worlds or cultures, of which one is clearly a dystopia and the other a (possibly imperfect) utopia, *The Telling* presents two contrasting dystopian societies, Terra and Aka. In a series of flashbacks, the reader learns that Sutty has become an observer partly to flee from the fundamentalist theocracy of the Unist on Terra. Ironically, because of the relative difference in time spans occasioned by near-light-speed travel (seventy-some years have actually elapsed in the much shorter time it took Sutty to journey from Terra to Aka), she reaches Aka after a "Cultural Revolution" has taken place and the now-ruling Corporation has erased nearly all traces of the past system of spiritual beliefs and knowledge, called the Telling. A secular fundamentalism dedicated to science, technology, and consumerism characterizes the new society. The two worlds then mirror one another, and Sutty has simply traded religious fundamentalism for secular.

With her mission compromised, Sutty is sent by Ekumen envoy Tong Ov on a journey outside Dovza City to the rural villages, where a remnant of the old culture may have survived. There, she learns of a pocket of resistance, at first through small details in behavior and environment. After winning the confidence of the clandestine culture and apparently evading the surveillance of a Corporation agent known as a monitor, she embarks on a third journey, this time to Mount Silong, one of the biggest *umyazu* (temple or monastery) and the last repository of books and historical treasures. Sutty's official, albeit covert, mission to find and record lost traces of the planet's past also becomes a private and personal quest. In order for her to understand the Akan past, she must come to terms with her own history and painful memories, particularly the death of her lover Pao at the hands of Terran religious fundamentalists. In her quest to recover and preserve an endangered history, she discovers that she needs to do her own telling. In a series of challenging meetings, Sutty and Yara, the agent who has followed her to Silong, reveal to one another their painful pasts and are thus able to maintain their positions with respect and understanding. The novel ends on the critical question of how Sutty and the Ekumen might intervene to save the old culture.

In an interview, Le Guin stated that "what happened to the practice and teaching of Taoism under Mao . . . was the initial impetus of the book. . . . The atrocity, and my long ignorance of it, haunted me. I had to write about it, in my own sidelong fashion" (Le Guin, "Driven"). The novel becomes, then, her own telling of Taoism and her own attempt to resist its destruction (Lindow 73). However, the novel's themes and its open and fragmentary structure provide a larger commentary on the global rise of materialism and fundamentalism in the last few decades. *The Telling* shows a similar shift in both worlds Le Guin describes: the suppression of an ancient belief on planet Aka, together with the rise of materialism, and the dominance of a fundamentalist religion and suppression of politics on Terra. The novel, therefore, provides an extrapolated dystopia of our world. But hope is maintained within the novel: in its structure, its settings, its themes, and, most clearly, its open ending.

Against this bleak setting, Le Guin juxtaposes a fragmentary and open narrative that uses the theme of Sutty's quest for history and memory to counter dystopian pessimism with hope and responsibility. The novel offers a powerful story of utopian resistance against oppression. Its unresolved ending, with the bargaining meeting between representatives of the Ekumen and the Corporation, opens the door to a possible utopia. Such a strategy, together with the fragmentary nature of the novel, provides a "utopian" resistance, also at the level of form, to the dystopian fundamentalism of the events narrated. In fact, Sutty's recovery of the Telling enriches the novel's events with stories, almost parables, that resist a traditional pattern of reading and explication. The central element of these stories is their ambiguity, as they challenge both Sutty's and readers' certainties, suggesting that there is no single truth and that it is dangerous to allow one idea to become the only idea. Moreover, the very presence of the stories also represents another feature of the critical dystopia, since, by blurring the genre, they present another form of opposition and resistance.

A second way to maintain hope within the story is represented by the setting. Sutty's journey upriver allows her to find a utopian enclave where she discovers fragments of what once was "a way of thinking and living developed and elaborated over thousands of years" (Le Guin, *Telling* 98). The Telling is "a religion of process" (102) that is "very different from Terran religions, since it entirely lack[s] dogmatic belief, emotional frenzy, deferral of reward to a future life, and sanctioned bigotry" (121). Against the double dystopian setting, Le Guin then posits enclaves of resistance as exemplified by the physical space of the umyazu, the nature of the Telling, and the *maz*—professionals whose work is "telling: reading aloud, reciting, telling stories, and talking about the stories" (115) in order to pass on such a heterogeneous system of belief.

Hope is further maintained within the novel through the themes of historical awareness and memory. The Telling and the library of Silong resist their official erasure with knowledge and a utopian, collective process of memory:

> History, memory, and the telling of tales are subversive elements in that they promote hope and the potential for change. In living their culture, the people of the Telling challenge the hegemonic discourse of the Corporation and create for themselves a way to attain freedom. . . . Utopia then is maintained in the very choice to make memory and history the central subjects of the book. (Baccolini, "Useful" 126–27)

Sharing knowledge, one of the principles of the Ekumen, is promoting awareness both of the past and of who we are, thus becoming a necessary step to foster change or open up possibilities. The themes of history, memory, and storytelling represent an alternative to the false, imposed, and singular story of the regime, and these themes become instruments of resistance that create the utopian dimension of Le Guin's book: "Unlike in classical dystopia, where the *art of memory* remains trapped in an individual, regressive nostalgia, in *The Telling* and in other critical dystopias the *culture of memory* allows for the formation of a collective resistance" (Baccolini, "Useful" 127; italics in orig.).

Finally, the ending also offers another site of resistance and utopian possibility within the novel. *The Telling* ends as negotiations between representatives of the Ekumen and the Corporation are just about to start—negotiations that have been facilitated by the confrontation at Mount Silong between Sutty and Yara. In these meetings concerning their past, the two "engage in a utopian process of memory and telling" (Baccolini, "Useful" 128) that brings them both to understand and accept the past and acknowledge their responsibility without the need to resort to forgiveness or, worse, denial. This process also allows Sutty to move toward individual and collective action at the bargaining table. By interweaving the recovery of the Telling with Sutty's and Yara's sharing of their different and yet similar pasts, Le Guin is able to set in motion a memory process that becomes both liberating and utopian, in that it enacts a possible change. The macro- and micro-histories Sutty and Yara learn allow them to share their past histories, transcend prejudice, challenge fundamentalist thought, and move toward change. They are able to move from paralyzing pain and hatred to mutual respect, but with no need for forgiveness for the crimes and violence experienced. The novel's structure, themes, and open ending emphasize, then, the utopian dimension of the story. Its closing image, of Sutty at the bargaining table negotiating the survival of the library at Silong, reinforces the utopian process of memory:

> But it was not the Monitor's, it was Yara's face that she held in her mind as the bargaining began.
> His life, that was what underwrote her bargaining. His life, Pao's life. (Le Guin, *Telling* 264)

Thus Le Guin's critical dystopia becomes a site of resistance, hope, and political renewal.

Le Guin's work has always combined utopian and dystopian elements critically, increasingly moving toward the critical dystopia:

> Sometimes I think I am just trying superstitiously to avert evil by talking about it; I certainly don't consider my fictions prophetic. Yet throughout my whole adult life, I have watched us blighting our world irrevocably, irremediably, and mindlessly—ignoring every warning and neglecting every benevolent alternative in the pursuit of "growth" and immediate profit. It is quite hard to live in the United States in 2001 and feel any long term hopefulness about the unrelenting use of increasingly exploitative and destructive technologies. (Le Guin, "Driven")

And yet, in so doing, she has maintained a utopian horizon by constantly exposing the need for a radical change in society that can be achieved through collective struggles and individual political agency. These themes are reflected in the narrative structures of her work as well as in her multiple settings and her blurring of utopia and dystopia. In turn, they also reflect the contemporary critical debates within post-structuralist, postcolonialist, and gender studies. One dichotomy that needs to be deconstructed in our own society—and thus in future worlds as well—is that between reason and imagination, rationality and spirituality, and high and low culture. In particular, Le Guin's work indicts the Western binary system that, far from being neutral, is functional to the maintenance of white male domination as well as of any fundamentalism. The difficult encounter between different cultures and traditions, be it about gender, class, sexual preference, religion, ethnicity, "race," or politics, is what allows Le Guin to flesh out her critique of contemporary society. Through the eyes of flawed travelers, Le Guin encourages us readers to think critically about our own societies, opens up possibilities of radical change, teaches us to understand what is necessary to begin to articulate our desires, and reveals the shortcomings and limits of utopia, thus stressing the importance of maintaining utopia as impulse and not as blueprint.

Works Cited

Atwood, Margaret. "Orwell and Me." *The Guardian*. Guardian News and Media, 16 June 2003. Web. 11 Apr. 2012.

Baccolini, Raffaella. "Gender and Genre in the Feminist Critical Dystopias of Katharine Burdekin, Margaret Atwood, and Octavia Butler." *Future Females, the Next Generation: New Voices and Velocities in Feminist Science Fiction Criticism*. Ed. Marleen Barr. Lanham, MD: Rowman, 2000. 13–34.

_____. "'It's Not in the Womb the Damage Is Done': Memory, Desire and the Construction of Gender in Katharine Burdekin's *Swastika Night*." *Le trasformazioni del narrare*. Ed. E. Siciliani, A. Cecere, V. Intonti, and A. Sportelli. Fasano, Italy: Schena, 1995. 293–309.

_____. "'A Useful Knowledge of the Present Is Rooted in the Past': Memory and Historical Reconciliation in Ursula K. Le Guin's *The Telling*." Baccolini and Moylan 113–34.

Baccolini, Raffaella, and Tom Moylan, eds. *Dark Horizons: Science Fiction and the Dystopian Imagination*. New York: Routledge, 2003.

Baggesen, Søren. "Utopian and Dystopian Pessimism: Le Guin's *The Word for World Is Forest* and Tiptree's 'We Who Stole the Dream.'" *Science Fiction Studies* 41.1 (1987): 34–43.

Bernardo, Susan M., and Graham J. Murphy. *Ursula K. Le Guin: A Critical Companion*. Westport, CT: Greenwood, 2006.

Boothman, Derek. "The Sources for Gramsci's Concept of Hegemony." *Rethinking Marxism* 20.2 (2008): 201–15.

Cavalcanti, Ildney. "Articulating the Elsewhere: Utopia in Contemporary Feminist Dystopias." Diss. U of Strathclyde, 1999.

Grewell, Greg. "Colonizing the Universe: Science Fictions Then, Now, and in the (Imagined) Future." *Rocky Mountain Review of Language and Literature* 55.2 (2001): 25–47.

Le Guin, Ursula K. *The Dispossessed*. New York: EOS, 2001.

_____. "Driven by a Different Chauffeur: An Interview with Ursula K. Le Guin." By Nick Gevers. *SF Site*. SF Site, 2002. Web. 11 Apr. 2012.

_____. *The Left Hand of Darkness*. London: Futura, 1989.

_____. "The Ones Who Walk Away from Omelas (Variations on a Theme by William James)." *The Wind's Twelve Quarters*. New York: Harper, 1975. 251–59.

_____. *The Telling*. New York: Harcourt, 2000.

_____. *The Word for World Is Forest*. New York: Tor, 1972.

Levitas, Ruth. *The Concept of Utopia*. Oxford: Lang, 2010.

Lindow, Sandra J. "Sometimes It Takes a Leap: Decision Making and the Tao within the Work of Ursula K. Le Guin." *Foundation* 90 (2004): 71–80.

Moylan, Tom. *Demand the Impossible: Science Fiction and the Utopian Imagination*. New York: Methuen, 1986.

_____. *Scraps of the Untainted Sky: Science Fiction, Utopia, Dystopia*. Boulder, CO: Westview, 2000.

Sargent, Lyman Tower. "The Problem of the 'Flawed Utopia': A Note on the Costs of Eutopia." Baccolini and Moylan 225–31.

_____. "The Three Faces of Utopianism Revisited." *Utopian Studies* 5.1 (1994): 1–37.

Thibodeau, Amanda R. "Gender, Utopia, and Temporality in Feminist Science Fiction: (Re)reading Classic Texts of the Past, in the Present, and for the Future." Diss. U of Miami, 2011.

Totalitarian Technocracies_____

Dystopian fiction emerged as a distinct genre at the beginning of the twentieth century, although the label, as Russell Jacoby explains, was not widely used until later: "In the mid-twentieth century, J. Max Patrick, a coeditor of an anthology of utopian writings, coined the term 'dystopia' as the contrary of utopia" (7). If utopia, which literally means "nowhere," is commonly understood as good place, then dystopia, as utopia's opposite, means "bad place." This distinction, however, is inherently subjective. For example, George Orwell's *Nineteen Eighty-Four* (1949) is a classic dystopian novel, and from the perspective of its sympathetic protagonist, Winston Smith, Oceania—the society presented in *Nineteen Eighty-Four*—is a terrible place. But to Winston's acquaintance and coworker Tom Parsons, Oceania is a utopia and remains one even after he finds himself under arrest. In *1985* (1978), his critique of *Nineteen Eighty-Four*, Anthony Burgess emphasizes Oceania's redeeming qualities:

> Consider the situation for eighty-five per cent of the community—the proles. There is a war going on, but there is no conscription. . . . There are pubs, with beer sold in litre glasses, there are cinemas, a state lottery, popular journalism and even pornography. . . . There is no unemployment, there is enough money, there are no oppressive regulations—indeed, there are no laws at all. The entire population, prole and Party alike, is untroubled by crime and violence on the democratic model. . . . There are no worries about inflation. One of the major issues of our time, racial intolerance, is lacking. . . . There are no stupid politicians, time-wasting political debates, ridiculous hustings. The government is efficient and stable. There are even measures devised to eliminate from life the old agonies of sex and the oppressions of family loyalty. No wonder the system is universally accepted. (42–43)

Burgess makes clear that despite the motives of Oceania's rulers, the nation's stability is proof that the masses either welcome their governance or are not sufficiently troubled by it to rebel. The most troubling and intriguing aspect of dystopias, as Allan Weiss points out, is that they often reflect the people's will:

> Contrary to the impression some historians of dystopian fiction . . . seem to have, dystopian regimes are not so much imposed from above as sought from below. . . . The common image of a dystopian society is that it is the exact opposite of a utopia. . . . Instead, the two genres mirror each other in many ways, particularly in that most residents of dystopias are happy or at the very least satisfied, and the (supposed) rebels are anomalies in their societies. (127–28)

Few would trade our world for the one described by Orwell, but part of the reason we feel this way is because the story is artfully presented so that we identify with Winston, a disaffected intellectual. The difference between a dystopia and a utopia is largely a matter of personal preference. When we refer to a work of literature as dystopian, we mean that the community in question would probably be unappealing to most, but not all, of the author's intended readers.

Although the two genres are not entirely distinct, it is important, if tricky, to distinguish utopian and dystopian literature from science fiction. Margaret Atwood, a recipient of the Arthur C. Clarke Award for science fiction and the author of influential dystopian novels, argues that dystopias and utopias address the known, while science fiction imagines the unknown: "I said I liked to make a distinction between science fiction proper—for me, this label denotes books with things in them we can't yet do or begin to do, talking beings we can never meet, and places we can't go—and speculative fiction, which employs the means already more or less to hand, and takes place on Planet Earth" ("*Handmaid's Tale* and *Oryx*" 513). Dystopian, utopian, and other forms of speculative fiction project exaggerated models of current political and socioeconomic trends into the future, frequently in order to inform, warn, or advise readers. Although scientific developments sometimes feature prominently in this literature, such technology always advances the underlying societal philosophy that the author either endorses or critiques; it never figures as an independent concern, as it often does in science fiction.

Nevertheless, although they do not emphasize science, authors of dystopian fiction are interested in scientists and the role they should play in society. This is because scientists are presented as ideal political leaders in the seminal late nineteenth- and early twentieth-century utopias of H. G. Wells. Today, Wells is primarily known for his science fiction, but his utopian writings were so pervasive and compelling that the disparate works that comprise the canon of dystopian fiction are largely united in their resistance to them. As Ken Davis notes, citing Mark Hillegas, "Wells, particularly in his later 'utopian' works, virtually created the twentieth-century dystopian movement by providing the chief models which such writers as Eugene Zamiatin, Aldous Huxley, and George Orwell reacted so strongly against" (123). The history of dystopian fiction is therefore also the history of how engagement with Wells's theories, concepts, and predictions developed from respectful questioning to parody to outright dismissal of his ideas. My analysis will focus chronologically on the most influential dystopias of the last hundred years, namely Jack London's *The Iron Heel* (1907), Yevgeny Zamyatin's *We* (1924), Aldous Huxley's *Brave New World* (1932), Orwell's *Nineteen Eighty-Four* (1949), and Atwood's *The Handmaid's Tale* (1985), *Oryx and Crake* (2003), and *The Year of the Flood* (2009), all of which draw upon the utopias of Wells. The fact that modern scientific thought is so often harnessed by entities with goals unrelated to the public good makes the warnings offered by dystopian writers especially pertinent. In short, an appreciation of the ongoing relevance of dystopian fiction depends on an understanding of the work of H. G. Wells.

Wells argues that scientists make ideal rulers because their rational, dispassionate ways of thinking allow them to resist attractive but socially destabilizing concerns like religious fundamentalism, nationalism, militarism, and—above all—individualism. According to Wells, only "scientific Puritans" (*Shape* 375) can steward humanity's transition from factionalism to global utopia and then be relied upon to relinquish power. Although this idea is strongly implied in *A Story of the Days to Come* (1899) and other late nineteenth-century novels by Wells, it is explicitly articulated in *Anticipations of the Reaction of Mechanical and Scientific Progress upon Human Life and Thought*, his best-selling philosophical work of nonfiction, published in 1902:

> A world-wide process of social and moral deliquescence is in progress, and . . . a really functional social body of engineering, managing men, scientifically trained, and having common ideals and interests, is likely to segregate and disentangle itself from our present confusion of aimless and ill-directed lives. . . . This class will become, I believe, at last consciously *the* State, controlling and restricting very greatly the . . . non-functional masses with which it is as yet almost indistinguishably mingled. (81–86; italics in orig.)

This faith in a utopian technocracy was a lifelong belief of Wells's, one that he never seriously questioned, even as cultural and historical developments of the twentieth century such as Stalinism and Fascism undermined its validity. As Orwell explains, "Unfortunately the equation of science with common sense does not really hold good. . . . Much of what Wells has imagined and worked for is physically there in Nazi Germany. The order, the planning, the State encouragement of science, the steel, the concrete, the aeroplanes, are all there, but all in the service of ideas appropriate to the Stone Age. Science is fighting on the side of superstition" ("Wells" 143). Here, Orwell observes that a scientific state can have a primitive outlook and nefarious aims. Although they refuse to pay tribute to it, dystopian writers such as Orwell are not especially troubled by technology; they simply argue that technocrats are no less corruptible than anyone else.

These authors also deride Wells's notion that scientific training can reduce and even eclipse our baser instincts. At the close of *The Shape of Things to Come* (1933), the world government voluntarily dissolves, having realized that through generations of scientific education, organization, and development, human nature has irrevocably improved:

> We have made war impossible; we have liberated ourselves from the great anti-social traditions that set man against man; we have made the servitude of man to man through poverty impossible. The faculties of health, education and behaviour will sustain the good conduct of the race. The controls of food, housing, transport, clothing, supply, initiative, design, research, can do their own work. There is nothing left for a supreme government to do. Except look at the world it has made and see that it is good. And bless it. (392)

The biblical allusion to Genesis at the end of this quotation is fitting, since it implies that science has the godlike power to recreate us, a dubious notion that Atwood directly contests in *Oryx and Crake* and *The Year of the Flood*. There is much to be said for scientific thinking and its potential to elevate civilization. But dystopian writers remind us that most people are ultimately driven by their feelings rather than their intellect, even when their passions cause them to act against their own self-interest. Orwell elucidates a common theme in dystopian fiction: history has shown that even those who agree with Wells either unknowingly remain susceptible to atavistic impulses or cannot understand why others do:

> What is the use of pointing out that a World State is desirable? . . . All sensible men for decades past have been substantially in agreement with what Mr. Wells says; but the sensible men have no power and, in too many cases, no disposition to sacrifice themselves. . . . The energy that actually shapes the world springs from emotions—racial pride, leader-worship, re-

ligious belief, love of war—which liberal intellectuals mechanically write off as anachronisms, and which they have usually destroyed so completely in themselves as to have lost all power of action. ("Wells" 140–41)

It is the threat, but also the potentially redemptive power, of this primal energy that dystopian writers are concerned with. They accept that the rational thought, however appealing, that characterizes utopian literature cannot undermine and often cannot compete with irrational tendencies, which is why dystopias are so dynamic, while utopias, even to the sympathetic reader, often seem sterile and static.

Certainly visceral energy permeates Jack London's pulpy, melodramatic dystopia *The Iron Heel*, the twentieth century's first major dystopian novel. London is best remembered for his naturalistic fiction, but he was also a committed socialist who feared the rise of an authoritarian plutocracy as corporate money came to corrupt and dominate the American political system. In this novel, the capitalist elite seize power and form a hereditary oligarchy informally known as the Iron Heel. The story is presented as a personal account authored in secret by a female revolutionary named Avis Everhard. Avis's exact fate is a mystery because her manuscript, which is discovered and annotated centuries after the overthrow of the Iron Heel, truncates abruptly. Following London's lead, other dystopian writers employ the same strategy: Atwood frames the narrative of her protagonist Offred in an almost identical way in *The Handmaid's Tale*, and even Orwell mimics this device to some extent by concluding *Nineteen Eighty-Four* with a scholarly appendix. Embedding the main narrative imbues the story with hope by allowing the author to indicate that the totalitarian order will ultimately fall, without obliging him or her to show precisely how.

The Iron Heel's plot centers on the love between Avis, a sheltered young woman of privilege, and Ernest Everhard, a rugged, working-class intellectual and socialist politician. The two are key figures in an ill-fated uprising to overthrow the Iron Heel, a regime whose philosophy anticipates the modern Fascist state minus the anti-Semitism and obsession with ethnic purity. While conceding that it is not great literature, Orwell highlights *The Iron Heel*'s sociopolitical value:

> On several points London was right where nearly all other prophets were wrong . . . he foresaw, for instance, that peculiar horror of totalitarian society, the way in which suspected enemies of the régime *simply disappear*. But the book is chiefly notable for maintaining that capitalist society would not perish of its "contradictions," but that the possessing class would be able to form itself into a vast corporation . . . , sacrificing many of its privileges in order to preserve its superior status. ("Introduction" 24; italics in orig.)

These insights about a capitalist society in which great wealth is concentrated in a few hands, while meaningful in Orwell's day, are especially relevant to our world of multinational corporations, governmental deregulation, cuts in social-welfare programs, privatization, and tax breaks for the rich. But London also questioned Wells's trust in the persuasiveness and vigor of scientific thinking.

Writing at the height of Wells's popularity and influence, London shows the older author considerable deference. We are told by the annotator that some of Wells's writings survived the Iron Heel's reign and are revered as classics: "Wells was a sociological seer, sane and normal as well as warm. . . . Many fragments of his work have come down to us, while two of his greatest achievements, 'Anticipations' and 'Mankind in the Making,' have come down intact" (London 159). Clearly, Wells's utopian writings provided source material for the *The Iron Heel*, which is why, apart from Avis, most of the primary socialist characters are scientists or have received the benefit of science education. Ernest Everhard sees himself as a philosopher, calling philosophy "the widest science of all" (11). Avis's father, John Cunningham, a physicist whose scientific training has fostered an open and tolerant mind, is particularly impressed with Ernest's scientific aptitude, saying, "He has a splendidly disciplined mind. He would have made a good scientist if his energies had been directed that way" (18). Like Wells, London roots socialism in scientific thought. It is through their dispassionate, scientific dispositions that John and Avis reconcile themselves to the loss of property and status that accompanies political dissent. A scientific perspective allows Avis to describe her father's attitude toward the slum where they end up living in almost laughably sanguine terms:

> He had become enamoured of proletarian life. He looked upon our slum neighborhood as a great sociological laboratory, and he had embarked upon an apparently endless orgy of investigation. . . . Also, he worked at odd jobs, and the work was play as well as learned investigation, for he delighted in it and was always returning home with copious notes and bubbling over with new adventures. He was the perfect scientist. (150)

In keeping with Wellsian thought, science in *The Iron Heel* is the fount of social harmony.

Unfortunately, Ernest, John, and Avis are incapable of convincing others that both a proletarian victory in the coming class warfare and the triumph of socialism are scientific inevitabilities. When Avis makes fruitless entreaties to investors, lawyers, and executives on behalf of an impoverished, injured laborer, Ernest tells her that these men are incorrigible due to their lack of scientific knowledge: "The weakness in their position lies in that they are merely business men. They are not philosophers. They are not biologists nor sociologists. If they were, of course all would be well. A business man who was also a biologist and a sociologist would know, approximately, the right thing to do for humanity. But, outside the realm of business, these men are stupid" (London 46). Here, London echoes Wells, saying "all would be well" if everyone had scientific knowledge. Zamyatin, Huxley, Orwell, and Atwood will all take issue with this claim, but even London impliedly concedes that few people have the benefit of scientific training, particularly in the early twentieth century, and without that education, the socialist position, no matter how well articulated, fails to resonate. In a key scene, Ernest attempts unsuccessfully to persuade prominent members of the middle class who are feeling the pressure of patrician policies to align themselves with the socialist cause. As he bids them goodbye, Ernest ruefully says, "I only wish you fellows knew a little something about evolution and sociology. . . . We would be saved so much trouble if you did" (104). Through Ernest's words, London posits a window of opportunity during the formative years to impart the scientific knowledge on which the appeal of socialism depends. Once missed, that opportunity is gone forever. Though he admired Wells, London's work respectfully questions not the validity but the efficacy of his theories.

Among dystopian authors, direct disagreement with Wells did not emerge until after the First World War, when, as Orwell rightly concludes, people saw that scientific thinking could produce mass death as easily as a better life:

> The ultimate subject-matter of H. G. Wells's stories is, first of all, scientific discovery. . . . He is saying all the time, if only that small shopkeeper could acquire a scientific outlook, his troubles would be ended. And of course he believes that this is going to happen, probably in the quite near future. A few more million pounds for scientific research, a few more generations scientifically educated, a few more superstitions shoveled into the dustbin, and the job is done. . . . [T]he war of 1914–18 . . . succeeded in debunking both Science, Progress and civilized man. . . . Science was something that created bombing planes and poison gas, civilized man, as it turned out, was ready to behave worse than any savage when the pinch came. ("Rediscovery" 203)

This notion that a scientific outlook would not necessarily produce a just, rational, prosperous society is a central concern of Yevgeny Zamyatin's *We*, a novel written shortly after World War I and the Russian Revolution. Clarence Brown points out that Zamyatin, a socialist with a degree in engineering, was well acquainted with the writings of H. G. Wells:

> That *We* has even a faintly English tone to it is not due, of course, to the Englishmen who followed it but to the Englishman, H. G. Wells, who preceded Zamyatin and everyone else in the peculiar genre in which they were all working. Zamyatin knew the works of Wells intimately. . . . But if the visionary Wells gave everyone the idea, he was repaid by the usual black ingratitude. Zamyatin, Huxley, and Orwell all wrote savage satires of the idea of a scientific utopia. (xx)

We, like *Brave New World*, can be considered an anti-utopian novel rather than a dystopian one because it parodies the kind of planned, painless, cooperative community celebrated by Wells. People in *We* have no individual identities; they are merely numbers in identical uniforms who see themselves as insignificant cells comprising the all-important body politic. This sacrifice of individuality to the universal collective is presented in idealistic terms by Wells, who discusses it in his preface to the 1914 edition of *Anticipations*: "This Collective Mind is essentially an extension of the spirit of science to all human affairs, its method is to seek and speak and serve the truth and to subordinate oneself to one's conception of a general purpose" (xvi). Wells asserts that the Collective Mind will liberate humanity; Zamyatin and Huxley contend that it reduces so-called civilization to a glorified ant farm.

The reluctant hero of *We* is D-503, the designer of the *Integral*, a spacecraft that will be used to bring the "beneficial yoke of reason" to "unknown creatures on alien planets, who may still be living in the savage state of freedom" (Zamyatin 3). D-503's narrative is an official record meant to extol the virtues of his "utopian" community to these free aliens. By presenting the story as a bureaucratic account drafted by a gifted scientist, Zamyatin tests Wells's claim that scientists can better withstand atavistic impulses. Though a loyal, happy citizen of the One State, where every number enjoys the right of sexual access to every other number, D-503 falls inexplicably in love with I-330, a revolutionary who introduces him to a community of free humans living beyond the city walls and makes him aware that a sizeable minority of numbers secretly prefers freedom to guaranteed happiness. D-503 joins the resistance, demonstrating that his commitment to scientific order cannot contain his emotional passions. When open revolution breaks out, the Benefactor, One State's perpetual ruler, announces that surgery to remove the imagination must be immediately performed on all numbers to make them perfectly uniform, like the machines that science has allowed them to mass produce. In *We*, the scientific principles of cooperation, conformity, and efficiency threaten to end rather than advance humanity.

We is not an outright dismissal of Wells's Collective Mind. Throughout the novel, D-503 recognizes the benefits of life in One State and on several occasions nearly betrays the rebellion. But through D-503's story, Zamyatin shows that we cannot transcend our irrational tendencies with a scientific mindset, and perhaps we should not want to.

Aldous Huxley's *Brave New World* makes the same point in a similar way. Jacoby observes that Huxley, unlike Zamyatin, was troubled by mass production and consumerism, rather than the warfare and political upheaval that characterized the second and third decades of the twentieth century:

> While Huxley does allude to Soviet Communism in *Brave New World*, which features a character named Lenina, neither communism nor Nazism much bothered him. . . . The fetish of youth, the dangers of consumerism, the manipulations of the human psyche: these worried him, especially as he observed them in America of the 1920s. After all, the American auto manufacturer Henry Ford, who pioneered mass production, pervaded *Brave New World*. . . . Huxley feared a technological and Americanized future. (9)

Ford's assembly-line production method, which is applied to nearly every aspect of life in *Brave New World*, was a commonsensical application of the kind of scientific thinking espoused by Wells, and, as in *We*, it succeeds in making most people happy, if not free. Although Orwell doubted the predictive value of *Brave New World*, he valued its satirical stab at Wells's idea of a utopia: "In Aldous Huxley's *Brave New World*, a sort of post-war parody of the Wellsian Utopia, . . . the hedonistic principle is pushed to its utmost, the whole world has turned into a Riviera hotel. . . . No society of that kind would last more than a couple of generations, because a ruling class which thought principally in terms of a 'good time' would soon lose its vitality" ("Prophecies" 31). But the world controllers of *Brave New World* do not pamper their citizenry to give them a good time; they have realized that control through satiety can be as effective as, if not more so than, control through repression. As Huxley puts it in his essay "Brave New World Revisited" (1958), "In *1984* the lust for power is satisfied by inflicting pain; in *Brave New World*, by inflicting a hardly less humiliating pleasure" (259).

In Huxley's World State, we meet Mustapha Mond, a world controller who was a physicist but abandoned the pure science he might have practiced in exile to gratify this "lust for power." Through this character, Huxley refutes the notion that scientific training facilitates self-regulation, a point that he emphasizes in "Brave New World Revisited":

> To the question *quis custodiet custodes?*—Who will mount guard over our guardians, who will engineer the engineers?—the answer is a bland denial that they need any supervision. . . . [T]heir heart is pure because they are scientists. . . . Alas, higher education is not necessarily a guarantee of higher virtue, or higher political wisdom. And to these misgivings on ethical and psychological grounds must be added misgivings of a purely scientific character. Can we accept the theories on which the social engineers base their practice, and in terms of which they justify their manipulations of human beings? (260)

Brave New World suggests that we cannot accept the scientific theories that social engineers use to justify their socioeconomic manipulations. By taking this position, Huxley set himself in opposition to Wells, who, as Donald Watt recounts, attacked the novel for its supposed betrayal of science: "The book . . . moved H. G. Wells, says Gerald Heard, to write Huxley an angry letter charging treason to science. . . . Wells was joined by Wyndham Lewis, who referred to the novel as 'an unforgivable offence to Progress'" (16). Huxley, of course, was not attacking science itself, merely Wells's theory that a ruling class of scientists would necessarily be equipped to bring about paradise on earth; and though it is in many ways a radically dissimilar book to *Brave New World*, Orwell's *Nineteen Eighty-Four* provides a similar critique of this veneration of the scientific perspective.

Of all dystopian writers, George Orwell is perhaps the most forthright in acknowledging his debt to Wells and the scope of Wells's influence on the modern world: "Thinking people who were born about the beginning of this century are in some sense Wells's own creation. . . . I doubt whether anyone who was writing books between 1900 and 1920, at any rate in the English language, influenced the young so much. The minds of all of us, and therefore the physical world, would be perceptibly different if Wells had never existed" ("Wells" 143). *Nineteen Eighty-Four* illustrates a possible consequence of liberal-minded intellectuals tolerating and even supporting the dictatorial policies of supposedly socialist nations like the Soviet Union. As a socialist, Orwell knew that socialists could not attack the human-rights abuses of right-wing regimes while ignoring injustices perpetrated by the Left, and he was troubled by those who interpreted the perversion of socialism he presents in *Nineteen Eighty-Four* as an attack on socialism itself:

> My recent novel is NOT intended as an attack on Socialism or on the British Labour Party (of which I am a supporter). . . . I believe . . . that totalitarian ideas have taken root in the minds of intellectuals everywhere, and I have tried to draw these ideas out to their logical consequences.

The scene of the book is laid in Britain in order to emphasize that the English-speaking races are not innately better than anyone else and that totalitarianism, *if not fought against*, could triumph anywhere. ("Letter" 502; italics in orig.)

Margaret Atwood, a Canadian, may well have set her three dystopian novels in the United States to make a similar implied argument against American exceptionalism.

Nineteen Eighty-Four provides more than a critique of (mis)applied socialism; like *Brave New World*, it opposes the Wellsian assertion that scientists are uniquely equipped for political leadership. O'Brien, Winston's sadistic inquisitor (who is assisted by a technician in a white coat), presents Winston's fate in scientific terms, saying, "Posterity will never hear of you. . . . We shall turn you into gas and pour you into the stratosphere" (257). O'Brien also uses scientific diction to celebrate his own anticipated immortality: "You are thinking that my face is old and tired. You are thinking that I talk of power, and yet I am not even able to prevent the decay of my own body. Can you not understand, Winston, that the individual is only a cell? The weariness of the cell is the vigor of the organism. Do you die when you cut your fingernails?" (267). Orwell shows that scientific terminology is as plastic as religious rhetoric: it can be used to justify or inculcate anything.

O'Brien also exposes the fiction that people always believe what is scientifically proven, the inaccuracy of which is made evident today by the controversy surrounding climate change:

You must get rid of those nineteenth-century ideas about the laws of nature. We make the laws of nature. . . . Nothing exists except through human consciousness. . . . The earth is the center of the universe. The sun and stars go round it. . . . For certain purposes, of course, that is not true. When we navigate the ocean, or when we predict an eclipse, we often find it convenient to assume that the earth goes around the sun. . . . But what of it? Do you suppose it is beyond us to produce a dual system of astronomy? The stars can be near or distant, according as we need them. Do you suppose our mathematicians are unequal to that? Have you forgotten doublethink? (267–68)

By linking acceptance of fixed laws of nature to the nineteenth century, Orwell implicitly links such fixed laws to Wells, a man who he claimed was "too sane to understand the modern world" ("Wells" 145). Through O'Brien, Orwell asserts that scientists practice doublethink—the ability to hold two contradictory ideas simultaneously—like everyone else.

Indeed, many of the most dreaded and admired aspects of Oceania are taken straight out of Wells's scientific thought. Newspeak, Oceania's simplified English that restricts thought and meaningful discourse, is the successor to Basic, an 850-word reduction of English developed by a Cambridge University linguist, said to "spread like wildfire" in the World State of Wells's *The Shape of Things to Come* (431–32). The nationalism that Orwell so feared in British society is a point of pride for Wells: "There is plentiful material from the comparatively orderly and prosperous period between 1890 and 1930. Great Britain then constituted the healthiest and most law-abiding community in the world" (*Shape* 437). Furthermore, the analogy used by O'Brien to equate himself to a cell in the immortal body politic represents the ideal mindset for a citizen of Wells's World State: "The body of mankind is now one single organism of nearly two thousand five hundred million persons, and the individual differences of every one of these persons is like an exploring tentacle thrust out to test and learn. . . . We are all members of one body . . . and more and more plain does it become to us that it is not our little selves, but Man the Undying who achieves . . . through us" (445). In many ways, Orwell's dystopian Oceania reflects Wells's utopian World State.

Just as Orwell drew heavily upon Wells, the contemporary author most indebted to Orwell—and thus indirectly to Wells—is Margaret Atwood. As Larry Caldwell points out, "Margaret Atwood's *The Handmaid's Tale* (1985) is particularly intriguing . . . because of its obvious, self-conscious, even ironic debt to Wells and especially to Orwell" (340). *The Handmaid's Tale* foresees what its narrator, in a passing reference to Wells, deems "the true shape of things to come" (Atwood, *Handmaid's Tale* 46): a right-wing takeover of America in the name of religion, prompted by declining birthrates, environmental degradation, and fear of Islamic terrorists. In *The Handmaid's Tale*, under a literal application of Mosaic law, fertile women in the newly created state of Gilead are treated as chattel, farmed out to prominent men for procreative purposes. Illustrating Orwell's proposition that science could fight on the side of superstition, the high-ranking commander in *The Handmaid's Tale*, a founding member of the regime, actually describes himself as a scientist: " 'I was in market research, to begin with,' he says diffidently. 'After that I sort of branched out.' . . . 'You might say I'm a sort of scientist,' he says. 'Within limits, of course' " (185). In a country that traditionally prided itself on free speech and inquiry, science has moved from being a tool of corporate bureaucracy to serving a fundamentalist dictatorship.

Ironically, these limitations on science set by the ruling technocrats actually subvert the society's most urgent need. Although the nation is suffering from infertility, its commanders prohibit modern obstetrics:

> It used to be different, [the doctors] used to be in charge. A shame it was, said Aunt Lydia. Shameful. What she'd just showed us was a film, made in an olden-days hospital: a pregnant woman, wired up to a machine, electrodes coming out of her every which way so that she looked like a broken robot, an intravenous drip feeding into her arm. . . . Once they drugged women, induced labor, cut them open, sewed them up. No more. No anesthetics, even. Aunt Elizabeth said it was better for the baby, but also: *I will greatly multiply thy sorrow and thy conception; in sorrow thou shalt bring forth children.* (114)

In Gilead, physician-controlled childbirth procedures have been replaced by midwifery, the only childbirth model available regardless of

---

the demands of a given pregnancy. Just as London argues that the scientific perspective can fail to persuade people, here it loses out entirely, even among former scientists, to religious faith.

Atwood examines many of the same disturbing trends in the first two installments of her MaddAddam trilogy, *Oryx and Crake* and *The Year of the Flood*. Coral Ann Howells goes so far as to read *Oryx and Crake* as a thematic sequel to *The Handmaid's Tale*:

> *Oryx and Crake* might be seen as a sequel to *The Handmaid's Tale*. The pollution and environmental destruction which threatened one region of North America in the earlier novel have escalated into worldwide climate change through global warming in the latter, and the late twentieth-century Western trend towards mass consumerism which Gilead tried to reverse by its fundamentalist doctrines and its liturgy of "moral values" has resulted in an American lifestyle of consumerist decadence in a high-tech world which is ultimately death-doomed by one man's megalomaniac project of bioterrorism. (161)

Again, though, the threat in these books is not so much technology as the fallibility of those who develop and employ it. In both novels, which offer differing narrative perspectives on the same scenario, the humanities are entirely devalued as a rising generation acquires scientific training to develop profitable technologies for unregulated multinational corporations. Atwood's trilogy centers on Crake, a young man who discovers that his father was murdered for attempting to reveal a corporate policy of seeding illnesses into medication to create more illness and thus more demand for health-care products. Rather than blame the specific individuals involved or even the predatory corporations they willingly serve, Crake locates the root of his father's cruel fate in a global market system that consistently puts profits ahead of people. Realizing that this ruinously amoral system has arisen through a combination of greed, popular consent, and indifference to the suffering of others, Crake judges humanity, finds it worthy of extermination, and attempts to replace it with genetically engineered creatures, which he develops under the pretense of providing designer babies to the ultra-wealthy. *Oryx and Crake* and *The Year of the Flood* present scientists locked in an apocalyptic struggle between those who serve the corporations and those who, like the MaddAddam ecoterrorists, seek to undermine corporate consumerism by dismantling the global infrastructure. Foreseeing a very different future than Wells, Atwood portrays what can happen to a society that puts the highest premium on scientific innovation.

The speculative fiction of the last hundred years anticipates what transpires when societies are put under extreme pressure. Although freedom to do as one wishes is appealing in times of stability and prosperity, the desire for freedom from what threatens us takes hold in a crisis. The question then becomes, who best to govern when the desire for "freedom from" predominates, as sooner or later it must? For Wells, the answer is scientists; but for the major authors of dystopian fiction, it is humanists, grounded in art, emotion, and imagination as well as critical thought.

Works Cited

Atwood, Margaret. *The Handmaid's Tale*. Boston: Houghton, 1986.

_____. "*The Handmaid's Tale* and *Oryx and Crake* in Context." *PMLA* 119.3 (2004): 513–17.

_____. *Oryx and Crake*. New York: Anchor, 2003.

_____. *The Year of the Flood*. New York: Doubleday, 2009.

Brown, Clarence. "Zamyatin and the Persian Rooster." Introduction. *We*. By Yevgeny Zamyatin. Trans. Brown. New York: Penguin, 1993. xi–xxvii.

Burgess, Anthony. *1985*. Boston: Little, 1978.

Caldwell, Larry W. "Wells, Orwell, and Atwood: (EPI)Logic and Eu/Utopia." *Extrapolation* 33.4 (1992): 333–45.

Davis, Ken. "*The Shape of Things to Come*: H. G. Wells and the Rhetoric of Proteus." *No Place Else: Explorations in Utopian and Dystopian Fiction*. Ed. Eric S. Rabkin, Martin H. Greenberg, and Joseph D. Olander. Carbondale: Southern Illinois UP, 1983. 110–24.

Howells, Coral Ann. "Margaret Atwood's Dystopian Visions: *The Handmaid's Tale* and *Oryx and Crake*." *The Cambridge Companion to Margaret Atwood*. Ed. Howells. New York: Cambridge UP, 2006. 161–75.

Huxley, Aldous. *Brave New World and Brave New World Revisited*. New York: Harper, 2005.

Jacoby, Russell. *Picture Imperfect: Utopian Thought for an Anti-utopian Age*. New York: Columbia UP, 2005.

London, Jack. *The Iron Heel*. Westport, CT: Hill, 1980.

Orwell, George. "Introduction to *Love of Life and Other Stories* by Jack London." Orwell and Angus, *In Front* 23–29.

_____. "Letter to Francis A. Henson." Orwell and Angus, *In Front* 502.

_____. *Nineteen Eighty-Four*. New York: Harcourt, 1977.

_____. "Prophecies of Fascism." Orwell and Angus, *My Country* 30–33.

_____. "The Rediscovery of Europe." Orwell and Angus, *My Country* 197–207.

_____. "Wells, Hitler and the World State." Orwell and Angus, *My Country* 139–45.

Orwell, Sonia, and Ian Angus, eds. *In Front of Your Nose, 1945–1950*. By George Orwell. New York: Harcourt, 1968. Vol. 4 of *The Collected Essays, Journalism and Letters of George Orwell*.

_____. eds. *My Country Right or Left, 1940–1943*. By George Orwell. New York: Harcourt, 1968. Vol. 2 of *The Collected Essays, Journalism and Letters of George Orwell*.

Watt, Donald. Introduction. *Aldous Huxley: The Critical Heritage*. Ed. Watt. London: Routledge, 1997. 1–37.

Weiss, Allan. "Offred's Complicity and the Dystopian Tradition in Margaret Atwood's *The Handmaid's Tale*." *Studies in Canadian Literature* 34.1 (2009): 120–41.

Wells, H. G. *Anticipations of the Reaction of Mechanical and Scientific Progress upon Human Life and Thought*. Mineola, NY: Dover, 1999.

_____. *The Shape of Things to Come*. London: Penguin, 2005.

_____. *A Story of the Days to Come. 3 Prophetic Science Fiction Novels of H. G. Wells*. Ed. E. F. Bleiler. New York: Dover, 1960.

Zamyatin, Yevgeny. *We*. Trans. Natasha Randall. New York: Mod. Lib., 2006.

Compare/Contrast: Media Culture, Conformism, and Commodification in Ray Bradbury's *Fahrenheit 451* and M. T. Anderson's *Feed*

M. Keith Booker

Ray Bradbury's *Fahrenheit 451* (1953) is in many ways a classic dystopian novel, somewhat in the vein of Yevgeny Zamyatin's *We* (1924) or George Orwell's *Nineteen Eighty-Four* (1949). However, among the founding texts of the modern dystopian genre, Bradbury's book probably has the most in common with Aldous Huxley's *Brave New World* (1932), in that both attribute the dystopian conditions they describe to the dehumanizing effects of a consumer capitalism that gradually converts everything into commodities, including human beings. In addition, Huxley presents the works of Shakespeare in opposition to the mind-numbing popular culture that reinforces consumerism in his future dystopia; similarly, Bradbury envisions books—or at least the kind of thoughtful, detailed examination of complex issues that can be found in the best books—as the most powerful potential antidote to dehumanizing consumerism.

Of course, *Fahrenheit 451* is now more than half a century old, and consumer capitalism has evolved considerably over that period of time—sometimes in ways the book seems to have anticipated, sometimes in ways it clearly did not. Meanwhile, M. T. Anderson's *Feed* (2002) is a much more recent dystopian novel that, though intended for a young-adult audience, explores more contemporary consumer capitalism in ways that can quite profitably be compared with such explorations in Bradbury's novel. Perhaps the most obvious of the parallels between the two books involves the role of the media in maintaining and promoting consumer capitalism. Both novels also set their consumerist dystopias against a background of coming apocalypse, in ways that usefully illustrate the differences in popular anxieties that informed the American societies from which the two books arose.

Bradbury's book presents a future dystopian society in which books have been officially banned due to fears that they might encourage an independence of thought that would be inimical to social tranquility. The protagonist is Guy Montag, a "fireman" whose job it is to seek out any existing books and destroy them by fire, along with the houses in which they are found. It is important to keep in mind that *Fahrenheit 451* is very much a text of its time; its elaboration of attempts to eliminate the individual imagination by banning books is typical of 1950s fears of forced conformism, while the entire text is set against a Cold War–style fear of nuclear holocaust. Indeed, such a holocaust occurs at the end of the book, which is probably its darkest aspect, made all the darker by the fact that Bradbury seems to regard this nuclear devastation as a positive event—a cleansing destruction of the oppressive anti-book society he describes, presumably clearing the way for a subsequent resurgence in book culture, even though it is not at all certain how nuclear war would facilitate such a resurgence.

The oppressive future America of *Feed*, on the other hand, operates in more sophisticated ways. Books, for example, are not banned; they have simply been rendered quaint and uninteresting in relation to the much hipper electronic cultural forms of the era. Meanwhile, there is a "Global Alliance" of countries aligned against the US quest for world dominance, posing a potential threat of cataclysmic conflict. However, the real threat looming over this society seems to be environmental, as the natural world has been largely destroyed by the excesses of precisely the same consumerist forces that remain dominant in the enclosed, artificial world in which its characters live. The circumscribed nature of this world is partly physical: the rich live in homes that are enclosed by individual domes to provide a livable (and programmable) environment, while the less fortunate live in neighborhoods enclosed in collective domes. One wonders, in fact, whether there might be even poorer people who struggle to live with no domes whatsoever, forced to encounter the toxic natural environment directly, but the logic of the book dictates that Titus, the privileged adolescent narrator/protagonist of the novel, would never encounter members of this underclass or probably even know of their existence, so readers have no way of learning about them either.

If *Fahrenheit 451*, while remaining relevant in the twenty-first century, is very much a book of the 1950s, the principal issues at stake in *Feed*, then, are very much of the early twenty-first century. In addition to the fact that the main apocalyptic fear is associated with environmental devastation rather than nuclear war, the central trope of the novel involves the eponymous "feed," a never-ending barrage of entertainment and information that is pumped directly into the minds of individuals via chips implanted in their brains, typically in infancy. As a result, individuals of Titus's generation, at least, have no experience of a world without the feed to guide them through it, as well as very little sense of their own identities apart from the ever-present voice of the feed inside their heads. Their identities are largely shaped by the feed, which constantly monitors their behavior and interests so that it can tailor its content, especially advertising, to individual tastes, even as it plays a central constitutive role in developing those tastes. Titus and his friends are thus quite dependent on the feed, a fact that becomes clear in their disorientation and discomfort early in the book when a hacker attack temporarily cuts them off.

Of course, this notion of a media-dominated society in which a never-ending stream of increasingly mindless (yet ever more powerful) imagery is pumped into the minds of individual citizens is an old dystopian trope, dating back at least to *Brave New World*. This motif is central to *Fahrenheit 451* as well, though with a distinctively 1950s flavor, in that the main media threat comes from a version of television, widely regarded during that decade as a destructive force that would lead to the dumbing down of American culture. Thus, while virtually everyone in the book has been taught to think and feel (or, more accurately, not to think and feel) in very much the same way, individuals find it virtually impossible to establish genuine communication with one another, preferring to sit dumbly alone in front of television screens rather than seek out human companionship.

Both *Fahrenheit 451* and *Feed* present us with strongly capitalist dystopias in which the oppressive system described largely involves the use of the media to further the consumerist agenda of the powers that be. Indeed, a comparison of these two texts provides, among other things, an interesting way to track the historical development of this phenomenon over the second half of the twentieth century. The feed, for example, is more than anything a marketing tool, constantly pumping advertising into the minds of individuals, who can then order the products advertised directly through the feed, in a more sophisticated version of today's online shopping. Meanwhile, in Bradbury's dystopian world, anything and everything is up for sale, including Jesus Christ himself, who is often shown on television endorsing commercial products. The character Faber, a former English professor who serves as a sort of voice of reason in the novel, notes that Christ is "a regular peppermint stick now, all sugar crystal and saccharine when he isn't making veiled references to certain commercial products that every worshipper *absolutely* needs" (Bradbury 88; italics in orig.).

Somewhat in the mode of the dystopian society of Huxley's *Brave New World*, Montag's America has replaced books with a never-ending stream of electronic broadcasts designed both to support the society's ruling ideology and, more simply, to keep the minds of individuals occupied and passive. To this end, all citizens carry small radio receivers so that they can receive these broadcasts at all times. Meanwhile, their homes are dominated by immersive three-dimensional television broadcasts that provide programming designed to compensate for the lack of any real emotional existence. Montag's own wife, Mildred, is particularly devoted to these programs, the characters in which she regards as members of her family.

This incessant flow of banal popular culture seems designed precisely to numb the minds of the populace, preventing them from experiencing any real thought or feeling, rather than stimulating these experiences, as we are accustomed to thinking of great works of literature as doing. At the same time, this popular culture has a leveling effect that tends to make all of its consumers think and feel in the same superficial ways, thus encouraging conformist behavior. As Jack Zipes notes,

> Bradbury wants to get at the roots of American conformity and immediately points a finger at the complicity of state and industry for using technology to produce television programs, gambling sports games, amusement parks, and advertising to block self-reflection and blank out the potential for alternative ways of living which do not conform to fixed national standards. (185)

Anderson's feed, of course, is much more advanced in its ability to literally get inside the heads of consumers. Meanwhile, the corporate-sponsored programming on the feed is reinforced by most of the input that individuals receive from the world around them, which is equally dominated by corporations. From the point of view of the young people on whom the book focuses, the most important of these corporate institutions is the educational system, which, by the time of the events of the book, has been completely privatized, leading to educational practices that drop virtually all pretense of doing anything but preparing students to become ideal consumers who will respond as expected to the cues they receive from the feed and other corporate sources.

The power of this system is indicated in the characterization of Titus, who resembles the typical dystopian protagonist in that he initially sees no problem with the system in which he lives, then meets and becomes fascinated by a girl (Violet) who has a number of problems with the system. Violet thus plays very much the same role in *Feed* that young Clarisse McClellan plays in *Fahrenheit 451*. However, while the free-thinking Clarisse inspires Montag to begin to challenge the premise of his work as a fireman and his society as a whole, Titus seems so thoroughly indoctrinated by the feed that he is never really able to conjure up any genuine resistance to its message, or to the system that this message helps perpetuate. And this remains the case even as this system leads to Violet's death; in the book's final scene, Titus stands beside Violet's deathbed, and though her death has literally been caused by the feed, her fate does little to inspire Titus to oppose the system, which goes on broadcasting unchecked into his brain. Detecting at this point that Titus is "feeling blue," Titus's feed segues this fact into an ad for the "Blue-Jean Warehouse," which is having a massive going-out-of-business sale in which "everything must go!" (Anderson 299). In fact, the book ends with four additional invocations of this last phrase, each in smaller type than the one before, which cannot help but call attention to the potential double message here. As Clare Bradford notes, this ending, beyond the literal advertising cliché, suggests a declaration that in order for conditions to improve, the entire technology-based society in which Titus and his friends live must be swept away to make room for a new beginning. Read this way, while it lacks the literally apocalyptic occurrence that ends *Fahrenheit 451*, *Feed* suggests a similarly pessimistic view of our modern world, with a similar need for a cleansing destruction of all that exists. In this particular sense, in fact, *Feed* is even more pessimistic than *Fahrenheit 451*; however problematic and misguided as a solution, the longed-for nuclear holocaust does come in the latter text, while *Feed* offers no real hope of escape from technological domination, other than a total environmental collapse from which there would likely be no recovery.

Jennifer Miskec also sees a thoroughgoing rejection of modernity in Anderson's text. Comparing *Feed* with Cory Doctorow's *Little Brother* (2008), Miskec concludes that "while Anderson longs for a time without technology, Doctorow endeavors to promote a critical eye toward our technology-centered society" (73). In particular, Miskec notes that in *Little Brother*, technology can serve as a tool of either oppression or resistance, while in *Feed*, technology seems to serve only the powers that be. *Feed* again resembles *Fahrenheit 451* in its suggestion that the best hope for resistance to high-tech oppression lies in a return to older, presumably more "human" forms of culture.

A general suspicion of technology, and the expectation that advanced technology is inevitably dehumanizing, is fairly typical of recent science fiction, though Bradbury was unusual among the science-fiction writers of his generation for the consistency with which he figured technology and modernity in general in a negative light. One might compare here his other major early Cold War work, *The Martian Chronicles* (1950), in which human colonists from a ravaged Earth get a fresh start on Mars, only to bring their consumerist mentalities with them and subsequently ravage that planet as well. Bradbury's favorite proposed alternative to modernity—a rather stereotypical vision of an old-time small-town America that never really existed—is highly problematic, sometimes even juvenile, leading science-fiction author and critic Thomas Disch to call Bradbury "a lifelong child impersonator of a stature equal to that of Pee-Wee Herman" (81).

Having said that, *Fahrenheit 451* is nevertheless a very special book, especially for book lovers, for whom the vision of books as a crucial tool against oppression has to be heartening. Of course, one could argue that a book that recommends the reading of books is the ultimate example of preaching to the choir, given that it can best deliver its message to those who already understand the value of reading. Bradbury's book, however, has a special value, both as a historical document (because it so vividly reflects many of the characteristic concerns of the 1950s) and as an example of thoughtful meditation on the future (because its anticipation of the future looks so prescient to us more than half a century later).

On the other hand, if Bradbury seems to have anticipated the growing power of media culture, he appears to blame consumers themselves for preferring such a culture, while paying little attention to the power of the culture industry to mold the tastes of its audiences. Thus, in the future dystopia of *Fahrenheit 451*, the oppressive conditions are maintained largely because the majority of the population seem to prefer it that way, finding television more entertaining than books in any case. Faber, again seemingly acting as Bradbury's spokesman, notes that "the firemen are rarely necessary. The public itself stopped reading of its own accord. You firemen provide a circus now and then at which buildings are set off and crowds gather for the pretty blaze, but it's a small sideshow indeed, and hardly necessary to keep things in line" (Bradbury 94).

In any case, the book burnings of *Fahrenheit 451* are clearly intended partly as entertainment, designed to procure the complicity of the general population in the burning of books and the persecution of readers. Their purpose is more symbolic than it is literally to destroy all books, which have already been rendered ineffectual by the general population's lack of interest in reading them. Bradbury, of course, also uses the book burnings as a symbol to make his own points, knowing that the image of burning books has a great deal of power in our society. In so doing, however, he seems to use the popularity of book burnings as an indictment of the kind of popular taste that would appreciate such a spectacle, rather than as a suggestion of the power of the government to manipulate individual tastes. The masses, in short, lack the intellectual power to appreciate the books that are being burned. As Zipes notes, "The dystopian constellation of conflict in *Fahrenheit 451* is not really constituted by the individual versus the state, but the intellectual versus the masses" (191).

In addition, Bradbury has Montag's supervisor in the fire department, Captain Beatty, explain to Montag that although the burning of books is now official policy, it actually began as a popular movement on the part of various minorities to ban books that they found to be offensive, with the resulting pressure causing authors to try to produce inoffensive works in order to avoid such controversies and thus reach larger audiences. This trend led to the production of more and more superficial works until finally full-length books fell out of fashion altogether, replaced by comic books, magazines, and television—all of which, according to Beatty, came about as a result of the insipidity of popular taste (Bradbury 61).

Granted, Beatty may not be an exemplary figure, but Bradbury's 1979 afterword to the book makes very much the same point, arguing that the giants of the Western literary tradition—including Shakespeare, Dante, Milton, and apparently himself—would not have been able to reach the heights they did if they had allowed "the minorities, be they dwarf or giant, orangutan or dolphin, nuclear-head or water-conservationalist, pro-computerologist or neo-Luddite, simpleton or sage, to interfere with aesthetics" (183). If minorities do not like the books produced by such writers, concludes Bradbury, they should write their own.

This contempt for the masses and for minorities is one of the least attractive aspects of Bradbury's book, and the contempt expressed in the book (again through Faber) for the "unmoving cattle of the majority" is highly problematic. Nevertheless, the critique of mass culture in *Fahrenheit 451* is very much in tune with any number of critiques of the massification of American culture in the 1950s from both the Right and the Left, most of them triggered especially by the rise of television in that decade. What is most impressive about *Fahrenheit 451* is that it appeared so early in the 1950s, anticipating so many trends in American popular culture at a time when television was only just beginning to become a significant cultural force in the United States.

This is not, of course, to say that there is no opposition to the official view in *Fahrenheit 451*. There remains a substantial minority of individuals who secretly hold on to their books, and thus presumably to their humanity. Indeed, it is this very fact that makes Montag's job as a fireman possible. Of course, this job continually puts Montag into contact with books and "book people," ultimately resulting in his own rejection of the official culture of his society and acceptance of book culture.

In the final analysis, however, it would be a mistake to see Bradbury's book as positioning television as commodified culture against books as emancipatory culture in any simplistic way. After all, books have not been entirely banned in Bradbury's dystopia: comic books and sex magazines are still allowed. It is, Bradbury stipulates, the content of a medium that determines its effect, not the physical form itself. Thus Faber explains to Montag that it is not the books themselves that are powerful but the things in the books. Further, he argues that the same things could be put into television programming, should someone only choose to do so. "The same infinite detail and awareness could be projected through the radios and televisors, but are not. . . . Books were only one type of receptacle where we stored a lot of things we were afraid we might forget. There is nothing magical in them at all. The magic is only in what books say, how they stitched the patches of the universe together into one garment for us" (Bradbury 89–90).

This important suggestion that television could be as profound as books, if only those in control of programming chose to make it so, is reminiscent of the important cultural critic and theorist Raymond Williams's comments in one of the first serious book-length critical studies of television as a medium, published in 1974. Williams, echoing Bradbury's dystopian formulation of television, argues that television broadcasting "can be diagnosed as a new and powerful form of social integration and control. Many of its main uses can be seen as socially, commercially and at times politically manipulative" (17). At the same time, Williams repeatedly warns us against the simple-minded "technological determinism" of assuming that the poor quality of television programming is determined by the characteristics of television as a medium. Instead, Williams insists that television programming has developed in the way it has, not because of properties inherent in the technology, but in response to certain specific social, economic, and political stimuli. For Williams, then, television retains powerful utopian dimensions: change the stimuli and television itself can change. Thus, the content of television programming and the evolution of television as a medium are not simply driven by the available technology but are in fact "a matter of social and cultural definition, according to the ends sought" (137).

Williams's comments help us to see that Bradbury does not necessarily reject television out of hand, simply a particular kind of television programming. Williams's remarks also suggest that Anderson, while outlining the negative consequences of an excessive reliance on technology in *Feed*, does not necessarily recommend doing away with technology altogether. It is certainly the case that Anderson presents us with a wrecked and ruined future world and that unrestrained uses of technology have no doubt contributed in central ways to this condition.

The world of *Feed* features extremely advanced technologies. In addition to the crucial feed technology itself and the enclosed environments in which people live on earth, travel to the moon has become routine (though still expensive), mostly for recreational purposes. Meanwhile, those who can afford it, like Titus and his family, travel about in the flying cars that were once a central icon of science fiction's visions of futuristic technologies, although they have since become widely regarded as a key example of naive and unrealistic expectations of future technological development.

One of the crucial messages of *Feed*, in fact, involves the idea that the extremely advanced level of technology available in this society does not seem to have been wisely used in either a physical or a social way. Despite this technology, the earth's environment has still been destroyed, and little effort seems to be under way to correct that situation. Meanwhile, if anything, technology development seems to have widened the gap between the rich and the poor by granting the former access to much better technologies than the latter—a sharp contrast to the vision of science-fiction classics such as the *Star Trek* television series, in which technological advancement has enabled a truly egalitarian society based on universal affluence. Indeed, one suspects that the particularly iconic nature of the technology represented in *Feed* (perhaps especially the flying cars) is meant precisely to call attention to itself and signal to readers that the technology here has a satirical function. For example, why can a society that features such cars not do something to improve the environment? One answer, of course, might be that environmental decay has reached a tipping point and there is simply nothing to be done. Still, this society is so decadent and irresponsible that people seem almost to enjoy having a ruined natural environment, as it provides a setting for hazardous recreations whenever the bored inhabitants venture out of their enclosed, protected worlds. Thus, late in the novel, Titus's father accompanies other executives from his company on a "corporate adventure," a whale-hunting trip (emblematic of the human destruction of nature) in which they heartlessly kill a whale that has been "laminat[ed]" in order to allow it to live in the caustic ocean waters (Anderson 280–81).

Of course, one reason why the citizens of the world of *Feed* seem so clueless about what is happening to their world is that the feed itself insulates them from it. Also crucial here is perhaps the greatest failure of this society to make use of its available technology: they have a truly dismal education system, despite the fact that the feed technology should provide spectacular opportunities to educate children by pumping knowledge directly into their brains. Instead, in a particularly pointed instance of social commentary in the novel, this society has abandoned public education altogether, ceding that important function to corporate management. And, of course, this corporate-run education system is interested less in educating students than in stupefying them, preparing them to become ideal consumers: passive and unquestioning recipients of the corporate messages that the feed will supply to them throughout the rest of their lives. Thus, despite their immediate access to unlimited amounts of information, the inhabitants of this future society have very little understanding of that information, as Titus makes clear when he explains that "everyone is supersmart now. You can look things up automatic, like science and history, like if you want to know which battles of the Civil War George Washington fought in and shit" (Anderson 47).

Feed, while largely intended for a young-adult audience, is thus somewhat more sophisticated than *Fahrenheit 451* in its understanding of the way popular culture works, perhaps because Anderson had access to the results of an additional fifty years of American media culture, while that culture was still in its formative stages when Bradbury wrote *Fahrenheit 451*. In any case, and for whatever reason, Anderson seems to understand better than Bradbury that while mass audiences might enjoy mind-numbing popular culture, they do so largely because this is the kind of culture they have been conditioned to appreciate.

Feed suggests that this conditioning is so effective that book burnings such as those envisioned in *Fahrenheit 451* are entirely unnecessary. If the firemen are rarely necessary in Bradbury's book, they are never necessary in Anderson's. Books have not been banned in Anderson's future America, just as having the feed chips implanted in one's brain is not required. Yet the culture is such that books have been rendered largely irrelevant, while the installation of feed chips is nearly universal—at least for those who can afford it. Thus, while Anderson's dystopia does allow for a certain amount of resistance to the mainstream culture, that resistance has been rendered almost entirely ineffectual. Even Titus, who is not exactly well informed, knows that his world is dominated by profit-seeking corporations, and he grants that he and everyone else know that these corporations are "evil"; they simply do not care, because the corporations are "the only way to get all this stuff, and it's no good getting pissy about it" (Anderson 48–49).

Meanwhile, Anderson's alternative to the privatized education and commodified information of this future America is in many ways very much the same as Bradbury's alternative to television: good old-fashioned books. Violet, as it turns out, is the daughter of a countercultural professor who has brought her up to challenge the received values of her materialistic society and who, among other things, greatly values the wisdom to be found in books. If Violet is somewhat like Clarisse in *Fahrenheit 451*, her father plays the role of Faber.

However, in a somewhat amusing commentary on the arc of American society in the half century between Bradbury's book and Anderson's, Violet's father is a professor not of English but of "dead" computer languages like FORTRAN and BASIC.

The nearly illiterate Titus is initially amazed to find that Violet can actually write—with a pen, on paper—a skill that has been rendered almost obsolete by the digitalization of virtually all communication (65). Later, when Titus goes to visit Violet in her home (so modest compared to his family's fancy abode), he discovers a world that seems to him just plain weird, a home that functions almost as a museum of the written culture of the past: "The place was a mess. Everything had words on it. There were papers with words on them, and books, and even posters on the wall had words" (135). Violet's father even intentionally speaks in florid and archaic ways in order to combat the debasement of the English language via the feed, though this makes him seem all the more like a harmless kook, rather than a subversive threat to the system (137). One senses, in fact, that his particular form of rebellion will do little to halt the decline of the language—or anything else. He has certainly been marginalized in this society, as, to an extent, has Violet, who never quite fits in with Titus and his friends because of her somewhat old-fashioned attitudes.

Partly because of the expense and partly because of ideological objections, Violet was not implanted until the age of seven, which has caused her implant not to integrate itself into her consciousness as effectively as it does with most children. As a result of this fact, as well as her general upbringing, Violet is less blindly addicted to the feed than are the other teenagers in the book. For example, she amuses herself by conducting completely random and eccentric searches on the feed to try to defeat its attempts to build a personalized customer profile for her. Ultimately, though, she suffers from her marginal position; the hacker attack that temporarily cuts Titus and his other friends off from the feed early in the book initiates a deterioration in Violet's feed that leads to a fatal brain disease. Meanwhile, the corporation that provided her implant refuses to accept any responsibility for her condition or provide any treatment for it, making clear the heartless and inhumane attitudes of the corporate masters of this future world.

As the book ends, these masters are still firmly in control, with no end to their rule in sight—at least not from internal opposition, even though it seems clear that environmental decay, foreign enemies, or some combination of the two will surely bring about the ultimate demise of feed-fed America. Anderson's book is thus ultimately more chilling than Bradbury's. The subtly oppressive society of *Feed* has individuals far more thoroughly in its grip than does the more overtly oppressive society of *Fahrenheit 451*, and it seems far less likely to be superseded by something better. Both books, though, detail very similar phenomena involving the crucial role of the media in the growing commodification of every aspect of American life, which only became more intense in the time between the writing of the two books.

Works Cited

Anderson, M. T. *Feed*. Cambridge, MA: Candlewick, 2004.

Bradbury, Ray. *Fahrenheit 451*. New York: Ballantine, 1979.

Bradford, Clare. "'Everything Must Go!' Consumerism and Reader Positioning in M. T. Anderson's *Feed*." *Jeunesse: Young People, Texts, Cultures* 2.2 (2010): 128–37.

Disch, Thomas M. *The Dreams Our Stuff Is Made Of: How Science Fiction Conquered the World*. New York: Free, 1998.

Miskec, Jennifer. "*Feed* vs. *Little Brother*: The Same, Only Different." *Radical Teacher* 90.1 (2011): 72–73.

Williams, Raymond. *Television: Technology and Cultural Form*. New York: Schocken, 1975.

Zipes, Jack. "Mass Degradation of Humanity and Massive Contradictions in Bradbury's Vision of America in *Fahrenheit 451*." *No Place Else: Explorations in Utopian and Dystopian Fiction*. Ed. Eric S. Rabkin, Martin H. Greenberg, and Joseph D. Olander. Carbondale: Southern Illinois UP, 1983. 182–98.

CRITICAL READINGS

Science, Politics, and Utopia in George Orwell's *Nineteen Eighty-Four*_____

Tony Burns

Introduction

This chapter will address George Orwell's understanding of the relationship between science and politics in his novel *Nineteen Eighty-Four* (1949) and in his essays and journalism. I shall begin by saying something about the broader theme of science and politics in the history of utopian and dystopian literature, and the ways in which that theme has been handled by historians of utopian/dystopian thought and literature, before turning to make just a few remarks about Orwell and *Nineteen Eighty-Four* and how they fit into this broader picture.

Science and Politics in the History of Utopian/Dystopian Thought and Literature

As M. Keith Booker has rightly observed, "science has played a major role in the history of utopian thinking," and especially in "the modern turn from utopia to dystopia" (5). From the time of Plato onward, one of the issues that have been of interest to writers associated with the utopian/dystopian literary tradition has been the role of "experts" in society, that is, the political implications of the fact that knowledge and expertise are a monopoly held in the hands of a relatively small, elite group of people—such as the philosophers of the ancient world, the priesthood associated with the Catholic Church in medieval Europe, and the scientists of the modern era—who are regarded as the producers of knowledge.

Over two thousand years ago, in his *Republic* (which, rightly or wrongly, is often considered to be the first great work of utopian literature), Plato suggested that a society ruled by experts, in his case philosophers, would undoubtedly be a good thing. Much later, in western Europe from roughly the seventeenth century onward, a number of utopian writers were to take the same view, only in their case it was scientists who ought to rule, not philosophers. Since that time, what Krishan Kumar has termed the idea of a "scientific utopia" or a "utopia of science" has been a core theme for writers working within the utopian/dystopian tradition (*Utopianism* 46–47, 53–59).

For example, an optimistic belief in the potential benefits of science and scientific knowledge was central to the seventeenth-century utopian thinking of Sir Francis Bacon, whose *New Atlantis*, published in 1627, postulated the existence of a utopian society ruled not by philosophers but by scientists. More recently, in the first half of the twentieth century, science was also associated with the utopian writings of H. G. Wells, who thought that history was taking humanity in the direction of a harmonious and benevolent cosmopolis or "World State" that would be ruled by scientists in order to promote the welfare and happiness of all (Wagar). Wells's utopianism can fairly be accused of *scientism*— that is to say, a naive or overoptimistic belief in the benefits of science; the belief that science and rule by scientists can provide the solution to all of mankind's problems. It is this type of thinking in general, and that of Wells in particular, that was the main target of attack for the authors of some of the great works of dystopian literature published in the first half of the twentieth century, including both Yevgeny Zamyatin's *We* (1924) and Aldous Huxley's *Brave New World* (1932) (Hillegas). My main claim here is that it is also fruitful to read Orwell's *Nineteen Eighty-Four* in this way—not so much as a critique of utopianism, or even of the utopianism of Wells, but more specifically as a critique of scientism and of the idea of a scientific utopia as Wells understood it.

There has been at least some discussion of the general theme of the scientific utopia, but not by any means as much as one would expect or as much as the topic merits, given its obvious importance. The works of Alexandra Aldridge, René Dubos, Nell Eurich, Everett Mendelsohn, and Helga Nowotny are especially significant in this regard. There has been even less discussion of this theme as it is played out in the writings of Orwell; for example, in a recent brief bibliographical essay devoted to "Eutopias and Dystopias of Science," Lyman Tower Sargent refers to the works of Zamyatin and Huxley cited above but does not even mention Orwell. Perhaps even more surprising is the fact that despite Everett Mendelsohn and Helga Nowotny's edited collection on this subject being entitled *Nineteen Eighty-Four: Between Science and Dystopia* (1984), it does not contain a single chapter devoted to Orwell's work. René Dubos's general survey of the theme of science and utopia does not mention Orwell at all, so there is nothing to say about it, other than that the omission is disappointing.

Nell Eurich's *Science in Utopia: A Mighty Design*, published in 1967, is a sustained discussion of the idea of the scientific utopia and its history from the seventeenth century onward. Eurich's main focus is on works of utopian rather than dystopian literature, and she says little about Orwell. Nevertheless, what she does say is certainly of some interest. Eurich maintains that "in the first quarter of the 17th century," a number of utopian theorists, including Johann Valentin Andreae, Francis Bacon, and Tommaso Campanella, came "to the conclusion that the new age of mankind was to be the result of science and the new learning." According to Eurich, although this new approach to utopian theorizing and writing, which was based on a "creative adoption of scientific discoveries" of the seventeenth century, "did not instantly blot out all other views of utopia," nevertheless it did prove "to be the main road to the future" (102) that utopian thought and writing has traveled since that time—at least until the emergence of the genre of dystopian fiction in the early years of the twentieth century, which Eurich associates especially with *Brave New World* and *Nineteen Eighty-Four*.

More to the point for present purposes, however, is the fact that Eurich associates Orwell not only with a dystopian critique of utopianism but more specifically with a critique of a certain kind of utopianism: the "utopianism of science" she writes about in her book. For example, according to Eurich, one of the main themes of Orwell's novel is the way in which "the individual" in contemporary society is increasingly coming to be "controlled by the new [scientific] knowledge," which is held "in the hands of a few leaders" (260). Eurich notes, for example, that *Nineteen Eighty-Four* depicts a world in which science is "sterile," because "no empirical or questioning habits of thought are permitted." She emphasizes the significance of Winston Smith's observation in his diary that "the official language of Oceania, 'Newspeak,' has no word for 'science'" (259). More generally, she maintains that Orwell is particularly interested in the idea that "science is taking over the reins of control" in contemporary society and "becoming all powerful, to the detriment of man," thereby reducing him to "the status of a robot." For Orwell, based on Eurich's account of his views, the result of "the progress Bacon anticipated" in his *New Atlantis* is "man the automaton" (260).

Eurich claims that *Nineteen Eighty-Four* is best seen specifically as a critique of the idea of a scientific utopia. According to her, this critique lies at the heart of Orwell's novel, marking the terminus of a process of historical development that started with the scientific utopias of Andreae, Bacon, and Campanella; in Eurich's own words, "these 17th-century utopists stand at the beginning of a line of thought for which Orwell and Huxley demonstrate the end" (260). Her book hints at a possible reading of *Nineteen Eighty-Four* that both merits and requires further discussion. What Eurich does not do, however, is provide her thesis with an adequate defense. Nor would it be possible to do so, of course, in just the three pages of text that she devotes to this issue.

Alexandra Aldridge's *The Scientific World View in Dystopia* (1984) is the most systematic attempt made so far to address the relationship between science and politics in twentieth-century works of dystopian literature. However, although Aldridge's book does contain chapters on Wells, Zamyatin, and Huxley, it does not have a separate chapter devoted to the work of Orwell and *Nineteen Eighty-Four*. Surprisingly, Aldridge does not consider *Nineteen Eighty-Four* to be a work of dystopian literature (78–80). Consequently, she considers it as falling outside the bounds of her study and dismisses Orwell's work in a two-page appendix, the purpose of which is not to offer her readers an account of how Orwell and *Nineteen Eighty-Four* fit her general thesis but rather to justify her exclusion of the novel from her examination of the issue. Like Sargent, then, Aldridge cannot see how Orwell's *Nineteen Eighty-Four* could be connected to a discussion of utopias and dystopias of science.

As noted above, Mendelsohn and Nowotny's *Nineteen Eighty-Four: Between Science and Dystopia* does not have a chapter on Orwell. Nevertheless, it does contain a general survey by J. C. Davis devoted to the general theme of science and utopia in the history of utopian thought and literature in the early modern period; this survey does at least mention *Nineteen Eighty-Four*, though only twice, and in passing (39, 47).

Davis's essay addresses the general issue of the compatibility or incompatibility of science and utopianism. According to Davis, utopian writers have a tendency to associate the notion of utopia with that of a perfect and therefore static society, because one cannot improve on perfection (34). At the same time, however, he argues that science is a dynamic, not static, phenomenon. The pursuit of scientific knowledge has a history, and there is no reason to think that in this area there will ever be an "end" of history, a situation in which final or absolute knowledge has been attained and no further improvement or progress is possible. One of the main points adduced by Davis in his contribution is that there is, therefore, a contradiction or "dilemma" inherent in the very idea of a scientific utopia (21). Davis argues that science, understood as an inherently dynamic phenomenon, and utopia, understood as a static society in which there is "complete social stability," are incompatible with one another. In his view, the pursuit of "scientific knowledge" in the strict sense of the term, or properly understood, is necessarily "subversive of utopia" (34). Davis notes, however, that this is not the view of science that was taken by the authors of the scientific utopias of the seventeenth century, all of whom believed that science delivers the final and absolute truth regarding the issues with which it deals. He maintains that in a number of early scientific utopias, such as Campanella's *City of the Sun* (1623), "we are shown the results of scientific inquiry, fixed, complete, finished, an immutable orthodoxy in which there is no longer any role for scientific research" (33; see also Kumar, *Utopia* 35–37).

Davis's general thesis regarding science and utopia in the history of utopian literature is of great interest, but he says relatively little about how this theme is played out in works of twentieth-century dystopian fiction, mentioning the issue only in passing. Moreover, when alluding to it, his preferred text for purposes of illustration is *Brave New World*, not *Nineteen Eighty-Four*. Davis notes, for example, that in Huxley's text, the world controller Mustapha Mond "sees science as a menace to stability" (37). As far as Orwell is concerned, Davis confines himself to the single observation, expressed in a footnote, that in *Nineteen Eighty-Four*, "Newspeak has no word for science" (47). Davis makes no sustained attempt to consider the relevance of *Nineteen Eighty-Four* to his general thesis about the relationship between science and utopianism. Nor, turning this around, does he consider the relevance of his general thesis for readers of Orwell's *Nineteen Eighty-Four*. There is, therefore, much more that could be said about this issue.

It is fairly clear that the works of Zamyatin and Huxley can and should be read as critiques of the idea of a scientific utopia, in one sense of the term. However, as we saw above when commenting on the work of Lyman Tower Sargent and Alexandra Aldridge, it has seemed much less clear to a number of commentators that Orwell's *Nineteen Eighty-Four* can and should also be read in this way. In the next section, I shall say just a few things that seem to me to be relevant in this regard.

Science and Politics in Orwell's *Nineteen Eighty-Four*

As with the dialogue between John Savage and Mustapha Mond in Huxley's *Brave New World*, it is fruitful to think of that between Winston Smith and O'Brien in Orwell's *Nineteen Eighty-Four* as capturing the essence of what the novel is about. What exactly do Winston Smith and O'Brien disagree about in their dialogue? It is arguable that the questions at issue between them are philosophical questions having to do, not overtly and explicitly with social affairs or politics, but rather with our knowledge of the natural world—that is, with natural science.

Orwell has a reputation as a writer who had little time or aptitude for theoretical abstractions. Stephen Ingle, for example, has claimed that Orwell "had no great capacity for philosophical thought" (124). Samuel Hynes has claimed that "the evolution of modern science held none of the fascination for Orwell that it did for H. G. Wells" (14). And George Woodcock has argued that Orwell "did not have a scientific mind" and that "the abstractions of mathematics," in particular, "made little appeal to him" (170).

Nevertheless, it is arguable that *Nineteen Eighty-Four* is a deeply philosophical novel. In it, Orwell addresses issues that are usually discussed in the philosophy of science. Examples of such questions include the following: What is knowledge? What constitutes scientific knowledge? How is scientific knowledge produced? Do the beliefs associated with scientific knowledge necessarily provide a true explanation of things? If so, what is it that makes those beliefs true? Are they true because they correspond to or reflect external reality, or for some other reason? How do we know that they are true? And so on.

At the same time, however, it must also be conceded that Orwell is primarily interested in the ethical and political implications of the positions that can be and have been taken up with respect to these questions. Given that the literary treatment of such issues is often associated with the genre of science fiction, it is not at all surprising that many commentators have for this reason claimed that Orwell's *Nineteen Eighty-Four* is a work of science fiction (Amis 17, 78, 91, 153; Bould 1, 17; Roberts 209).

Perhaps the best way to illustrate this point is to refer not to Orwell's use of the example of the proposition that $2 + 2 = 4$, but rather to what he says about a different issue taken from the discipline of astronomy. Here I have in mind the disagreement between Winston Smith and O'Brien over the issue of heliocentrism, the question of whether the earth revolves around the sun or the sun around the earth. When discussing this issue, O'Brien maintains to Winston Smith that "the earth is the centre of the universe" and "the sun and the stars go around it." He concedes that "for certain purposes," it is "convenient to assume" that the opposite is true, "that the earth goes round the sun" and not vice versa. "But," he says, "what of it?" The fact that this is so does not undermine the validity of either claim, each of which can justifiably be considered to be "true," depending on the circumstances (213).

In this interchange between Smith and O'Brien, Orwell explicitly alludes to the debate that took place between Galileo Galilei, a key figure in the first scientific revolution of the seventeenth century, and the Catholic Church, whose priesthood had been the dominant "knowledge producers" in Europe throughout the medieval period and still were at that time. Church orthodoxy defended the view of Aristotle and Ptolemy that the earth stood at the center of the universe and the sun revolved around it, whereas Galileo, due to empirical observations, shared the view of the astronomer Copernicus that the opposite was the case. Because this view challenged church orthodoxy, Galileo was called to Rome, where he was interrogated by the Inquisition and his views were declared heretical. Having been shown the instruments of torture used by the Inquisition, Galileo recanted and promised that he would never express his views publicly again.

In the twentieth century, the issue of Galileo's conflict with the church was much discussed by authors with an interest in the philosophy and politics of science, some creative writers and some not (Kuhn; Feyerabend, *Against Method* and *Science*). The passage from *Nineteen Eighty-Four* cited above indicates that Orwell attached great importance to this issue, which he also refers to on a number of occasions in his essays ("Prevention" 83, 89, 91; "Literature" 162–63). For instance, he says at one point that "a totalitarian state" of the kind depicted in *Nineteen Eighty-Four* "is in effect a theocracy," and that "its ruling caste," just like that of the Catholic Church at the time of Galileo, "in order to keep its position, has to be thought of as infallible" ("Prevention" 86). Booker has rightly observed that "many of the Party's objections to science" expressed by O'Brien in *Nineteen Eighty-Four* "echo those of the medieval Church" (70).

In this respect, as in so many others, Orwell may be seen as following the lead of Zamyatin, who also refers to the example of Galileo's conflict with the church, both in his novel *We* (168) and in his essays ("On Literature"; see also Burns, *Political Theory* 4, 84, 87–89, 91–94, 99–102). Although it is not even mentioned by Eurich, Zamyatin's *We* is of course widely considered to be the prototype for any critique of the idea of a scientific utopia.

Like Zamyatin before him, Orwell thought of Galileo as the archetypal example of a modern scientific "heretic" (Zamyatin, "On Literature" 108), and he portrays Smith in just this way in *Nineteen Eighty-Four*. Connecting the debate between Smith and O'Brien in the novel to the debate between Galileo and Cardinal Bellarmine, the Grand Inquisitor who interrogated him, is a striking way of illustrating its significance for the novel as a whole. From this point of view, O'Brien can be thought of as putting Smith and his views on mathematics, science, and philosophy "to the question," just as the Inquisition did to Galileo. In both cases, what lie at the very heart of the debate are philosophical issues relating to the notions of science and scientific knowledge, and in both cases, these philosophical issues are also thought of as being questions of politics.

In particular, these issues have to do with power, specifically the nature of power and its different forms and uses. These include, of course, the means of physical coercion or torture, something that Orwell considered to be central to totalitarianism. However, they also include such things as the ability to engineer consent by various mechanisms of thought control, including ideological manipulation. Orwell evidently agreed with Sir Francis Bacon that knowledge, specifically scientific knowledge, is power. However, not surprisingly, his understanding of the meaning of this phrase and its political significance was somewhat different from that of his seventeenth-century predecessor, just as it is somewhat different from that of a later figure such as Michel Foucault, who also has a great deal to say about the issue of knowledge and power.

Evidence that Orwell had a keen interest in questions of this kind is also to be found in his essays. For example, in an essay entitled "What Is Science?" published in 1945, Orwell says a number of things about science and politics that are significant for our efforts to understand his concerns in *Nineteen Eighty-Four*. In this essay, Orwell is interested in the politics of science, especially the issue of the possible uses and abuses of power by scientists in contemporary society. Like the nineteenth-century anarchist Mikhail Bakunin in his essay "On Authority," and more recently Jean-Francois Lyotard in his *The Postmodern Condition* (1979), Orwell in this essay discusses "the danger of a 'scientific hierarchy'" emerging in contemporary society ("What Is" 26). Orwell objects here to the attitude of mind that earlier I termed scientism, upon which scientific utopias are often thought to be based. According to those who embrace this attitude, scientific knowledge can provide the solution to all of mankind's problems. Such people, in Orwell's own words, think that the world "would be a better place if the scientists were in control of it" (28).

As we have seen, Orwell associates this attitude with one form of utopianism, the scientific utopianism of the later Wells, and he is extremely critical of it (Orwell, "Wells"). He argues that those who think this way assume that "if one has been scientifically trained one's approach to *all* subjects will be more intelligent than if one had had no such training" (Orwell, "What Is" 27; italics in orig.). Consequently, they also assume that "a scientist's political opinions" or his or her "opinions on sociological questions, on morals, on philosophy, perhaps even on the arts, will be more valuable than those of a layman." Orwell is skeptical about these assumptions. He asks whether it is "really true that a 'scientist,' in this narrower sense, is any likelier than other people to approach non-scientific problems in an objective way" and answers that "there is not much reason for thinking so" (28).

This essay also provides us with a good understanding of what Orwell considers to be the "scientific attitude," or the basic approach to all questions he associates with modern science from the time of Galileo onward. Orwell argues that this attitude involves a certain "way of looking at the world." In his view, a scientific education means, or "ought to mean," the "implanting of a rational, sceptical, experimental habit of mind"—that is to say, "acquiring a *method*—a method that can be used on any problem that one meets" ("What Is" 29; italics in orig.). To think scientifically is to employ a certain "method of thought which obtains verifiable results by reasoning logically from observed fact" (27). Unlike the anarchist philosopher of science Paul Feyerabend, then, Orwell is not by any means "against method."

Elsewhere, Orwell associates the scientific attitude with what he calls "the liberal habit of mind," which he contrasts with that of "totalitarianism." He maintains that those who, like Galileo, share this habit of mind think of scientific truth "as something outside yourself, something to be discovered, and not as something you can make up as you go along" ("As I Please" 111). In Orwell's opinion, those who have the scientific attitude think that "correct knowledge" or scientific truth is something that is valuable for its own sake, or "as a matter of course" ("Prevention" 86). Such people are, Orwell maintains, prepared to concede "that a fact may be true even if you"—or anybody else, such as the Catholic Church in the seventeenth century or the Communist Party in the Soviet Union under Stalin—"don't like it" ("As I Please" 109).

It is clear from this that in Orwell's view, the intellectual climate in totalitarian states, like that of Oceania in *Nineteen Eighty-Four*, is not conducive to science or the practice of scientific research. For Orwell just as much as for Feyerabend, science can only flourish in a free society. It is also clear, turning the point around, that in Orwell's view, the pursuit of scientific knowledge—associated as it is with the liberal values of individualism, freedom of thought, and freedom of speech or expression—necessarily poses a threat to the order and stability of any totalitarian state. It is for this very reason that in *Nineteen*

Eighty-Four, Newspeak has no word for science, and "the empirical method of thought, on which all the scientific achievements of the past were founded, is opposed to the most fundamental principles of Ingsoc" (Orwell, *Nineteen Eighty-Four* 156).

J. C. Davis refers to Orwell's *Nineteen Eighty-Four* as being similar to other "twentieth century 'scientifically' based social constructs" (that is, works of dystopian fiction), such as Zamyatin's *We* and Huxley's *Brave New World*, because it contains a "rebel" against an allegedly utopian world of science and reason. According to Davis, in the case of all three of these works of dystopian literature, this act of rebellion "is not only profoundly anti-social or criminal" but "also anti-scientific" (39). In Davis's opinion, then, although it is indeed fruitful to read *Nineteen Eighty-Four* as a contribution to a discussion of the general issue of science and politics in utopia or as a critique of the idea of a scientific utopia, nevertheless the significance of our doing so is that its author, who on this reading is assumed to sympathize with the views expressed by Smith and not with those of O'Brien, is thereby revealed as being not only an anti-utopian thinker but also an antiscientific one. Indeed, according to Davis's interpretation, Orwell's (alleged) rejection of utopianism in *Nineteen Eighty-Four* can be connected to his (alleged) rejection of science. Davis suggests that it is precisely because Orwell is hostile to science that he is also hostile to Wells's utopianism.

In my view, however, this interpretation of Orwell is mistaken, not least because it associates the views of Orwell with those of O'Brien rather than those of Smith. Orwell was not antiscience. This is very clear from the very positive things that he says about science in the essay cited above. It seems to me that Booker is much closer to the mark when he says that although for Orwell, "certain mechanical applications of technology lend themselves directly to political oppression," nevertheless in his view "science itself remains a potentially liberating realm of free thought" (70). Against Davis, it might be argued that Orwell was opposed not to science per se but to scientism, which is not at all the same thing. Nor is Orwell's antipathy toward scientism necessarily associated with anti-utopianism. It would be more accurate to say that Orwell objects not to utopianism as such but simply to the idea of a scientific utopia as it is to be found in the writings of Wells.

Like Zamyatin, Orwell has a tendency to associate the idea of a scientific utopia with totalitarianism. Turning this idea around, however, we may say that, again like Zamyatin, Orwell associates totalitarianism not with science itself but rather with a certain way of thinking about science and scientific truth. We have seen that Orwell associates the "liberal attitude of mind," which in his view is also that of science and of scientists, with the notion of truth (see Conant, "Freedom," "Rorty"; Rorty, *Contingency* 169–88, "Response."). In his view, the idea of science, properly understood, has to do with the pursuit of a certain kind of truth that is valued for its own sake. What Orwell is thinking of here is the notion of objective truth.

To illustrate this, in *Nineteen Eighty-Four* Orwell uses the well-known example of the proposition that "two plus two make four" (67–68, 200–207, 222–24). Part of what Orwell has in mind when referring to this proposition as an example of an objective truth is that in his view, the truths of science, like the proposition $2 + 2 = 4$, are both timeless and universal. According to Orwell, if a proposition does indeed express a scientific truth or a fact, then what it expresses does not depend on one's perspective or point of view; rather, it must be true for anybody and everybody, in all societies at all times and in all places. Orwell believed that it makes no sense to claim that $2 + 2 = 4$ is true only for men but not for women, or only for fascists but not for communists, or only in twentieth-century Europe but not in ancient Greece—just as, in his view, it would make no sense to say that Newton's law of gravity operates in England but not anywhere else, or that it did not operate until Newton discovered it.

In short, so far as the concept of truth is concerned, Orwell's understanding of science is objectivist and not relativist. It is also that of a common-sense "realist" (Clark; van Inwagen). Orwell suggests that for relativists, there can be no difference between what is really true, on the one hand, and what is merely believed to be true on the other. As Orwell has O'Brien point out in *Nineteen Eighty-Four*, a logical consequence of O'Brien's commitment to relativism is that "whatever the Party holds to be truth, *is* truth" (200; italics in orig.). According to Orwell, for O'Brien and for relativists generally, it is thinking that some opinion or belief is true that makes it so. Against this view, Winston Smith (and, it may be assumed, Orwell himself) holds the objectivist belief that in the natural sciences, truth is something that is discovered rather than constructed or created. It cannot, therefore, be altered or changed by any individual or group, no matter how powerful they are. Orwell would, I think, have had sympathy for Hugo Grotius's view, expressed long ago, that not even God almighty could create a world in which the proposition $2 + 2 = 4$ is not true (Grotius 155; also Arendt 236).

There are numerous occasions on which Orwell maintains that totalitarianism should be associated with relativism and the rejection of the idea of objective truth in science. For example, in a letter to H. J. Wilmett, written in 1944, Orwell associates totalitarianism with "a tendency to disbelieve in the existence of objective truth" ("Letter" 177). To illustrate the point, he refers to the fact that "a number of German scientists" before the Second World War "swallowed the monstrosity of 'racial science'" ("What Is" 28). On another occasion, Orwell laments the fact that "the very concept of objective truth is fading out of the world" ("Looking Back" 295). Indeed, there are times when Orwell gives his readers the impression that he identifies these two things with each other, suggesting that all scientific relativists are totalitarians and that all totalitarian thinkers are scientific relativists. In *Nineteen Eighty-Four*, it is O'Brien who is portrayed as being both a relativist in science and a defender of totalitarianism, whereas Smith is portrayed as being both an objectivist, so far as the issue of scientific truth is concerned, and a defender of liberal political ideals. Rightly or wrongly, then, Orwell associated both the idea of a scientific utopia and that of totalitarianism with relativism.

Orwell's views on this subject can fruitfully be compared with those expressed by Zamyatin in *We*, who also uses the example of $2 + 2 = 4$ in his critique of the idea of a certain kind of scientific utopia (76). However, Zamyatin comes to quite different conclusions from those drawn by Orwell. In Zamyatin's opinion, it is the modern scientific worldview, especially its notion of objective truth, that provides the philosophical underpinnings of totalitarian politics. Zamyatin contrasts this attitude with that of relativism, which in his opinion provides the theoretical basis for a quite different form of libertarian or anarchist politics. As I have argued elsewhere, Zamyatin's views on the relationship between science and politics are similar to those of Lyotard and certain other postmodernists (Burns, "Science and Politics"), or of what Paul R. Gross and Norman Levitt have termed "the academic left."

In the second half of the twentieth century, the broad issue of science in society, or the politics of science, was addressed both in Germany, by the Marxist theoreticians associated with the Frankfurt school, and in France, by poststructuralists and postmodernists who rejected all forms of Marxism and whose thinking has been associated with anarchism (Call; May; Newman). As Thomas McCarthy has observed in an essay comparing the thought of Foucault with that of the Frankfurt school, although they disagree about other things, nevertheless in this particular area the concerns of these two groups of thinkers are surprisingly similar. For example, in both cases we find a powerful critique of scientism.

A number of those writing about the politics of science today, especially those who are sympathetic to the postmodern or poststructuralist way of thinking about natural science, are relativists insofar as the issue of scientific truth is concerned, whilst also being committed to a form of anarchist politics. To these commentators at least, Orwell's "liberal" views on this subject are counterintuitive, if not plain wrong. So far as the relationship between science and politics is concerned, in their opinion, it is Zamyatin's critique of the idea of a scientific utopia, and not that of George Orwell, that is to be preferred.

Works Cited

Aldridge, Alexandra. *The Scientific World View in Dystopia*. Ann Arbor: UMI, 1984. Studies in Speculative Fiction.

Amis, Kingsley. *New Maps of Hell: A Survey of Science Fiction*. North Stratford, NH: Ayer, 2000.

Arendt, Hannah. *Between Past and Future: Eight Exercises in Political Thought*. Harmondsworth: Penguin, 2006.

Bacon, Francis. *New Atlantis*. *Three Early Modern Utopias:* Utopia, New Atlantis, *and* The Isle of Pines. Ed. Susan Bruce. Oxford: Oxford UP, 2008. 149–86.

Bakunin, Mikhail. *The Political Philosophy of Bakunin: Scientific Anarchism*. Ed. G. P. Maximoff. Glencoe, IL: Free, 1953.

Booker, M. Keith. *The Dystopian Impulse in Modern Literature: Fiction as Social Criticism*. Westport, CT: Greenwood, 1994.

Bould, Mark. "Introduction: Rough Guide to a Lonely Planet, from Nemo to Neo." *Red Planets: Marxism and Science Fiction*. Ed. Bould and China Miéville. London: Pluto, 2009. 1–28.

Brandom, Robert B., ed. *Rorty and His Critics*. Oxford: Blackwell, 2000.

Burns, Tony. *Political Theory, Science Fiction, and Utopian Literature: Ursula K. Le Guin and* The Dispossessed. Lanham, MD: Lexington, 2008.

_____. "Science and Politics in *The Dispossessed*: Le Guin and the 'Science Wars.'" *The New Utopian Politics of Ursula K. Le Guin's* The Dispossessed. Ed. Laurence Davis and Peter Stillman. Lanham, MD: Lexington, 2005. 195–215.

_____. "Zamyatin's *We* and Postmodernism." *Utopian Studies* 11.1 (2000): 66–90.

Call, Lewis. *Postmodern Anarchism*. Lanham, MD: Lexington, 2002.

Clark, Stephen R. L. "Orwell and the Anti-Realists." *Philosophy* 67.260 (1992): 141–54.

Conant, James. "Freedom, Cruelty, and Truth: Rorty versus Orwell." Brandom 268–341.

_____. "Rorty and Orwell on Truth." *On* Nineteen Eighty-Four: *Orwell and Our Future*. Ed. Abbott Gleason, Jack Goldsmith, and Martha C. Nussbaum. Princeton, NJ: Princeton UP, 2005. 86–111.

Davis, J. C. "Science and Utopia: The History of a Dilemma." Mendelsohn and Nowotny 21–48.

Dubos, René. *The Dreams of Reason: Science and Utopias*. New York: Columbia UP, 1961.

Eurich, Nell. *Science in Utopia: A Mighty Design*. Cambridge, MA: Harvard UP, 1967.

Feyerabend, Paul. *Against Method: Outline of an Anarchist Theory of Knowledge*. London: Verso, 1975.

_____. *Science in a Free Society*. London: Verso, 1978.

Foucault, Michel. *Power/Knowledge: Selected Interviews and Other Writings, 1972–1977*. Ed. Colin Gordon. New York: Pantheon, 1980.

Gross, Paul R., and Norman Levitt. *Higher Superstition: The Academic Left and Its Quarrels with Science*. Baltimore: Johns Hopkins UP, 1994.

Grotius, Hugo. *The Rights of War and Peace*. Ed. Richard Tuck. Vol. 1. Indianapolis: Liberty, 2005.

Hillegas, Mark. *The Future as Nightmare: H. G. Wells and the Anti-Utopians*. Oxford: Oxford UP, 1967.

Hynes, Samuel. Introduction. *Twentieth Century Interpretations of 1984: A Collection of Critical Essays*. Ed. Samuel Hynes. Englewood Cliffs, NJ: Prentice, 1971. 1–19.

Ingle, Stephen. *The Social and Political Thought of George Orwell: A Reassessment*. London: Routledge, 2006.

Kuhn, T. S. *The Structure of Scientific Revolutions*. 2nd ed. Chicago: U of Chicago P, 1970.

Kumar, Krishan. *Utopia and Anti-Utopia in Modern Times*. Oxford: Blackwell, 1987.

_____. *Utopianism*. Milton Keynes: Open UP, 1991. Concepts in the Social Sciences.

Lyotard, Jean-François. *The Postmodern Condition: A Report on Knowledge*. Trans. Geoff Bennington and Brian Massumi. Manchester: Manchester UP, 1984.

May, Todd. *The Political Philosophy of Poststructuralist Anarchism*. University Park: Pennsylvania State UP, 1994.

McCarthy, Thomas. *Ideals and Illusions: On Reconstruction and Deconstruction in Contemporary Critical Theory*. Cambridge, MA: MIT P, 1991.

Mendelsohn, Everett, and Helga Nowotny, eds. Nineteen Eighty-Four: *Science between Utopia and Dystopia*. Dordrecht: Reidel, 1984.

Newman, Saul. *The Politics of Postanarchism*. Edinburgh: Edinburgh UP, 2010.

Orwell, George. " 'As I Please,' *Tribune*, 4th February, 1944." Orwell and Angus vol. 3, 109–11.

_____. "Letter to H. J. Wilmett, 18th May, 1944." Orwell and Angus vol. 3, 177–79.

_____. "Literature and Totalitarianism." Orwell and Angus vol. 2, 161–65.

_____. "Looking Back on the Spanish War." Orwell and Angus vol. 2, 286–306.

_____. *Nineteen Eighty-Four*. Harmondsworth: Penguin, 1968.

_____. "The Prevention of Literature." Orwell and Angus vol. 4, 81–95.

_____. "Review of *We* by Yevgeny Zamyatin." Orwell and Angus vol. 4, 95–100.

_____. "Wells, Hitler and the World State." Orwell and Angus vol. 2, 166–72.

_____. "What Is Science?" Orwell and Angus vol. 4, 26–30.

Orwell, Sonia, and Ian Angus, eds. *The Collected Essays, Journalism and Letters of George Orwell*. By George Orwell. 4 vols. Harmondsworth: Penguin, 1970.

Roberts, Adam. *The History of Science Fiction*. Basingstoke: Palgrave, 2005.

Rorty, Richard. *Contingency, Irony, and Solidarity*. Cambridge: Cambridge UP, 2008.

_____. "Response to Conant." Brandom 342–50.

Sargent, Lyman Tower. "Eutopias and Dystopias of Science." *Imagining the Future: Utopia and Dystopia*. Ed. Andrew Milner, Matthew Ryan, and Robert Savage. Spec. issue of *Arena* 25/26 (2006): 357–74.

van Inwagen, Peter. "Was George Orwell a Metaphysical Realist?" *Philosophia Scientiae* 12.1 (2008): 161–85.

Wagar, W. Warren. *H. G. Wells and the World State*. New Haven, CT: Yale UP, 1966.

Woodcock, George. *The Crystal Spirit: A Study of George Orwell*. Harmondsworth: Penguin, 1970.

Zamyatin, Yevgeny. "On Literature, Revolution, Entropy and Other Matters." *A Soviet Heretic*. Ed. and trans. Mirra Ginsburg. London: Quartet, 1991. 107–12.

_____. *We*. Trans. Bernard Guilbert Guerney. Harmondsworth: Penguin, 1972.

Need It All End in Tears? The Problem of Ending in Four Classic Dystopias_____

Andrew Milner

Academic science-fiction studies have tended to stress the close affinity between science fiction and the much older genre of utopia. Darko Suvin famously argues, in his groundbreaking *Metamorphoses of Science Fiction* (1979), that "utopia is . . . the *sociopolitical subgenre of science fiction*" (61; italics in orig.). Carl Freedman echoes this view when he writes that science fiction "reinvents the older genre and energizes it with the kind of concrete utopian potentiality" available to a scientific age (78). Fredric Jameson's *Archaeologies of the Future* (2005) repeatedly and explicitly endorses Suvin's position (xiv, 57, 393, 410, 414–15), and Suvin's position also clearly informs the work of both Tom Moylan and Raffaella Baccolini. Jean Baudrillard posited the connection rather differently, regarding utopia and science fiction as functionally equivalent, mutually exclusive periodizing devices (121), but nonetheless stressed the affinity between the genres. Raymond Williams saw them as analytically distinct but cognate, because they are similarly concerned with the "presentation of *otherness*" and similarly dependent on "the element of discontinuity from ordinary 'realism'" (*Problems* 198; italics in orig.).

Strictly speaking, a utopia is neither a better nor a worse place, but rather a no place. As the verse epigraph supposedly written by the Utopian poet laureate Anemolius and included in all four of the earliest editions of *Utopia* makes clear, Thomas More's neologism was a Greek pun in Latin on *ou topos*, meaning no place, and *eu topos*, meaning good place:

> Utopia priscis dicta ob infrequentiam,
> Nunc civitatis aemula Platonicae,
>
> . . . .
> Eutopia merito sum vocanda nomine.

("No-Place" was once my name, I lay so far;
But now with Plato's state I can compare,

. . . .

"The Good Place" they should call me, with good cause.)
(18–19)

Until the mid-nineteenth century, however, the vast majority of utopias were at least as eutopian as More's own. The dystopia is a relatively recent form, the emergence of which coincides roughly with that of science fiction itself. Surprisingly, however, academic science-fiction studies tend to exhibit a distinct prejudice against dystopian fiction. The prejudice is at work, for example, in Suvin's argument that "SF will be the more significant and truly relevant the more clearly it eschews . . . the . . . fashionable static dystopia of the Huxley-Orwell model" (*Defined* 88). It informs Williams's dismissal of science-fiction dystopias as "putropias"—literally, putrefactions of utopia—predicated upon an elitist structure of feeling that counterposes "the isolated intellectual" to the "at best brutish, at worst brutal" masses ("Science Fiction" 357–58). In Jameson, the antipathy is yet more extreme. He sees George Orwell's *Nineteen Eighty-Four* (1949) as "the face of anti-Utopianism in our own time" (200), the mark of a more general "dystopian [awakening]" that is a "collective [response] of the bourgeoisie" to "the possibility of a workers' state" (201).

Following a line of argument first developed by Lyman Tower Sargent (7), Baccolini, Moylan, and Jameson each distinguish between the critical dystopia, which functions by way of warning, and the anti-utopia, which functions as a direct refutation of eutopia. The critical dystopia is eutopian in intent and import and thereby a "negative cousin" of eutopia (Jameson 198). Suvin posits a slightly different distinction between the " 'simple' dystopia" (*Defined* 385), which need have no relation to eutopia; the anti-utopia, which he understands in much the same fashion as Sargent; and the "Fallible Dystopia," which is concerned to demonstrate that "no dystopian reality is nightmarishly perfect, and that its seams may be picked apart" (395). All are agreed, however, that the most famous examples of the twentieth-century science-fiction dystopia, such as Karel Čapek's *R.U.R.* (1920), Yevgeny Zamyatin's *We* (1924), Aldous Huxley's *Brave New World* (1932), and Orwell's *Nineteen Eighty-Four*, tend toward the anti-utopia rather than the critical or fallible dystopia. This view seems to me in each case mistaken.

A common charge against eutopia is that its characters enjoy little in the way of individual existential experience and that the form thereby suffers from a certain necessary boredom. This is much less true, however, of eutopian films or novels than of works of eutopian philosophy or politics. Insofar as eutopian texts do work as fictions, they are often obliged to attempt this kind of existential plausibility; hence the persistence in eutopian fictions of such strategies as the sexual romance within eutopia (William Morris's 1890 work *News from Nowhere* more or less successfully, Edward Bellamy's 1888 novel *Looking Backward* unsuccessfully, most other eutopian novels with varying degrees of success), the view of eutopia from its distant borders (a common motif in Iain M. Banks's Culture novels, Ursula K. Le Guin's Hainish stories, and the different versions of the *Star Trek* television franchise), and the threat to eutopia from outside those borders (Banks again, Marge Piercy, Kim Stanley Robinson). Both Suvin and Williams define eutopia as a community imagined as more perfect (Suvin, *Metamorphoses* 45; Williams, *Problems* 196). If this is so, then it follows that a eutopian work's extratextual political point will vary between negative critique of the real and positive inspiration to create the better-than-real. The nearer any particular novel or film approximates the latter, the more it will attempt the kind of existential plausibility that will render both the fiction and the eutopia credible to the reader or filmgoer. No doubt Suvin is right to insist that utopia is an estranged, as distinct from naturalistic, form (*Metamorphoses* 18). But novels and films must necessarily work in a register very different from that of the truly nonfictional eutopias of political philosophy; they must work effectively as art or entertainment and must therefore be more directly implicated in naturalistic literary or cinematic conventions than Suvin or Jameson allows.

The worse worlds of dystopian fiction are similarly implicated, but by way of an extratextual political function as warning rather than inspiration. Dystopias are unlikely to be charged with boredom, given that their stories of human beastliness tend to have widespread appeal to conventional cultural taste. The equivalent problem is how to represent naturalistically plausible dangers that are sufficiently terrible to pose existentially plausible threats, but insufficiently so to demoralize the reader or viewer. Insofar as its serious purpose lies in a capacity to warn, the central dilemma of dystopian fiction is that the more grimly inexorable the fictive world becomes, the less effective it will be as a call to resistance. Hence Williams's judgment that "the very absoluteness of the fiction" in Orwell becomes "an imaginative submission to . . . inevitability" (*Orwell* 125–26). If the dystopia is intended as either critical or fallible, then it will be obliged to deploy mechanisms that offset this inevitability, one of which is clearly the contrapuntal ending. Which leads us to what I will term the problem of ending in dystopia. How, then, is this resolved in our four classic dystopias?

The Czech script for Čapek's play *R.U.R. (Rossum's Universal Robots)* was first published in book form in 1920, while the play was first performed in Prague on January 2 and 3, 1921 (Čapek, *R.U.R.: Kolektivní* 117). Different English-language versions were performed in 1922 by the New York Theatre Guild and in 1923 by the Reandean Company at St. Martin's Theatre in London. Later that year, distinct British and American translations were published in book form. The play bequeathed to science fiction one of its most famous devices: the robot, a word deriving from the Czech *robotá*, meaning "hard labor," with Rossum intended as an English-sounding proper name connoting the Czech common noun *rozum*, meaning "reason." Čapek's robots are human in form, what we would now term androids, but mechanically manufactured nonetheless. The original Czech version of *R.U.R.*

was organized into a comic prologue and three acts, but Paul Selver's English translation, as adapted for the London stage by Nigel Playfair, had three acts and an epilogue. All are set in the near future on an anonymous island housing the offices and factory of the eponymous Rossum's Universal Robots, an English- or American-sounding corporation that has acquired a global monopoly on the manufacture of artificial workers.

Whilst the first act is comic, the two that follow are distinctly dystopian. The second traces the initial human responses to the beginnings of a robot revolution, while the third shows the besieged humans attacked and finally overwhelmed. In *R.U.R.*, the unregulated pursuit of corporate profit through the global marketing of high technology leads to absolute disaster: the destruction of the human race, an outcome neither anticipated nor sought by any individual or corporation but produced nonetheless by the logic of capitalist competition. Faced with catastrophe, Domain, the plant director, justifies the project retrospectively as a noble attempt to triumph over the servitude of labor. But Alquist, the company's clerk of works, and with him Čapek, will have none of it: "Old Rossum only thought of his godless tricks, and the young one of his millions. And that's not what your R.U.R. shareholders dream of, either. They dream of dividends. And their dividends are the ruin of mankind" (Čapek, *R.U.R.: A Play* 66). With this theme, Čapek introduced into twentieth-century science fiction one of its two major dystopian topoi. The other was the overweeningly intrusive totalitarian state, introduced into Russian by Zamyatin in *We* and into English by Orwell in *Nineteen Eighty-Four*. For the most obvious of contextual reasons—Stalinism in Russia, Fascism in Italy, Nazism in Germany—the dystopian imaginings of the middle decades of the twentieth century were preoccupied with the problem of totalitarianism. But in *R.U.R.*, Čapek confronted the problem of a globalizing, corporate-capitalist, scientific-industrial complex, which would acquire renewed urgency only in the science fiction of the late twentieth and early twenty-first centuries.

In *R.U.R.*, humanity is led to extinction through a combination of unbridled capitalism and hubristic technology, the robots to near-extinction through their cruel determination to exterminate their human masters. Its logic appears to proceed remorselessly, then, toward their mutual self-destruction. Only one human remains alive at the end: Stavitel Alquist, RUR's head of construction, retained by the robots in an attempt to reproduce themselves in the absence of the humans who had sole possession of the secrets of their creation. His theatrical function, however, is to bear witness to the play's ultimately optimistic conclusion that life will continue, even if humanity will not. So Čapek's play insists, against everything we know both of biology and of his own fictional robotics, that altruistic heterosexual love between Primus, the male robot, and Helena, the robotess, will eventually produce new life. Hence Alquist's last speech, in which he pronounces them a new Adam and Eve, quoting directly from the book of Genesis and then citing the song of Simeon from Luke: "Now, Lord, lettest Thou Thy servant depart in peace, according to Thy will, for mine eyes have seen Thy salvation" (Čapek, *R.U.R.: A Play* 104). No matter what the sterilities of human and capitalist robotics or inhuman and communist robots, the play concludes that love and life will ultimately triumph. The rhetoric is Judeo-Christian, but the solution, that life will always win out, is essentially pantheist. This might well be seen as possessing a peculiarly contemporary relevance to our own time, insofar as it anticipates recent deep-ecological speculation about the earth's capacity to survive the depredations of our species. For Čapek, however, it was merely a way to produce an optimistic resolution where none seemed readily available.

Zamyatin's *Мы* was written in Russian in 1920–21. It was first published in an American English translation as *We* in 1924 and in French translation as *Nous autres* in 1929, but was not published in British English until 1972 and not in Russia until 1988. The novel is set in the twenty-sixth century amid the gleaming glass towers of a technologically advanced collectivist state established in the aftermath of a ruinous "200-Years War . . . between the City and the Country" (Zamyatin 21). The French translation clearly provided Orwell with a model for *Nineteen Eighty-Four*, but Zamyatin's novel is far more a critique of scientific rationalism than one of political totalitarianism, and its "One State" is ruled by science and mathematics as much as by the dictatorial Benefactor. The novel's central protagonist is D-503, the designer of the *Integral* space probe, and like all the other members of this society, he is merely one "Number" amongst many (3–4). Like the routines of all of these numbers, his daily routines are precisely and arithmetically ordered by the Table of Hours (11). Formally, the novel itself also comprises a series of forty laboratory records. D-503 is seduced into rebellion, both sexually and politically, by I-330, who can be read on one level as the model for Orwell's Julia. Both are sexually proactive women whose affections prompt the male protagonist into political resistance to the state, and both will eventually be betrayed by the protagonist. D-503's last record reports his subjection to the Benefactor's "Great Operation" to eliminate the imagination and his subsequent impassive witness to I-330's torture under "the Bell" (224–25). It is a moment of simultaneous defeat and betrayal that clearly provides a template for that moment in *Nineteen Eighty-Four* when "*I sold you and you sold me*" (Orwell, *Nineteen Eighty-Four* 307).

But there are important differences between the two novels. Where the structure of Orwell's three rival totalitarian states (Oceania, Eurasia, and Eastasia) is essentially both fully enclosed and self-sealing, Zamyatin's One State is both encircled by the wilderness beyond "the Green Wall" and threatened from within by the Mephi underground. Furthermore, I-330 is a much stronger character than Julia. She is a leader of the Mephi, and as such, she also provides the novel with its chief intellectual antagonist to state positivism. D-503's loyalty to the mathematical foundations of the One State is only finally undermined by her insistence that there cannot logically be any final number, and therefore any final revolution (Zamyatin 168). There are, no doubt, clear homologies between the destruction of Julia and Winston in

Nineteen Eighty-Four and that of I-330 and D-503 in *We*. But there is no equivalent in Orwell to D-503's illicit child by O-90, a child who will be born and brought up outside the state. Although the Benefactor continues to rule the One State at the conclusion of Zamyatin's novel, this rule has been challenged by the Mephi much more effectively during the course of the narrative than is Big Brother's by either the Brotherhood or Winston's vague hopes for the "proles."

The contrast is at its keenest in the two novels' respective accounts of the mathematics of totalitarianism. Whilst Orwell's O'Brien eventually succeeds in forcing Winston to see five fingers, I-330's insistence that there is no final number haunts D-503 right through to "The End" in record 39: "Listen to me, I tell you! You have to tell me this. There where your finite universe ends—what's there . . . beyond?" (Zamyatin 223; ellipsis in orig.). This is not quite the end, in fact, since record 40 is still to come. But even there, in the novel's closing paragraphs, Zamyatin reminds us that the Green Wall has been successfully breached, that the One State is actually already in retreat: "In the western quarters there is still chaos, roaring, corpses, animals, and, unfortunately, quite a lot of Numbers who have betrayed reason. But on Fortieth Avenue, which runs crosstown, they've managed to build a temporary wall of high-voltage waves" (225). The particular defeats suffered by D-503 and I-330 are therefore contextualized and mitigated by the continuing possibility of infinite revolution. As Suvin concludes, "the defeat in the novel *We* is not the defeat of the novel itself, but an exasperated shocking of the reader into thought and action" (*Metamorphoses* 259).

Like Zamyatin's *We*, Huxley's *Brave New World* is set in the twenty-sixth century, in an affluent and technologically sophisticated dystopia. But where the One State anticipates Orwell's Oceanian sexual puritanism, Huxley's novel explores the dystopian possibilities of the mass commodification of pleasure. It is directed at "the hedonistic principle," Orwell observed, at a world "turned into a Riviera hotel," and is thus a "brilliant caricature" of "the present of 1930"—that is, the 1920s. From our vantage point in the twenty-first century, we might well want to add the present of 1990, 2000, and 2010, but for Orwell, writing in 1940, it cast "no light on the future" (*My Country* 46). Huxley began writing in 1931 and the novel was first published in London the following year. He had originally intended it to be a straightforward anti-utopia, a direct refutation of what he called "the horror of the Wellsian Utopia" (Huxley, *Letters* 348). But in the process of composition, it acquired many other targets, ranging from American capitalism and Russian Communism through eugenics and state planning to sexual, pharmacological, and media-induced hedonism, Keynesian economics, and Lawrentian primitivism, most of which he would later explore far more positively. An important part of the novel's distinctive character, simultaneously both a strength and a weakness, is its capacity to represent many different sides of many different questions more or less sympathetically. As each of these becomes in turn an object of satire, so the anti-eutopia becomes transformed into a scattershot critique of twentieth-century modernity.

Both *We* and *Brave New World* famously end with a death, but in the latter, the death is a media-saturated suicide rather than a political execution:

"Mr Savage!"

Slowly, very slowly, like two unhurried compass needles, the feet turned towards the right; north, north-east, east, south-east, south, south-south-west; then paused, and after a few seconds, turned as unhurriedly back towards the left. South-south-west, south, south-east, east . . . (Huxley, *Brave* 237)

If the Savage were the hero of the novel, and his resistance to the pseudo-Wellsian World State properly heroic, then the ending would, of course, be tragic. But it is much closer to bathetic comedy, since he is neither hero nor protagonist: he does not appear until chapter 7, the forms of his rebellion are absurdly excessive, his final public self-flagellation is so ludicrous as to be almost comic, and his previous home on the Savage Reservation is no less drug obsessed and socially conformist than the civilization he rejects. Structurally, the role of central protagonist is better performed by Bernard Marx. But intelligent though he undoubtedly is, Bernard is both self-important and self-pitying, and therefore yet another target for the novel's humor.

This, surely, is the point; *Brave New World* is essentially a comic novel, a satire on the surrounding intellectual landscape, aimed at everything from Hollywood hedonism to Pavlovian psychology, Freudianism to Fordism (in the sense used in the novel and in that of more recent economics and sociology). As Huxley himself explained to his father, it is "a comic, or at least satirical, novel about the Future" (*Letters* 351). It is very different, in this respect, from each of our other dystopias: the first act of *R. U. R.* may be comic, to some extent reminiscent of George Bernard Shaw, but its dominant register soon becomes closer to that of Anton Chekhov or Henrik Ibsen; there are, no doubt, comic episodes in *We*, for example when D-503 imagines I-330 as a Valkyrie (193), but these are comparatively rare; and there is next to no comedy at all in *Nineteen Eighty-Four*.

The one character exempted from satire in *Brave New World* is the world controller for western Europe, Mustapha Mond. Significantly, the Savage only becomes a fully serious figure in the debate with Mond, in the novel's sixteenth and seventeenth chapters. This is the true philosophical core of the text, where Mond presents the case for both Enlightenment civilization in general and the utilitarian "felicific calculus" in particular,[1] while the Savage does the same for both Romantic culture and primitivist barbarism. Chapter 16 concludes with Bernard Marx's and Helmholtz Watson's banishment to an island reserved for those "too self-consciously individual to fit into community-life" (Huxley, *Brave* 178). Their fate is described to explicitly comic effect for Bernard, less so for Helmholtz, but there is no suggestion that the outcome will be especially intolerable for either. The World State provides the occasion for satirical amusement rather than terrified dread. Chapter 17 ends with the novel's interestingly ambivalent philosophical conclusion: "What you need," the Savage argues, "is something *with* tears for a change. Nothing costs enough here." "We prefer to do things comfortably," Mond retorts a little later. "But I don't want comfort," the Savage replies:

> "I want God, I want poetry, I want real danger, I want freedom, I want goodness. I want sin."
>
> "In fact," said Mustapha Mond, "you're claiming the right to be unhappy."
>
> "All right then," said the Savage defiantly, "I'm claiming the right to be unhappy."
>
> "Not to mention the right to grow old and ugly and impotent; the right to have syphilis and cancer; the right to have too little to eat; the right to be lousy; the right to live in constant apprehension of what may happen tomorrow; the right to catch typhoid; the right to be tortured by unspeakable pains of every kind." There was a long silence.
>
> "I claim them all," said the Savage at last.
>
> Mustapha Mond shrugged his shoulders. "You're welcome," he said. (186–87)

The last chapter, which narrates the Savage's self-exile, self-mutilation, and self-destruction, still remains, but the philosophical argument ends with this unresolved choice between what Huxley would later describe, in a 1946 foreword to the novel, as "an insane life in Utopia, or the life of a primitive in an Indian village, a life . . . in some respects . . . hardly less queer and abnormal" (7). In sum, the novel concludes with a set of highly elaborate comic and satiric trappings that are used to disguise the presence of an underlying philosophical impasse.

First published in London in 1949 and set in a very near future that has now both literally and metaphorically become our past, Orwell's *Nineteen Eighty-Four* is without doubt the best known of all anglophone literary dystopias. And most anglophone readers know exactly how it ends: with Winston Smith's betrayal of Julia in Room 101, hers of him, and their shared capitulation to Big Brother, the Party, and Ingsoc. "But it was all right," Winston finally assures himself, "everything was all right, the struggle was finished. He had won the victory over himself. He loved Big Brother." The novel then reads, in most subsequent editions as it did in the first, "THE END" (Orwell, *Nineteen Eighty-Four* 311). It does not end there, however, but continues, in the Penguin edition for over fourteen more pages (312–26), only finally reaching its actual ending at the conclusion to the appendix on Newspeak: "It was chiefly in order to allow time for the preliminary work of translation that the final adoption of Newspeak had been fixed for so late a date as 2050" (326). In their content, these lines appear to add very little, but in their form they are redolent with meaning. For, as Margaret Atwood observes, the appendix "is written in standard English, in the third person, and in the past tense, which can only mean that the regime has fallen, and that language and individuality have survived. For whoever has written the essay on Newspeak, the world of *1984* is over" (*Curious Pursuits* 337). Thomas Pynchon makes an analogous case in his foreword to the centennial edition of the novel. They are both almost certainly right: the appendix is internal to the novel, a fictional commentary on fictional events, rather than an author's or scholarly editor's account of how the fiction works. Furthermore, this ending has been anticipated in the main body of the text, when in the first chapter a footnote assures us, once again in standard English, in the third person, in the past tense, that "Newspeak was the official language of Oceania" (Orwell, *Nineteen Eighty-Four* 5). Atwood used a very similar device in the first of her own dystopian science-fiction novels, *The Handmaid's Tale*, which concludes with part of the proceedings of a "Symposium on Gileadean Studies," written long after the demise of the Republic of Gilead in what is clearly intended as a eutopian future (311–24). Moreover, she cheerfully confesses that *Nineteen Eighty-Four* provided her with the "direct model" for this ending (*Curious Pursuits* 337). If she is to be believed, then both Orwell's appendix and her "Historical Notes" work as framing devices by which to blunt the force of dystopian inevitability.

Comparing Zamyatin's *We* and Huxley's *Brave New World* in 1946, Orwell wrote that "in Huxley's book . . . no clear reason is given why society should be stratified in the elaborate way that is described. The aim is not economic exploitation, but the desire to bully and dominate does not seem to be a motive either. There is no power hunger, no sadism, no hardness of any kind" (*In Front* 97). By contrast, "it is th[e] intuitive grasp of the irrational side of totalitarianism—human sacrifice, cruelty as an end in itself, the worship of a Leader who is credited with divine attributes—that makes Zamyatin's book superior to Huxley's" (98). The political point of Orwell's dystopia, which he had begun to work on as early as 1943, was thus apparent. His own novel would need to be so unremittingly horrible as to expose the sheer ghastliness of totalitarianism, but would therefore require something external to itself to inspire belief in the possibilities for resistance. This is why Orwell's "THE END" could never provide the novel with its actual ending.

To recapitulate: Čapek's *R.U.R.* resolves the problem of dystopian ending by contriving an optimistic outcome essentially at odds with the play's main narrative; Zamyatin's *We*, by framing the particular defeats suffered by D-503 and I-330 with a surrounding context of infinite revolution; Huxley's *Brave New World*, by framing its philosophical impasse with comedy and satire; and Orwell's *Nineteen Eighty-Four*, by framing Winston and Julia's defeat within the context of the eventual overthrow of Ingsoc. The first seems to me the least persuasive, the second the most. But regardless of their effectiveness, these four endings suggest the outlines of a possible ideal typology of dystopian endings. This would be arranged around measures of internality and externality applied, firstly, to the formal question of narrative structure and, secondly, to the content of the dystopian imaginary worlds present in the fiction. The solution in *R.U.R.* is thus external to the main narrative in form—the fourth act is indeed an epilogue, just as the English translation supposes—and also in content, since its closing transcendental religiosity inhabits a very different conceptual space from that of the first three acts. The solution in *We* is internal to the text's main narrative and also to the fictional history of the imaginary world it describes. That in *Brave New World* is internal to the novel's main narrative but nonetheless external to the fictional history of AF 632, if only because satire necessarily implies a position outside the reality it satirizes. Conversely, that in *Nineteen Eighty-Four* is external to the main narrative but nonetheless internal to the fictional world of the novel. In all four cases, however, the effect is to transform what might have been an anti-eutopia into what is, in aspiration at least, a critical or fallible dystopia.

In summary, then, the solution in *We* is internal to both form (continuity with the main narrative) and content (continuity with the imaginary world represented in the fiction); in *R.U.R.*, it is external to both form and content; in *Brave New World*, it is internal to form but external to content; and in *Nineteen Eighty-Four*, it is external to form but internal to content. We know that Orwell read each of the other three texts, so we might plausibly infer that the appendix on Newspeak was a deliberate experiment in relation to the genre of dystopian science fiction. There is no trace of it in what remains of Orwell's manuscript (*Nineteen Eighty-Four: Facsimile*). In itself, this proves very little, given the latter's dilapidated state. But it suggests the possibility that Orwell's appendix really was written last, as the real "END" to the novel, a solution to a problem that became apparent only when the main body of the text was already very nearly complete. We might reasonably conclude, then, with Atwood and Pynchon, that readings premised on the assumption that *Nineteen Eighty-Four* ends at "THE END" are invariably radically misconceived.

Notes

1. The nineteenth-century English utilitarian philosopher Jeremy Bentham believed that the aim of all public policy should be the greatest happiness of the greatest number of people. The "felicific calculus" was his algorithm for calculating the degree of pleasure or happiness any action is likely to cause.

Works Cited

Atwood, Margaret. *Curious Pursuits: Occasional Writing, 1970–2005*. London: Virago, 2005.

_____. *The Handmaid's Tale*. London: Virago, 1987.

Baccolini, Raffaella, and Tom Moylan, eds. *Dark Horizons: Science Fiction and the Dystopian Imagination*. London: Routledge, 2004.

Baudrillard, Jean. *Simulacra and Simulation*. Trans. Sheila Faria Glaser. Ann Arbor: U of Michigan P, 1994.

Čapek, Karel. *R.U.R. (Rossum's Universal Robots): A Play in Three Acts and an Epilogue*. Trans. P. Selver. R.U.R. *and* The Insect Play. By Karel Čapek and Josef Čapek. Oxford: Oxford UP, 1961. 1–104.

_____. *R.U.R. Rossum's Universal Robots: Kolektivní drama o vstupní komedii a třech dějstvích*. Prague: Československý spisovatel, 1966.

Freedman, Carl. *Critical Theory and Science Fiction*. Hanover, NH: Wesleyan UP, 2000.

Huxley, Aldous. *Brave New World*. Harmondsworth: Penguin, 1955.

_____. *Letters of Aldous Huxley*. Ed. Grover Smith. London: Chatto, 1969.

Jameson, Fredric. *Archaeologies of the Future: The Desire Called Utopia and Other Science Fictions*. London: Verso, 2005.

More, Thomas. *Utopia: Latin Text and English Translation*. Ed. George M. Logan, Robert M. Adams, and Clarence H. Miller. Cambridge: Cambridge UP, 1995.

Moylan, Tom. *Demand the Impossible: Science Fiction and the Utopian Imagination*. New York: Methuen, 1986.

_____. *Scraps of the Untainted Sky: Science Fiction, Utopia, Dystopia*. Boulder, CO: Westview, 2000.

Moylan, Tom, and Raffaella Baccolini, eds. *Utopia Method Vision: The Use Value of Social Dreaming*. Bern: Lang, 2007.

Orwell, George. *In Front of Your Nose, 1945–1950*. Ed. Sonia Orwell and Ian Angus. Harmondsworth: Penguin, 1970. Vol. 4 of *The Collected Essays, Journalism and Letters of George Orwell*.

_____. *My Country Right or Left, 1940–1943*. Ed. Sonia Orwell and Ian Angus. Harmondsworth: Penguin, 1970. Vol. 2 of *The Collected Essays, Journalism and Letters of George Orwell*.

_____. *Nineteen Eighty-Four*. Harmondsworth: Penguin, 1989.

_____. *Nineteen Eighty-Four: The Facsimile of the Extant Manuscript*. Ed. P. Davison. London: Secker, 1984.

Pynchon, Thomas. Foreword. *Nineteen Eighty-Four*. By George Orwell. Centennial ed. New York: Plume, 2003.

Sargent, Lyman Tower. "The Three Faces of Utopianism Revisited." *Utopian Studies* 5.1 (1994): 1–37.

Suvin, Darko. *Defined by a Hollow: Essays on Utopia, Science Fiction and Political Epistemology*. Frankfurt: Lang, 2010.

_____. *Metamorphoses of Science Fiction: On the Poetics and History of a Literary Genre*. New Haven, CT: Yale UP, 1979.

Williams, Raymond. *Orwell*. 3rd ed. London: Fontana, 1991.

_____. *Problems in Materialism and Culture*. London: New Left, 1980.

_____. "Science Fiction." *Science Fiction Studies* 15.3 (1988): 356–60.

Zamyatin, Yevgeny. *We*. Trans. Clarence Brown. Harmondsworth: Penguin, 1993.

"They Got Me a Long Time Ago": The Sympathetic Villain in *Nineteen Eighty-Four, Brave New World,* and *Fahrenheit 451*_____

Rafeeq O. McGiveron

After Winston Smith is captured by the Thought Police in George Orwell's *Nineteen Eighty-Four* (1949), his last "flickering hope" (189) is extinguished when into his cell comes O'Brien, his mysterious, "curiously civilized" (13) coworker and supposed coconspirator against the dictatorship of the even more mysterious Big Brother. "They've got you too!" Smith gasps. Yet O'Brien's reply of "mild, almost regretful irony" unnerves more than any shrill demagogue's ever could: "They got me a long time ago" (197). As some of the best villains of dystopian literature demonstrate, the drive to crush the human spirit is not found only in blind ideologues and slogan-mongers; it can lure even the most discerning intellects.

Inner Party member O'Brien of *Nineteen Eighty-Four*, Controller Mustapha Mond of Aldous Huxley's *Brave New World* (1932), and Fire Captain Beatty of Ray Bradbury's *Fahrenheit 451* (1953) all enforce the orthodoxies of regimes that in one way or another destroy thought and emotion and individuality. Each, however, is implied to have been, in his younger days, something of a failed rebel himself and thus may be termed a "sympathetic" villain in both meanings of the word: each has some measure of sympathy for the dissident protagonist, and each, by virtue of his own tragic lost potential, receives more sympathy from the reader than a mindless drone ever could. Whether they rule by fear, the seductive lure of pleasure, or a combination of both, O'Brien, Mond, and Beatty are more than mere yes-men for their sinister governments. These sympathetic villains remind us chillingly that the face of dehumanization can be good natured and avuncular and oh-so-deceptively reasonable. It is the seeming reasonableness of their arguments that makes the slippery slope so dangerous.

Nineteen Eighty-Four

George Orwell's masterful *Nineteen Eighty-Four* is a dystopia whose flaws, at least to the outsider, are clear. Physically, the world is one of polluted and decaying cities, populated by unfed masses living in dingy conditions. These conditions are partially the result of the now-permanent war between the world's three great superstates but also partially because the effects of a nuclear war in the 1950s, in which hundreds of nuclear weapons were dropped on the major cities of Europe and America, have never been fully repaired. Orwell's portrayal of the nagging, niggling poverty of London, from the perpetually out-of-service elevators to the shortages of food and clothing whose quality is insufficient in any event, is detailed, evocative, and compelling. Yet had Orwell made his fictional world appear undesirable solely by focusing on physical conditions that naturally bring visceral protest, then, masterful though it is, the artistry would have been merely something of an intellectual shortcut. Do rationing and run-down living conditions necessarily indicate an oppressive government? Do the privations of Valley Forge, for example, brand Washington a cynical tyrant? Of course not. On the other hand, if the world of *Nineteen Eighty-Four* "is a bare, hungry, dilapidated place compared with the world that existed before 1914" (Orwell 155), then perhaps the revolution so praised in Party textbooks and slogans was not quite so revolutionary after all.

Orwell, however, is master not merely of the external but of the internal as well, and the intellectual and moral situation of *Nineteen Eighty-Four* is even worse than the physical. For example, while "the Party claim[s], of course, to have liberated the proles from bondage," protagonist Winston Smith notes that on the contrary, the conditions of the ignored proletarians actually may not have improved at all. Despite the high-sounding propaganda, after all, the "swarming disregarded masses" are essentially cattle who need only "work and breed," beset by "a whole world-within-a-world of thieves, bandits, prostitutes, drug peddlers, and racketeers of every description" that the government simply ignores (Orwell 60–62). Safely occupied by manual labor, sports, drinking, gambling, and other mundane matters, the proles are not even given—or, put another way, not subjected to—much government-sponsored education, for "it [i]s not desirable that the proles should have strong political feelings" (61–62).

Yet while the proles can be ignored, the Western superstate of Oceania actually directs almost as much violence and oppression at the more privileged members of its Party as it does at its external enemies. Always at war with either Eurasia or Eastasia, while at the same time conniving to betray its supposed ally and switch sides at the most advantageous moment, the government of Oceania considers "such acts as raping, looting, the slaughter of children, the reduction of whole populations to slavery, and reprisals against prisoners" to be "normal" and even "meritorious" when directed against the enemy of the moment beyond its borders (Orwell 153). At home, of course, Oceania is a police state little less brutal to its own citizens. Constant surveillance enables the ruthless suppression of any perceived unorthodoxy by means of torture and forced-labor camps, occasional purges and show trials of the prominent, and, most commonly, secret executions, after which the person is considered "*vaporized*" (20; italics in orig.). One executed by the Thought Police is therefore "an *unperson*. Any identifiable reference to him would [be] mortally dangerous" (130; italics in orig.).

Purposeful policies "have cut the links between child and parent, and between man and man, and between man and woman" (Orwell 220), so that "today there [a]re fear, hatred, and pain, but no dignity of emotion, or deep or complex sorrows" (28–29). "Hardly a week passe[s] in which the *Times* d[oes] not carry a paragraph describing how some eavesdropping little sneak—'child hero' [i]s the phrase usually used—had overheard some compromising remark and denounced his parents to the Thought Police" (24). Ideally for Party planners, children in the future would be produced by artificial insemination, but in the meantime, sex is to be used only for reproduction and is regarded grudgingly even then, "looked on as a slightly disgusting minor operation, like having an enema" (57). The elimination of privacy runs both ways, such that just as citizens can be watched around the clock by the ubiquitous two-way telescreens, those same constantly yammering telescreens enforce a government monopoly on public discourse (169–70). Finally, even the official language, Newspeak, has as its "whole aim . . . to narrow the range of thought" and thus "make thoughtcrime literally impossible, because there will be no words with which to express it" (46). Superficially, "nothing [i]s illegal, since there [a]re no longer any laws" (9), yet still any unauthorized thought, love, solitude, or even facial expression is considered *thoughtcrime*, *sexcrime*, *ownlife*, or *facecrime*.

Ruling over all, at the very apex of the victorious Party, is the ever-present persona of Big Brother, Stalin-like in his looks, his policies, and his cult of personality. The highest-ranking government official actually portrayed in the novel, however, is O'Brien, a member of the Inner Party whose exact position is unclear. Toward the end of the novel, O'Brien ends up being Smith's torturer, revealed as the man who for seven years has monitored his every move and who has lured him ever more deeply into thoughtcrime. Yet despite the calculated savagery of his tortures, still O'Brien has sympathy for Smith, and still he receives some measure of sympathy from the reader as well.

For fully four-fifths of *Nineteen Eighty-Four*, O'Brien appears to be a kindred spirit to Smith, then an actual coconspirator in the fabled Brotherhood that supposedly is "dedicated to the overthrow of the State" (15). Orwell's first description of him tantalizes the reader almost as much as Smith himself does the dissident longing for a companion:

O'Brien was a large, burly man with a thick neck and a coarse, humorous, brutal face. In spite of his formidable appearance he had a certain charm of manner. He had a trick of resettling his spectacles on his nose which was curiously disarming—in some indefinable way, curiously civilized. It was a gesture which, if anyone had still thought in such terms, might have recalled an eighteenth-century nobleman offering his snuff-box. (13)

Smith is "deeply drawn" to the enigmatic man, for "something in his face suggest[s] . . . irresistibly" that his "political orthodoxy [i]s not perfect" (13). In contrast to that of the man Smith knows as Mr. Charrington, that undercover member of the Thought Police who seems to undergo "a complete transformation" from only "tiny changes" of his face and posture (185), it seems unlikely that O'Brien's demeanor is solely a pose to draw out the wayward Smith. The "certain charm of manner," the "curiously disarming" and "curiously civilized" adjusting of his glasses, the "peculiar grave courtesy" and "disarming friendliness" (130), the face "so civilized" (144)—perhaps there is an occasional dash of art in the disarming aspect, but much appears unfeigned, and all generate in Smith a "wave of admiration, almost of worship" (144).

After an initial "interrogation" that includes a seemingly endless series of beatings by black-uniformed interrogators and the "formality" of confession to ever more outrageous charges (Orwell 198–200), O'Brien himself presides over the final treatments that "shall squeeze [Smith] empty, and then . . . shall fill [him] with [the Party]" (211). Even then, however, he is "gentle and patient," with "the air of a doctor, a teacher, even a priest, anxious to explain and persuade rather than punish" (203).

At one point, despite the agony he endures, Smith experiences a strange feeling of friendship, even love, for his calm, merciless, yet "almost kindly" (Orwell 225) tormentor:

If he could have moved he would have stretched out a hand and laid it on O'Brien's arm. He had never loved him so deeply as at this moment, and not merely because he had stopped the pain. . . . In some sense that went deeper than friendship, they were intimates; somewhere or other, although the actual words might never be spoken, there was a place where they could meet and talk. O'Brien was looking down at him with an expression which suggested that the same thought might be in his own mind. (208)

Perhaps Smith, "tortured . . . to the edge of lunacy" (208), is merely projecting his confused emotions onto the older man, but it seems just as likely that he is correct: O'Brien sees Smith not merely as an object or a victim but as a person rather too much like himself. Later, O'Brien explains with apparent candor, "I enjoy talking to you. Your mind appeals to me. It resembles my own mind except that you happen to be insane" (213).

O'Brien's definition of sanity, of course, is based upon *doublethink*, "the power of holding two contradictory beliefs in one's mind simultaneously" (Orwell 176), a self-deception both conscious and yet always striving for unconsciousness, so that one therefore might avoid the unsettling lingering knowledge that the truth is not actually what one is trying to claim it is. Yes, O'Brien's face shows intense enthusiasm for the process of Party brainwashing. And yes, O'Brien has absolutely no qualms about supporting the Party's quest for power for the sake of power. Such sentiments are repellent, naturally.

Still, O'Brien is neither merely a madman nor a blind yes-man. Because he is the only character we see in the novel with any real understanding of how the world of *Nineteen Eighty-Four* arrived at the state it is in, O'Brien is actually, morals aside, the one most similar to the reader in intellectual terms; his mind "resembles [our] own." As one of the agent provocateur coauthors of *the book*, the supposed "book without a title" that is "a compendium of all of the heresies" of the Brotherhood (Orwell 15)—and that, ironically, does indeed spell out the flaws of Oceania's police state with extraordinary thoroughness—O'Brien obviously understands history, psychology, and economics all too well to imagine that his own society is anything but "the exact opposite of the stupid hedonistic Utopias that the old reformers imagined. A world of fear and treachery and torment" (220). O'Brien knows that although Ingsoc, or English Socialism, "grew out of the earlier Socialist movement and inherited its phraseology," when the Party collectivized all the businesses, industries, and even houses of "the capitalist class," it gave the booty not to the public at large but to the Party itself, thus perpetuating the same inequalities it purported to abolish (170). He knows that the twenty-five-year war among the three superstates is, most fundamentally, "waged by each ruling group against its own subjects . . . not to make or prevent conquests of territory, but to keep the structure of society intact" (164); despite claims of glorious advances at the front and predictions of ultimate victory, no such victory will ever occur. He knows that whereas science increased the standard of living steadily in the first half of the twentieth century (156), now its sole focus is the strengthening of totalitarianism: research in mind control, torture, and weapons from the commonplace to the semi-fantastic (159–60). O'Brien thus recognizes fundamental truths toward which Smith has been groping uncertainly.

Was O'Brien himself ever actually a true rebel or thought-criminal, as Smith is? No, for, as he explains, during the process of reeducation that takes place in the sublevels of the windowless fortress of the Ministry of Love, "things . . . happen to you from which you could not recover, if you lived a thousand years" (Orwell 211). Clearly the powerful, nimble-minded O'Brien has never suffered that ordeal; his facility for *crimestop*, the "automatic, instinctive" creation of a mental "blind spot whenever a dangerous thought present[s] itself" (229), must be much better developed than Smith's. Yet he nevertheless has the penetrating mind that at least once had the capacity for rebellion, though he rejected the notion long ago. O'Brien gives "an impression of confidence and of an understanding tinged by irony" (144)—the latter being an exceedingly rare quality among the citizens of Oceania— and during Smith's torture, he looks down "gravely and rather sadly" (202). Though "they got [him] a long time ago," O'Brien's voice in explaining this is full of a "mild, almost regretful irony," the significance of which the reader can neither overlook nor forget.

Brave New World

Aldous Huxley's *Brave New World* is at the opposite end of the pleasure-pain spectrum from *Nineteen Eighty-Four*. Whereas Orwell wrote when the horrors of Nazi and Soviet tyranny were fully exposed to world consciousness, Huxley, in the interwar period, before even the rise of Hitler, imagined in the twenty-sixth century the common science-fiction trope that Orwell characterizes so well in *the book*: "a future society unbelievably rich, leisured, orderly and efficient—a glittering antiseptic world of glass and steel and snow-white concrete" (Orwell 155–56). The seeming playground of glass and steel and snow-white concrete is a figurative prison, however, for rather than having been worn down and enslaved by privation like the populace of Oceania, here the infantilized citizenry is enslaved by its very wealth and leisure. In terms of understanding human motivation, this is a masterstroke artistically, for despite the rise of the mid-century totalitarianisms that spied and starved and slaughtered at will, the seduction of pleasure is harder to notice and perhaps also harder to fight than any dictator's uniformed henchmen.

As in *Nineteen Eighty-Four*, however, Huxley shows that the price for this seeming utopia is the destruction of the human spirit: "'Stability,' said the Controller, 'stability. No civilization without social stability. No social stability without individual stability'" (42). Social stability here means a strict caste system founded in biology, while individual stability stems from the universal use of genetic engineering and even in vitro gestation, then education at a State Conditioning Centre after "decanting." The heretical *book* of *Nineteen Eighty-Four* considers all earlier dictatorships "half-hearted and inefficient" compared to the relentless Party (169), yet the Party may be compared to the World State of *Brave New World* in the same terms. The World State, after all, needs no telescreens, no spying helicopters, no Thought Police, no agent provocateurs, because thanks to genetic modification and subliminal programming, the overwhelming majority of its populace has neither the capacity nor the motivation to rebel.

Unlike the citizens of Oceania, those of Huxley's World State have every material comfort. First engineered at the very cellular level to be Alpha, Beta, Gamma, Delta, or Epsilon types and then relentlessly and unobtrusively conditioned with "hypnopaedia" so that "their minds would be made to endorse the judgment of their bodies" (Huxley 15), they are employed in jobs perfectly suited to their programmed temperaments, from creative and managerial through technical and then simpler factory work to the very menial. They are entertained by socially sanctioned promiscuity and various other amusements designed to both take up spare time and increase consumption, thus driving the economy. Stereoscopic motion-picture theaters provide "feely effects," from the "almost intolerable galvanic pleasure" of a kiss (170–71) to "a love scene on a bearskin rug" (34). And then whenever necessary, there is the drug *soma*, with "all the advantages of Christianity and alcohol; none of their defects" (53–54). In short, people's lives are made as "emotionally easy" as possible; the goal, in fact, is to keep the populace so pacified that they experience virtually no emotion at all (43–44).

As resident controller for western Europe, Mustapha Mond is uniquely qualified to be not only a maker and enforcer of World State policy but also an explainer of that policy, whether to eager young schoolboys or to outsiders such as the visiting Savage from the wilds of New Mexico—and ourselves. "Government's an affair of sitting, not hitting," he proclaims to a group of adolescent Alphas visiting the Central London Hatchery and Conditioning Centre. "You rule with the brains and the buttocks, never with the fists" (Huxley 49). This, of course, is because, as an underling matter-of-factly explains, any "hitting" essentially has already been done with oxygen deprivation in the Social Predestination Room: "The lower the caste . . . the shorter the oxygen" (13).

The purposeful creation of "simian" semi-morons kept in "the twilight of [their] own habitual stupor" (Huxley 59), "almost noseless" workers with misshapen skulls, laborers with grotesquely protruding jaws or induced dwarfism for better fit in the factory (162)—these are useful on the assembly line, whereas the "eyeless monsters" (13) created at less than seventy percent oxygen presumably are not. To the well-conditioned citizens of the World State, the situation seems unremarkable and ideal. When the Savage first sees a factory full of such mentally and physically deformed workers, however, he is set "violently retching" (163), and the reader finds it scarcely less disturbing.

O'Brien in *the book* spells out the historical, psychological, and economic imperatives that led to tyranny in his society, and Mond is more than able to do the same in his world. On the one hand, he begins with the famous "History is bunk" assertion of Henry Ford, who in *Brave New World* has been literally deified, and as Mond gestures loftily, the entirety of human history vanishes into oblivion: Greece, Rome, Jesus, Buddha, China—gone (Huxley 34). On the other hand, while Mond thus supports a program of forgetfulness as staggeringly ambitious as that of the Party of *Nineteen Eighty-Four* (though less bloodthirsty), he judiciously believes that, at least for these lucky few Alpha schoolboys—and, of course, for the reader—"now the time has come . . ." (34; ellipsis in orig.).

The World State's "campaign against the Past" (Huxley 51) has, Mond claims, an altruistic rather than a selfish goal, because society since the Industrial Revolution has become a machine made by, for, and of people who must focus on the present. The days of the hunter-gatherer and even the small farmer are gone. Goods, services, and above all food for the world's billions come only after coordinated effort overseen by government planners, and if the machine stops, "a thousand thousand thousand men and women [will] have starved to death" (42). Yet if the machine here keeps people superficially happy and well fed rather than miserable and fearful, as O'Brien's does, nevertheless it requires of its human cogs an obedience little less absolute: "Wheels must turn steadily, but cannot turn untended. There must be men to tend them, men as steady as the wheels upon their axles, sane men, obedient men, stable in contentment" (42). That, says Mond, is why "you're so conditioned that you can't help doing what you ought to do" (244).

Mond easily discards the long-dead ideals of the twentieth century as outmoded and foolish: "Liberty to be inefficient and miserable. Freedom to be a round peg in a square hole," he sniffs (Huxley 46). In contrast, without "family, monogamy, romance" and the resulting intensity of often-conflicting emotions (39), people now enjoy "self-indulgence up to the very limits imposed by hygiene and economics" (243). For the blithely happy citizens of the World State, there is, Mond croons hypnotically,

> no time, no leisure from pleasure, not a moment to sit down and think—or if ever by some unlucky chance such a crevice of time should yawn in the solid substance of their distractions, there is always *soma*, delicious *soma*, half a gramme for a half-holiday, a gramme for a week-end, two grammes for a trip to the gorgeous East, three for a dark eternity on the Moon; returning whence they find themselves on the other side of the crevice, safe on the solid ground of daily labour and distraction, scampering from feely to feely, from girl to pneumatic girl, from Electromagnetic Golf course to . . . (55–56; ellipsis in orig.)

This frenetic pace of promiscuity, sports, and *soma* is both pleasurable for the purposefully infantilized individual and necessary for the economy, for if "the wheels stop turning" (243), "the corpses of a thousand thousand thousand men and women would be hard to bury or burn" (42).

Yet although others may stay "safe on the solid ground of daily labour and distraction," the resident controller for western Europe cannot be so happily blinkered. "There [a]re those strange rumours of old forbidden books hidden in a safe in the Controller's study. Bibles, poetry—Ford knew what" (Huxley 34)—and of course those rumors are correct. Mustapha Mond has a great deal of sympathy for the few dissidents who still turn up in his otherwise-orderly society, for he understands their intellectual, moral, even spiritual frustration all too well.

A post-arrest interview with the genial Mond is "more like a caffeine-solution party than a trial," after all, and one with discernment cannot help being "reassured by the good-humoured intelligence of the Controller's face" (223–24).

Of course, Mond himself generates sympathy in the reader as well, for the secretly free-thinking man is the character in the novel most like ourselves. Before being saddled with the job of running one-tenth of the world, Mond had been a physicist, but a good enough physicist to realize that scientists in this regime were not seeking truth but merely following "a list of recipes that mustn't be added to except by special permission from the head cook" (Huxley 232). Given the choice, then, between exile and being co-opted into the very top of the ruling caste, Mond chose the latter, and despite his earlier unorthodox leanings, he is now the "head cook" of orthodoxy (232–33). Yet while he maintains the status quo because "truth's a menace, science is a public danger" (234), still he explains to the dissident whom he himself is about to exile that this so-called "punishment is really a reward," for the rebel is

> being sent to a place where he'll meet the most interesting set of men and women to be found anywhere in the world. All the people who, for one reason or another, have got too self-consciously individual to fit into community-life. All the people who aren't satisfied with orthodoxy, who've got independent ideas of their own. Every one, in a word, who's any one. I almost envy you. (233)

This lingering envy, far less ambiguous than the "almost regretful irony" of the enigmatic O'Brien of *Nineteen Eighty-Four*, shows the true humanity of the man who must dehumanize so many others. "Happiness," Mond explains with a sigh of regret, "is a hard master—particularly other people's happiness. A much harder master, if one isn't conditioned to accept it unquestioningly, than truth" (233). Others pay for rebellion with exile, but Mond, with the power of Zeus but the burden of Atlas, remains behind: "That's how I paid," he says with a smile. "By choosing to serve happiness. Other people's—not mine" (235).

Fahrenheit 451

The society of Ray Bradbury's *Fahrenheit 451* occupies something in the middle of the spectrum that has the openly brutal Party of *Nineteen Eighty-Four* on one end and the indulgently dehumanizing World State of *Brave New World* on the other. The secret police of the classic mid-twentieth-century dictatorships have their slightly watered-down equivalent in the book-burning "firemen," but here obedience to the established norms stems less from fear of the enforcers than from the pleasant lure of the distractions of commercialism. Set in roughly our own time rather than in the genetically engineered future of the seventh century "After Ford," *Fahrenheit 451* is the novel of the three that most closely resembles our world. Unlike the characters of Orwell and Huxley, those of Bradbury still might have time to change their grim future.

In an America that has "started and won two atomic wars since 1990" (Bradbury 73), books are banned, and they and any houses holding them are burned by the firemen. Book owners captured in the raids are taken "screaming off to the asylum" (33), while any who escape are hunted down by the firemen's eight-legged Mechanical Hound. On slow nights, seeking entertainment, the firemen let loose rats, or chickens, or cats, and then set the Hound on them and lay bets on which of them it will kill first (25). Middle-class women might take a nighttime drive out in the country, getting their kicks by driving fast and hitting rabbits and dogs (64), while teenagers either do the same thing to pedestrians (128) or enjoy violent entertainments at Fun Parks (30). Four-wall televisions carry the most predictable of soap operas and "snap ending" comedies, people often wear "Seashell" radios in their ears even when sleeping, and broadcast entertainment of all kinds is crammed with commercials. As disenchanted fireman Guy Montag tells a coconspirator, "We have everything we need to be happy, but we aren't happy. Something's missing" (82).

When Montag lies in bed with a fever after seeing a woman burn herself with her books rather than abandon her kerosene-soaked library, Fire Captain Beatty visits the shaken man's house. "I've seen it all," says Montag's superior sympathetically. "You were going to call for a night off." In a scene made exquisitely tense by the book hidden under Montag's pillow and by the nervous efforts of the fireman's empty-headed wife, Millie, to putter and straighten things, including the bedclothes, the innocent-seeming Beatty nods understandingly: "Every fireman, sooner or later, hits this. They only need understanding, to know how the wheels run. Need to know the history of our profession. . . . I'll let you in on it," he offers chummily (Bradbury 53–54).

In a sweeping monologue delivered between puffs of his pipe, the enigmatic Beatty covers American history since "a thing called the Civil War" (Bradbury 54), explaining that "technology, mass exploitation, and minority pressure carried the trick, thank God,"[1] such that print began to die off—except for "the comic books" and "the three-dimensional sex magazines, of course." Only after the populace stopped reading did government then wrap laws around the existing preferences so that, as Beatty puts it, now "you can stay happy all the time" (57–58). After all, "that's all we live for, isn't it? For pleasure? For titillation?" (59).

With this near-manic, almost pleading little speech, Beatty seems to the reader a man who knows too much trying to convince himself of too little. Here, too, he is in the middle between O'Brien, who once saw clearly enough to have rebelled but did not, and Mond, who did but turned back. Beatty at least dabbled, yet he also ended up turning away from the challenging path to dissidence. In any event, like the reader, and unlike the average citizen in the novel, he knows the uncertainties of complex thought, and he cautions that such thought can lead only to unhappiness. Someone focusing only on the here and now, he claims, "is happier than any man who tries to slide-rule, measure, and equate the universe, which just won't be measured or equated without making man feel bestial and lonely. I know, I've tried it; to hell with it" (Bradbury 61).

Certainly he has tried it, for the slyly taunting Beatty is "full of bits and pieces" (Bradbury 40) and can quote forbidden authors in rapid-fire succession to make Montag's guilty "head [whirl] sickeningly" (107). The captain's answer, therefore, is a hollow cheer: "So bring on your clubs and parties, your acrobats and magicians, your daredevils, jet cars, motorcycle helicopters, your sex and heroin, more of everything to do with automatic reflex" (61). He concludes with a plea as "tinged by irony" as anything Orwell's O'Brien has ever said:

> The important thing for you to remember, Montag, is we're the Happiness Boys, the Dixie Duo, you and I and the others. We stand against the small tide of those who want to make everyone unhappy with conflicting theory and thought. We have our fingers in the dike. Hold steady. Don't let the torrent of melancholy and drear philosophy drown our world. We depend on you. I don't think you realize how important *you* are, *we* are, to our happy world as it stands now. (61–62; italics in orig.)

Yet in truth, families in *Fahrenheit 451* are empty and loveless, suicide is endemic, and jet bombers circle ominously in the night. And even though he will not admit it, Beatty surely shares Montag's conviction that something is missing in all this.

Captain Beatty is thus a somewhat sympathetic character, rather like ourselves if only we had taken the easy, cynical path down the "happy" slide to moral and intellectual emptiness. He may not show the complete candor of Mustapha Mond—though he does have his own "slippery" (Bradbury 106) charm—yet neither does he torture his victims to the brink of death, as O'Brien does. He has attempted to "hint" to the straying Montag to turn away from his dangerous curiosity (113), and he "let[s] ride" (117) the first alarm against the man, but ultimately Beatty will stray from his duty no more than O'Brien or Mond, and he orders Montag to burn down his own house with a flamethrower.

In the end, however, as the man wanted for "crimes against the State" (Bradbury 124) stands before the smoldering ruins of his house still armed, Beatty, "with his most charming grin," goads Montag ever more snidely until the captain himself at last is incinerated (119). Montag is horrified, but after the shock wears off, he realizes that what he has done is not murder, or really even self-defense, but instead a form of suicide: "How strange, strange, to want to die so much that you let a man walk around armed and then instead of shutting up and staying alive, you go on yelling at people and making fun of them until you get them mad, and then . . ." (122; ellipsis in orig.). Yet perhaps, considering both the long years of book burning on his conscience and his knowledge of the good that his intellect might have done instead, choosing death over a continued hollow existence is not so strange after all. Mond will sigh, but Beatty will die.

Conclusion

The oh-so-understanding, patiently didactic, smilingly world-weary apologists for tyranny in *Nineteen Eighty-Four*, *Brave New World*, and *Fahrenheit 451* know all too well the reader's objections to their dehumanizing policies, for they, too, once were like us: well read, open minded, and discerning. They understand the history, psychology, and economics of their respective worlds, they know of human dignity and self-worth, and they understand the potentials of individual freedom— and they have turned away from true humanity, very consciously. Yet even as they serve governments that quash thought and emotion and individuality, often in the name of some greater societal good, they are not mere yes-men or slogan-mongers. O'Brien, Mustapha Mond, and Captain Beatty know full well where their so-called ideals lead, and, worse, they know how to convince, just as they themselves were "got[ten] . . . a long time ago." Life is easier without troubling emotions and thoughts, they croon, and they of course have just the right combination of punishments and rewards to propagate their view.

Yes, in our own world of the early twenty-first century, we are still a long way from having our very temperaments and sensibilities genetically engineered. And despite a few dictatorships that unfortunately still linger, events from the collapse of the Soviet bloc to the Arab Spring have brought much of the world beyond the grasp of the "traditional" Orwellian tyranny, and it can only be hoped that ever more peoples will step into freedom. Yet the same forces of market and mind that have brought about these welcome changes in our own world— the natural desires for goods, services, and information that will make life easier and more pleasant—also have the potential to lure the unwary to a slide into mere mindless consumerism, like Millie Montag, who seems to live only for television, by clichés, and on sleeping pills. George Orwell, Aldous Huxley, and Ray Bradbury could not know our exact present when they were writing, but even all these decades after the stories and characters were first imagined, their sympathetic villains still warn later generations against the seemingly reasonable arguments that would enslave us to others or to ourselves.

Notes
1. For a fuller discussion of these sometimes-misunderstood trends, see McGiveron.

Works Cited

Bradbury, Ray. *Fahrenheit 451*. New York: Del Rey, 1991.
Huxley, Aldous. *Brave New World*. New York: Harper, 1989.
McGiveron, Rafeeq O. "What 'Carried the Trick'? Mass Exploitation and the Decline of Thought in Ray Bradbury's *Fahrenheit 451*." *Extrapolation* 37.3 (1996): 245–56.
Orwell, George. *Nineteen Eighty-Four*. New York: Signet, 1984.

"The Wretched Refuse of Your Teeming Shore": Overpopulation and Social Breakdown in Harry Harrison's *Make Room! Make Room!*_____

Brian Ireland

Make Room! Make Room! is a 1966 science-fiction novel by Harry Harrison. Set in overpopulated New York City in 1999, the novel depicts a society stretched to the breaking point by overcrowding, food and water rationing, unemployment, and crime. New York's population of 35 million causes a huge strain on living space. People reside wherever they can find a space: if they are lucky, in overcrowded tenements reminiscent of the Five Points district in nineteenth-century New York; if they are less fortunate, in abandoned vehicles, in the rusting hulks of decommissioned ships, or, most commonly, on the streets. There are seven murders a day, and the beleaguered police force is often at the beck and call of corrupt politicians with links to crime syndicates. The plot, a deceptively straightforward detective story, was adapted by MGM for the film *Soylent Green* (1973), but with, as Gary Westfahl notes, an additional "horrific twist: the problem of feeding the masses has been solved by the secret recycling of human bodies into a ubiquitous processed foodstuff" (575). However, as shall be revealed, Harrison's original story line exposed something more horrific than the secret of *Soylent Green*, namely what a future United States might be like with a population of 344 million.

Make Room! Make Room! is a product of its time. Postwar science fiction was dominated by innovative and socially aware narratives and informed by scientific and social-science disciplines. This literature was particularly didactic, utilizing fantastic and speculative plots to instruct readers about moral, political, and social issues. Authors were attracted to dystopian scenarios, as these morally instructive tales warned readers that "something must . . . be done in the present to avoid the future" (Evans 33). These "new maps of hell" (Amis) presented readers with "challenging cognitive maps of the historical situation by way of imaginary societies" (Moylan xi). Additionally, *Make Room! Make Room!* is a product of historic American concerns about overpopulation, as well as a long-established urban-rural rivalry. The nuclear destruction of Hiroshima and Nagasaki that ended World War II ushered in a new age of anxiety about humanity's capacity to destroy itself and its environment. As Paul Boyer has shown, Americans reacted first with joy when news of the bombings was disseminated in the American media; however, that joy was soon tempered with the realization that if Japanese cities could be annihilated so easily and quickly, then so too could American. According to Boyer, "powerful currents of anxiety and apprehension surged through the culture" (8) as victory over Japan was "overshadowed by a growing fear of what might lie ahead" (9). In a *New Yorker* interview, for example, John W. Campbell, editor of *Astounding Science Fiction*, predicted that in a future nuclear war, "every major city will be wiped out in thirty minutes. . . . New York will be a slag heap. . . . Radioactive energy . . . will leave the land uninhabitable for periods ranging from ten months to five hundred years" (qtd. in Boyer 14).

Was survival possible? *Life* magazine thought so; the lead headline on the cover of its September 15, 1961, issue read, "How You Can Survive Fallout: 97 out of 100 People Can Be Saved." What might life be like, though, on a postapocalyptic Earth? Americans had seen the horrific physical effects of nuclear weapons in newsreel footage from Japan; they had read *Life*'s August 20, 1945, edition, which featured disturbing images of the aftermath of the Hiroshima and Nagasaki explosions, and which introduced Americans for the first time to the terrible beauty of an atomic mushroom cloud (Boyer 8). In addition, reports from the US government–funded Atomic Bomb Casualty Commission in Japan illustrated that children of irradiated pregnant women suffered from genetic damage (Hollingsworth). In 1956, Samuel Glasstone suggested that the effects of atomic warfare could include a so-called nuclear winter in which "debris entering the stratosphere may interfere with the transmission of radiant energy from the sun and so serve to decrease the temperature of the earth" (70). The result could be catastrophic disruption of the environment, climate, ecosystems, and human societies. Like no other invention, the atomic bomb gave Americans a sense of both power and vulnerability. As Tom Engelhardt has noted, "those two moments of blinding light had revealed in victory perils almost as terrifying as in defeat, holding out not the promise of an American Earth, but of no Earth at all" (55).

It would be an overstatement to claim that the threat of nuclear destruction was the catalyst for the environmental movement, but it did raise awareness of humanity's place in the natural environment. In particular, two related issues came to prominence in the 1960s: overpopulation and ecology. In 1962, Rachel Carson's *Silent Spring* revealed the long-term detrimental effects of pesticide use on birds, fish, insects, and plants. The book begins with a dystopian scenario: it is spring in a small American town, and no birdsong can be heard. Farm animals begin to die and the town's inhabitants fall ill. The cause? "The people had done it themselves," says Carson (3), by spraying their crops with a cocktail of harmful chemicals. Evocative and effective, *Silent Spring* stirred President John F. Kennedy's administration to investigate the dangers of pesticide use (Monteith 170). It also prefigured legislation such as the Wilderness Act and the establishment of the Land and Water Conservation Fund, both in 1964 (Anderson 67–68), and prompted a ban on the pesticide DDT. Most importantly, perhaps, Carson's work started a grassroots environmental movement (Lytle 57) and increased awareness of the interconnectivity between humanity and the environment.

In 1963, the world's population reached three billion, causing some to ask if the planet could support that many people and what would be the impact on the United States (Anderson 49). These were not new fears, however; for centuries, Americans had pondered the impact of waves of immigrants to their shores. In 1801, Thomas Jefferson congratulated Americans for choosing a land "with room enough for our descendants to the hundredth and thousandth generation" (qtd. in Boorstin 231), but in 1893, Frederick Jackson Turner argued that with a population density of two people per square mile (3), the United States had been settled and its frontier closed (38). Could it really be the case that in the ninety-two years between Jefferson's remarks and Turner's, the population had reached its full capacity? Clearly not. In fact, some were already complaining about overpopulation before Jefferson made his remarks. In 1797, for example, Massachusetts representative Harrison Gray Otis claimed, "When the country was new it might have been good policy to admit all. But it is so no longer" (qtd. in Barron 334). H. Niles, writing in 1817, was content to allow the ongoing flow of immigration, but he thought the Eastern Seaboard too overcrowded, stating, "We have room enough yet; let them come. . . . But the emigrants should press into the interior—in the present state of the times we seem too thick on the maritime frontier already" (359).

In the late 1820s, C. Basil Hall, a Scottish traveler in colonial America, wrote that "every one of the great towns" on the Eastern Seaboard suffered from overpopulation (165). Of course, Hall, a nobleman, was concerned only about supposed overpopulation of the impoverished classes, directing his criticism, for example, at the Orphan Asylum of Charleston for "holding out artificial means of subsistence to families, giv[ing] a hurtful degree of stimulus to the increase of population, already but too apt to run into excess" (165). Hall was, perhaps, influenced by Thomas Malthus's *Essay on the Principle of Population* (1798), wherein Malthus posited that the geometric rise in human population could not be matched by equivalent rises in food production. If left unchecked, he argued, hunger, famine, and social anarchy would be the outcome. Like Hall, Malthus believed that although charity to the poor might alleviate short-term distress, it was harmful in the long term, as it encouraged laziness and served to increase population. He argued that lower classes in particular should be encouraged to control their reproduction through moral restraint and sexual abstinence. One example Malthus cited in his essay was the population growth of colonial America, where the colonists settled almost entirely in towns on the Eastern Seaboard.

In the thirty years after the American Civil War, the nation almost trebled in population, with the arrival of eleven million new immigrants, many of them from the non-Anglo-Saxon nations of southern and eastern Europe. They looked different from extant Americans, did not speak English, and were often non-Protestant in religion. These traits marked them as non-American and possibly unassimilable. They arrived while the United States was in the throes of the Industrial Revolution, when strikes, economic depressions, and civil unrest were everyday occurrences. In this "time of disunity, of economic depression and labor strife, of immigrant urban workers . . . challenging a predominantly Anglo-Saxon Protestant economic and social elite" (Trachtenberg 16), Turner looked suspiciously at cities such as New York that he considered overpopulated with eastern European immigrants (316–17) and wondered how these new immigrants might be Americanized. He claimed that the underpopulated rural frontier, in contrast, acted as a safety valve for American democracy and social stability: "Whenever social conditions tended to crystallize in the East, whenever capital tended to press upon labor or political restraints to impede the freedom of the mass, there was this gate of escape to the free conditions of the frontier" (259).

Concern about overpopulation is interconnected with long-standing political, cultural, and economic competition between urban and rural America. Jefferson advocated an American "agrarian republic" in which democratic values would be protected, championed, and underpinned by the virtues and honesty of hardworking farmers (Kelsey 1172). He did not want the United States to replicate the European class system and the corruption he believed emanated from too much power held by city elites. This competition between urban and rural America often takes the form of a moral debate about values. For example, prohibition of alcohol in the 1920s can be attributed at least in part to rural America's distaste for urban "saloons"—licensed and legal drinking establishments that rural America often associated with a culture of crime, licentiousness, and moral depravity (Barrows and Room 413–14).

Race-based ideology often intersects with concerns about overpopulation. For example, the Immigration Act of 1924 excluded Asians and restricted the numbers of southern and eastern European immigrants. It was not until the 1965 Immigration and Nationality Act—which, not coincidentally, passed into law at the height of the civil-rights movement—that all ethnicity-based immigration quotas were eliminated (Foner and Fredrickson 120). Antiurban arguments have also had a racist subtext, often masked by arguments about the environment. Andrew Ross states, for example, that "at its worst, antiurban environmentalism is burdened by a rural nostalgia that barely submerges its racism. It perpetuates the monstrous image of the city as a greedy parasite, an overpopulated and dangerously polluted concrete jungle which has long transcended its appropriate biological limits" (101).

Frederick Jackson Turner's assertions about the frontier have fallen out of favor in recent years. In particular, historians have challenged his emphasis on the Anglo-Saxon experience of western movement, citing it as inadequate in accounting for the cultural multiplicity of the American West (Trachtenberg 17; Jones and Wills 43). In the early twentieth century, however, Turner's views went virtually unquestioned; every American history textbook published between 1926 and 1930 featured the western frontier as a major shaper of American history, and 80 percent of them agreed with Turner's views (Billington 2–4; Murdoch 79). In battles over resources, political rhetoric, and arguments about the nation's moral future, Turner's fears about assimilation and his reconstruction of an idealized Jeffersonian version of an agrarian America that had never actually existed continued to fuel antiurban sentiment, and in particular fears about overpopulation.

In the post–World War II years, the "atomic age" was characterized by competing emotions of hope and fear. Some believed that the application of atomic energy might provide correctives for many of mankind's problems. For example, in 1945, journalist John J. O'Neill looked forward to "cheap power; 'atomic-energy vitamin tablets'; the mining and smelting of various metals through radioactive beams; and the imminent availability of atomic-powered rockets, airplanes, ships, and automobiles" (Boyer 111). However, the fate of Hiroshima and Nagasaki also demonstrated the apocalyptic potential of splitting the atom. Americans in particular began to appreciate that they now had the scientific knowledge and technological capacity to fully exploit humanity's competing tendencies to both create and destroy. In turn, this led to a broader awareness of humanity's impact on the natural environment. For example, Americans were particularly receptive to Carson's *Silent Spring* in part because it was released during a national discussion about the potentially harmful effects of strontium 90 in baby milk (Lytle 324). It was dawning on some Americans that the choices they made in the present might have a huge impact on humanity's future. But would enough of them come to this realization? It was in this context, and specifically for this purpose, that Harrison wrote *Make Room! Make Room!*

Although not the author's most commercially successful novel, *Make Room! Make Room!* is perhaps his most exceptional achievement. Stan Nicholls calls it "a chilling portrayal of over-population" (55), while David Pringle considers it to be "[Harrison's] most sombre and admonitory work" (202) and Brian Aldiss describes it as "a highly credible portrait of an overcrowded New York" (Aldiss and Wingrove 299). Although a handful of overpopulation stories were published in the 1950s, of which Frederik Pohl's "The Census Takers" (1956) and Isaac Asimov's *The Caves of Steel* (1954) and *The Naked Sun* (1957) are perhaps the most well known, the major theme of science fiction in the postwar years was the atomic age (Boyer 257). By 1966, however, environmental concerns had become the primary science-fiction theme, replacing concerns about the nuclear bomb. The Cuban missile crisis of 1962 had taken the world to the brink of destruction, but its peaceful denouement indicated that political leaders were capable of reaching rational decisions in the face of imminent destruction, and an era of gradual rapprochement followed, evidenced by the Nuclear Test Ban Treaty of 1963 and the installation of a Moscow-Washington hotline to facilitate direct communication between the White House and the Kremlin. Americans were further reassured by President Kennedy's assurance that "in the final analysis, . . . we all inhabit this small planet. We all breathe the same air. We all cherish our children's future. And we are all mortal" (qtd. in Lytle 115). As a result, science-fiction writers looked to environmental topics for inspiration, and fears about overpopulation resulted in works such as Lester del Rey's *The Eleventh Commandment* (1962), Anthony Burgess's *The Wanting Seed* (1962), Brian Aldiss's *Earthworks* (1965), and John Brunner's *Stand on Zanzibar* (1968). As Lionel Shriver so aptly puts it, fears that "we are about to disappear!" were superseded by fears that "we are being overrun!" (153).

Harrison recalls that he first considered the topic in the late 1950s, after he had relocated his family from New York to Cuautla, a tiny, isolated settlement about one hundred kilometers south of Mexico City:

> I watched [overpopulation] develop there. We came back about 15 years after living there: the population had doubled. Why? Death control and no birth control. Malaria had been endemic, kept the population level. The new regime in its wisdom used aerial spray, killed all the mosquitoes in the swamps and wiped out malaria. Doubled the population in 15 years. You must have birth control. You can't have one without the other. (Harrison, "Instead of Having" 19)

Considering the extant political, international, and social climate, Harrison's pessimism about America's future is understandable. At the close of the 1960s, nine hundred thousand people in New York alone were on welfare, one person for every three working in private industry, and two-thirds of central Los Angeles had been concreted over for roads, garages, and parking lots. By 1970, the number of Americans living in or near cities made up nearly 70 percent of the population (Morison, Commager, and Leuchtenburg 706); by 1971, New York had the highest population density in the country, with twenty-six thousand people per square mile. And while population density did not necessarily cause crime, violent crime occurred more often in larger cities, with rates up to five times higher than in smaller cities and eleven times higher than in rural areas. Six major cities with populations over one million accounted for 10 percent of the total population of the United States but contributed 30 percent of the country's major violent crimes (Ehrlich and Freedman 11).

Given that "the treatment of imaginary societies in the best dystopian fiction is always highly relevant more or less directly to specific 'realworld' societies and issues" (Booker 19), Harrison chose to extrapolate from such data to create his dysfunctional New York. However, he wanted his future world to be recognizable, stating:

> Overpopulation had been a recurrent theme in sf for years, but the over-populated future had always been the far future and was about as relevant to life today as E. E. Smith's *Lensman.* My basic idea was a simple one: set a novel in the year 2000 just a few decades away, when the reader, and certainly the reader's children, would be around to see what the world would be like. ("Beginning" 92)

Eventually Harrison chose 1999 instead of 2000, but his point was the same: readers would be encouraged to think this future society was a real possibility rather than a distant flight of fancy. Harrison's future America is therefore made deliberately familiar; it is still a democracy, for example, although its citizens continue to make poor decisions. While this society is structured like a pyramid, with power residing in a minority at the top and the powerless masses at the bottom, Harrison has not so much imagined a new social order as he has recreated the current one, but with the elites more entrenched and the masses more exploited. Unlike in George Orwell's *Nineteen Eighty-Four* (1949), for example, the blame for humanity's predicament lies not with power-hungry dictatorships but with humanity itself, for not accepting responsibility for its actions. The implications of this are not wholly negative, though; Lyman T. Sargent points out, for instance, that "many dystopias are self-consciously warnings. A warning implies that choice, and therefore hope, are still possible" (26).

Make Room! Make Room!'s plot structure resembles that of a detective story; Kingsley Amis notes that "detective fiction and science fiction are akin," with "a closely similar exaltation of idea or plot over characterisation" and an invitation to the reader "to solve a puzzle" (34). Harrison's use of this generic plot format allows the reader access to all levels and aspects of his dystopian society. The main protagonist is Detective Rusch, and in the course of his homicide inquiry, many facets of this society are revealed—so much so that by the end of the novel, the reader (with a lot of signposts left by the author) is left wondering more about the circumstances that gave rise to this futuristic dystopia than about the murder investigation.

The victim is an ex-convict named "Big" Mike O'Brien, an intermediary between organized crime and corporate interests. O'Brien lives with his young mistress, a woman named Shirl Greene, in Chelsea Park, an exclusive and well-defended apartment complex that features a drawbridge, towers, and "crenelated battlements" (Harrison, *Make Room!* 51).[1] Billy Chung, an immigrant from Formosa, murders O'Brien during an attempted robbery. Chung is from this society's extensive underclass, the criminal poor who make up the majority of New York's population, and through his eyes is revealed the lowest stratum of society: a world that is squalid, impoverished, violent, and despairing. Meanwhile, the relationship between Shirl and O'Brien reveals the lives of the privileged, who use their wealth to distance themselves from the poor and partake of the dwindling supply of food, water, and consumer products. The elites employ the police, the courts, and the law to defend their position; for example, it is O'Brien's status that triggers a high-profile murder enquiry. Rusch resents this, as murder in this society is commonplace, averaging "seven murders a day, and ten on good days" (51). This is class warfare as described in the Marxist tradition, although Rusch does not realize his place in this schema until it is too late.

Rusch soon develops a romantic relationship with Shirl. When she is evicted from O'Brien's apartment, she moves in with Rusch and his roommate, Sol Kahn, who is seventy-five years old and still remembers a time before food shortages and the depletion of natural resources. Sol serves as the reader's link with his or her own time, and he is the character best able to articulate what has been lost. He hates the manufactured food because he knows what real food tastes like. He uses old-time slang that no one comprehends. No one understands why he is so passionate about birth control because they know only the world they have been born into. Sol is an anchor to the past, but he is also a conduit for Harrison's views; Harrison told actor Edward G. Robinson, who plays Sol in *Soylent Green*, "Very simply, you are *me* in this story" (Harrison, "Boom Two" 206). In one exchange between Sol and Shirl, for instance, Shirl's opinions are expressed not to counter Sol's point of view but to facilitate expository dialogue about the consequences of overpopulation. When Shirl refers to a proposed piece of birth-control legislation as the "Baby-killer Bill" and questions whether it is a violation of "natural law" and "an intrusion of privacy" (Harrison, *Make Room!* 159–62), Sol attacks the hypocrisy of organized religion, particularly the anti–birth control doctrine of the Catholic Church, arguing instead for the rational application of science and knowledge: "There should have been free discussion, tons of money for fertility research, world-wide family planning, educational programs on the importance of population control—and most important of all, free speech for free opinion" (176).

For the most part, though, Harrison makes his argument in a more subtle way, using a technique he calls "background as foreground." The background, he explains,

is what it's all about—the background is the foreground. In the book, which appears at first just to be an adventure story, I didn't draw attention to the setting—I just let it sink in slowly. When the reader is about two-thirds into it he suddenly becomes aware of the horrible reality of this terrible New York of the future and then it becomes obvious as to what the book is really about. ("Boom Two" 204)

For instance, readers know from the beginning that the murder took place during the course of a robbery, and unlike in a traditional detective narrative, there is no mystery to be revealed. As a result, the plot unfolds as a manhunt, which is resolved unsatisfactorily when Rusch inadvertently kills Chung. By this time, Rusch's superiors and O'Brien's organized-crime confederates have lost interest in the murder. As Paul Tomlinson has noted, for Harrison, the murder investigation is unimportant; it is simply a plot device "which sets the action in motion and gets the characters in trouble so that we can observe their reactions" (3). Rusch's reward for finding the killer is a demotion from detective to uniformed patrolman. In addition, Shirl leaves him for a richer man, and his roommate Sol dies of pneumonia. Rusch loses everything, and there is no happy ending to comfort the reader.

As the author intended, the plot winds down rather than building to a climax, in the process making the reader aware of the changes that have taken place between 1966 and 1999 and particularly their impact on ordinary people. In this scenario, overpopulation and subsequent overconsumption result in scarcity of resources, so for the majority on welfare, all aspects of everyday life are a struggle. Oil supplies are depleted, meaning privately owned cars are for the very rich only. There is no public transportation; those who have enough money can pay to be transported in a human-powered "pedicab." Water shortages mean that much of the nation's farmland has been reduced to dust bowl conditions reminiscent of the Great Depression of the 1930s. In the anti-urban tradition, resentful farmers destroy aqueducts to protest scarce water resources being diverted to the overpopulated cities. In another Depression-era allusion, this time to the Hoovervilles or shantytowns of the 1930s, tent cities have formed to house the poor; during the Depression, over twenty such enclaves existed in New York City alone (Silver 258). Prisoners are put to work breaking up concrete parkways to create more farmland. Drinking water is in short supply and has to be extracted from shared public taps. Food, most commonly manufactured from seaweed and plankton, is of poor quality and strictly rationed. Margarine is made from motor and chlorella oil. For a treat, people might buy Soylent Green, made from soybeans and lentils. Only the privileged elite can afford meat from the meatleggers, whose shops are defended by armed guards. Even shaving razors become a luxury item; Rusch complains about his dull, chipped blade and ponders when he might get a new one, thinking, "Maybe in the fall" (Harrison, *Make Room!* 12). Electricity supply is sporadic at best, and readers are shown how their future counterparts are forced to adapt to their circumstances; for example, the elderly and ill Sol must exert himself by pedaling a cycle-driven generator to create a current, and he uses heat from the sun to warm water for bathing and washing clothes.

As a result of such conditions, people in this society routinely suffer from diseases formerly endemic only in impoverished countries, such as dysentery and malaria. While not ill, Detective Rusch displays the negative physical effects of his starchy diet, such as thinning hair, pale skin, protruding ribs, and a potbelly. Such a life would be almost intolerable to affluent Americans in the 1960s, many of them products of the postwar baby boom; for the New Yorkers of Harrison's 1999, however, this is all they know. When Shirl comments that "everyone must be unthinking and selfish," Sol replies, "No—I think better of the human race. They've just never been told" (Harrison, *Make Room!* 162). Through Sol's didactic dialogue and Harrison's gradual revelation of the appalling reality of everyday life in this dystopian society, readers are made aware of the potentially horrific consequences of overpopulation and overconsumption and are thereby encouraged to mend their ways.

Harrison would return to the theme of overpopulation in later stories such as "A Criminal Act" (1967) and "Roommates" (1971), but *Make Room! Make Room!* is his definitive statement on the topic. Of course, few of his predictions have come to pass; in the afterword to a 2008 edition of the novel, the author admits that his predictions were "pretty bad in most of the general details" (*Make Room!* [2008] 232). However, *Make Room! Make Room!* is about ideas rather than prediction, as it extrapolates the future consequences of current circumstances (Ketterer 148). Paul R. Ehrlich, whose 1968 book *The Population Bomb* gave Thomas Malthus's views about overpopulation a new lease on life, wrote an introduction to some American editions of *Make Room! Make Room!*, stating:

> Projection of even the mid-range future of urban areas presents well nigh insuperable problems. . . . But the results of such projections, while instructive, are also preposterous. We know things won't work out that way as far as the numbers living in cities are concerned. Moreover, we are completely ignorant of future trends in urban living conditions. . . . *Make Room! Make Room!* presents a gripping scenario of where current trends may be leading. Such scenarios are important tools in helping us to think about the future, and in bringing home to people the possible consequences of our collective behavior. (Ehrlich viii–ix)

So while *Make Room! Make Room!* may make grim reading at times, the author's outlook is essentially optimistic, as he believes his readers will respond positively to rational analysis. At first glance, for example, Harrison's treatment of Chung is troubling. As stated earlier, fears about overpopulation can derive from racial fears about being "overrun"; Robert Scholes and Eric Rabkin argue that the trend toward overpopulation novels in the postwar years was caused at least in part by the American experience of the Korean War, which "made the West palpably aware of the sheer mass of Asian population" (150). Dystopian novels can act as outlets for such fears, occasionally featuring extremely racist and disturbing solutions to overpopulation and immigration issues, such as the race war in Andrew Macdonald's neo-Nazi novel *The Turner Diaries* (1978). There are, therefore, potential difficulties with Harrison's portrayal of Chung, an Asian immigrant, as a member of the criminal underclass and a murderer who is done away with by an Anglo-Saxon policeman. However, Harrison palliates this by revealing the horrific world in which Chung lives. The boy is a criminal only because society has criminalized him. He steals food to feed his family, sometimes goes without so that they can eat, and had not planned to murder O'Brien, who in turn is a career criminal through choice rather than circumstances. Harrison indicates through Chung that overpopulation and overconsumption are at the root of humanity's problems, and readers are encouraged to identify and sympathize with Chung's plight rather than blame him for the circumstances in which he lives and to which he has to adjust.

Furthermore, whereas many science-fiction writers offered "draconian legislation" (Scholes and Rabkin 150) as the solution to overpopulation—citizens in Alexie Panshin's *Rite of Passage* (1968) require permission from a "Eugenics Council" to have children; in William F. Nolan and George C. Johnson's *Logan's Run* (1967), citizens are euthanized when they reach age twenty-one—Harrison's solutions (education, knowledge, and rational thinking) are moderate and more in keeping with the liberal and tolerant values that characterized much of the 1960s, values that gave women the right to use birth control, assert more control over their lives, and thereby widen their potential horizons. This must have seemed like science fiction in 1966, but by the 1970s, at least in the United States, it had become science fact. By then, contraception had been decriminalized, the contraceptive pill was widely available, and attitudes toward family planning had shifted to a more liberal position. In 1973, the Supreme Court decision in *Roe v. Wade* legalized abortion, effectively ending what Margaret Sanger called a century-long "war against birth control." In that year, though, prominent science-fiction author Isaac Asimov was still suggesting a draconian measure like "mandatory sterilization" as the best method of population control (LeBlanc 69). Thankfully, Harrison's more benevolent viewpoint prevailed.

Notes

1. Unless otherwise stated, all references to Harrison's *Make Room! Make Room!* are to the 1973 Berkley edition.

Works Cited

Aldiss, Brian W., and David Wingrove. *Trillion Year Spree: The History of Science Fiction.* London: Paladin, 1988.

Amis, Kingsley. *New Maps of Hell: A Survey of Science Fiction.* London: Science Fiction Bk. Club, 1962.

Anderson, Terry H. *The Sixties.* 2nd ed. New York: Pearson, 2004.

Barron, Milton L. *American Minorities: A Textbook of Readings in Intergroup Relations.* New York: Knopf, 1957.

Barrows, Susanna, and Robin Room. *Drinking: Behavior and Belief in Modern History.* Berkeley: U of California P, 1991.

Billington, Ray Allen, ed. *The Frontier Thesis: Valid Interpretation of American History?* New York: Holt, 1966.

Booker, M. Keith. *The Dystopian Impulse in Modern Literature: Fiction as Social Criticism.* Westport, CT: Greenwood, 1994.

Boorstin, Daniel J. *The Lost World of Thomas Jefferson.* Chicago: Chicago UP, 1993.

Boyer, Paul S. *By the Bomb's Early Light: American Thought and Culture at the Dawn of the Atomic Age.* Chapel Hill: U of North Carolina P, 1994.

Carson, Rachel. *Silent Spring.* New York: Houghton, 2002.

Ehrlich, Paul. Introduction. Harrison, *Make Room!* 1973, vii–ix.

Ehrlich, Paul, and Jonathan Freedman. "Population, Crowding and Human Behaviour." *New Scientist and Science Journal* 50.745 (1971): 10–14.

Engelhardt, Tom. *The End of Victory Culture: Cold War America and the Disillusioning of a Generation.* New York: Harper, 1995.

Evans, Robert O. "The Nouveau Roman, Russian Dystopias, and Anthony Burgess." *Studies in the Literary Imagination* 6.2 (1973): 27–38.

Foner, Nancy, and George M. Fredrickson. *Not Just Black and White: Historical and Contemporary Perspectives on Immigration, Race, and Ethnicity in the United States.* New York: Sage, 2005.

Glasstone, Samuel. *The Effects of Nuclear Weapons.* Washington, DC: GPO, 1956.

Hall, Basil. *Travels in North America in the Years 1827 and 1828.* Vol. 3. Carlisle, MA: Applewood, 1830.

Harrison, Harry. "The Beginning of the Affair." *Hell's Cartographers: Some Personal Histories of Science Fiction Writers.* Ed. Brian W. Aldiss and Harry Harrison. London: Futura, 1976. 76–95.

_____. "Boom Two (1970–73)." *Future Tense: The Cinema of Science Fiction.* Ed. John Brosnan. New York: St. Martin's, 1978. 192–216.

_____. "Instead of Having a Rotten Job: The World according to Harry Harrison." Interview by Robert Neilson. *Albedo One* 11 (1996): 14–19.

_____. *Make Room! Make Room!* New York: Berkley, 1973.

_____. *Make Room! Make Room!* London: Penguin, 2008.

Hollingsworth, J. W. "Delayed Radiation Effects in Survivors of the Atomic Bombings: A Summary of the Findings of the Atomic Bomb Casualty Commission, 1947–1959." *New England Journal of Medicine* 263 (1960): 481–87.

Jones, Karen R., and John Wills. *The American West: Competing Visions.* Edinburgh: Edinburgh UP, 2009.

Kelsey, Timothy W. "The Agrarian Myth and Policy Responses to Farm Safety." *American Journal of Public Health* 84.7 (1994): 1171–77.

Ketterer, David. "The Apocalyptic Imagination, Science Fiction, and American Literature." *Science Fiction: A Collection of Critical Essays.* Ed. Mark Rose. Englewood Cliffs, NJ: Prentice, 1976. 147–55.

LeBlanc, Michael. "Judith Merril and Isaac Asimov's Quest to Save the Future." *Foundation* 35.98 (2006): 59–73.

Lytle, Mark H. *America's Uncivil Wars: The Sixties Era from Elvis to the Fall of Richard Nixon.* Oxford: Oxford UP, 2006

Malthus, Thomas. *An Essay on the Principle of Population.* London: Johnson, 1798.

Monteith, Sharon. *American Culture in the 1960s.* Edinburgh: Edinburgh UP, 2009.

Morison, Samuel Eliot, Henry Steele Commager, and William E. Leuchtenburg. *A Concise History of the American Republic.* 2nd ed. Oxford: Oxford UP, 1983.

Moylan, Tom. *Scraps of the Untainted Sky: Science Fiction, Utopia, Dystopia.* Boulder, CO: Westview, 2000.

Murdoch, David H. *The American West: The Invention of a Myth.* Reno: U of Nevada P, 2001.

Nicholls, Stan. *Wordsmiths of Wonder: Fifty Interviews with Writers of the Fantastic.* London: Orbit, 1993.

Niles, H. *Niles' Weekly Register.* Vol. 12. Baltimore: Franklin, 1817.

Pringle, David. *The Ultimate Encyclopedia of Science Fiction: The Definitive Illustrated Guide.* London: Carlton, 1997.

Ross, Andrew. *The Chicago Gangster Theory of Life: Nature's Debt to Society.* London: Verso, 1995.

Sanger, Margaret. "The War against Birth Control." *American Mercury* June 1924: 231–36.

Sargent, Lyman Tower. "The Three Faces of Utopianism Revisited." *Utopian Studies* 5.1 (1994): 1–37.

Scholes, Robert, and Eric S. Rabkin. *Science Fiction: History, Science, Vision.* Oxford: Oxford UP, 1977.

Shriver, Lionel. "Population in Literature." *Population and Development Review* 29.2 (2003): 153–62.

Silver, Nathan. *Lost New York.* New York: Houghton, 2000.

Tomlinson, Paul. Rev. of *Make Room! Make Room!* by Harry Harrison. *Make Room!* 2 (1985): 3.

Trachtenberg, Alan. *The Incorporation of America: Culture and Society in the Gilded Age.* New York: Hill, 1990.

Turner, Frederick J. *The Frontier in American History*. New York: Holt, 1921.

Westfahl, Gary, ed. *The Greenwood Encyclopedia of Science Fiction and Fantasy: Themes, Works, and Wonders*. Vol. 2. Westport, CT: Greenwood, 2005.

Rationalism, Revolution, and Utopia in Yevgeny Zamyatin's *We* _____

Peter G. Stillman

Yevgeny Zamyatin's *We* has only gradually become known in the English-speaking world. Written around 1920, *We* was first read in the Soviet Union at a literature society meeting. It was published in English translation in 1924 and then in Czech in 1927 (and not in the Soviet Union until 1988). The story seems part science fiction, part adventure tale; in it, a beautiful woman called I-330, seeking to advance her group's revolutionary aims, schemes to win the love of an important engineer of One State, D-503, and enlist him in seizing the spaceship he is building. But Zamyatin transforms the story into serious utopian political theory by engaging in many ongoing contemporary (and recurring) debates, criticizing important trends in twentieth-century thought and practice, and suggesting how to think about utopia and revolution.

Important Contemporary Contexts for *We*

In *We*, Zamyatin follows the mode of writing of H. G. Wells, a famous and prolific writer of science fiction, history, and utopias, beginning with *The Time Machine* in 1895. In a 1922 essay, Zamyatin praises Wells as a pioneer in the new genre of "socioscientific fantasy" ("H. G. Wells" 289). Wells did not write utopias, which, Zamyatin asserts, present "[s]tatic well-being" and "petrified paradisiac social equilibrium"; rather, he wrote stories with "dynamic" plots, "built on collisions, on conflict; the story is complex and entertaining" (288). Moreover, Wells's "sociofantastic novels" do not construct an ideal future so much as they "expos[e] the defects of the existing social order" (286). Zamyatin hoped that in the Soviet Union, Wellsian socioscientific fantasy was beginning to flourish; in his essay, he cites a few examples, including *We* (291).

Zamyatin's *We* is now frequently classed with Aldous Huxley's *Brave New World* (1932) and George Orwell's *Nineteen Eighty-Four*

(1949) as a classic antitotalitarian dystopian novel. But nascent Soviet totalitarianism seems not to have been Zamyatin's only or primary target. Rather, his book focuses on the tendencies, trajectory, and defects of modern industrial society in general, presenting One State as the logical political conclusion of modern mathematical rationalism and rationalized and efficient social organization, especially as suggested by Frederick Winslow Taylor. In his major work, *The Principles of Scientific Management* (1911), Taylor applies scientific analysis to the workplace with the goal of creating greater efficiency of labor. He concludes that workers need to have their tasks clearly defined and their activities limited to fulfilling those tasks, and thus must be managed to assure their performance of these tasks in a regularized and timely fashion. His ideas helped transform craftwork into mechanized and then automated tasks by promoting the assembly line as the method of production, emphasizing that each worker is a part of a larger process, and stressing that the entire process can be created and enforced only by management. "Taylorism" became synonymous with modern industrial practices of scientific management and assembly-line production. Some dystopian writers had been arguing against modern science and rationality since Jonathan Swift's *Gulliver's Travels* (1726) and against the machine society at least since E. M. Forster's "The Machine Stops" (1909); to that tradition, Zamyatin added his focus on the collectivism and authoritarianism of Taylor, the modern system of production, and contemporary industrialization.

Zamyatin also engaged in three debates especially active in nineteenth-century Russian literature but relevant throughout the West, the first of which focused on the Crystal Palace. Built to house a world exposition of technological and manufacturing progress in London in 1851, this temple to industrial productivity and technological innovation was primarily made of iron and glass, a monument to Western rationalism's clarity, transparency, and ability to use modern technology to conquer nature and satisfy human needs. The Crystal Palace became a cultural and intellectual symbol and battleground: a symbol of utopian aspirations in radical texts like Nikolai Chernyshevsky's *What Is to Be Done?* (1883) and a target for Fyodor Dostoevsky's conservative critique of modernity's empire of light, reason, and industry. Zamyatin joined the fray by designing his One State with the metaphors of the Crystal Palace.

A second debate centered on Dostoevsky's parable of the Grand Inquisitor, in which Jesus returns to earth during the Spanish Inquisition and meets the Grand Inquisitor, who arrests and interrogates him, accusing him of trying to bring freedom to mankind. But, the inquisitor says, people cannot endure freedom. Rather, they want happiness, and so the church, working with the devil, has struggled to bring them happiness and bread and security. For Dostoevsky, the quest for material well-being meant the evisceration of what is important about human beings. But modern technological society, like the inquisitor, offers people the happiness of satisfying their desires.

The third debate was the story of Adam and Eve in paradise. For Zamyatin, the Garden of Eden was a time of human happiness and innocence, disturbed by Mephistopheles (Satan) when he tempted Eve and Adam to eat the fruit of the tree of the knowledge of good and evil. D-503's friend R-13 sums up One State's stance: Adam and Eve, "in paradise, were given a choice: happiness without freedom, or freedom without happiness. . . . Those idiots chose freedom." For years, "they longed for the chains" (Zamyatin, *We* 61), and now One State has found a way to abolish freedom and restore happiness—to do God's work against the devil, to reestablish on earth the promise of that primordial myth of a peaceful, happy paradise where humans know neither choice nor evil (214).

One State: The Culmination of Dreams of Modern Western Industrial Civilization

As *We* begins, the reader meets D-503, the writer of the diary that constitutes *We*'s text. Living about a thousand years in the future, he is a leading engineer and mathematician, the builder of the spaceship *Inte-*

gral; he is also a committed member of his society, One State, which appears to him as a utopia of technological and scientific progress, happiness, and rational order. In his depiction of One State, Zamyatin distills and describes the fulfillment of a dream of modern Western industrial society: rationality applied to science and technology, issuing in machines, mechanization, and mass production, and resulting in a society capable of making its citizens' lives satisfied and happy.

After the Great Two Hundred Years' War between city and village, which resulted in the death of almost all the world's population, One State came into existence. One State builds on an idea of progress. D-503 traces a linear history "from nomadic to increasingly settled forms of existence. And does it not follow that the most settled form (ours) is at the same time the most perfect (ours)?" (Zamyatin, *We* 11). One essential element of One State is its Green Wall, which, D-503 writes, has "isolated our perfect mechanical world from the irrational, hideous world of trees, birds, animals" (93). Another is the scientific management of individuals and especially the daily timetable of each individual, the "Table of Hours," whose precise dictates coordinate everyone's schedule. "Every morning . . . at the same hour and the same moment, we—millions of us—get up as one. At the same hour," they all start work, eat, take a walk, go to the auditorium for phono-lectures, "go to the hall for the Taylor exercises," and go to sleep (12). Following the Table of Hours, "you feel yourself a part of a great, powerful, single entity" (33). So much is everyone a part of a larger whole that they all wear uniforms to indicate unity and everybody has a number instead of a name, fitting the utilitarian and regularized ethos. Deviants "are only breakdowns of minor parts which can easily be repaired without halting the eternal, grandiose movement of the entire Machine" (14).

One State is like a crystal, with its clarity and endlessly repeating patterns. The architecture and city planning reflect order, uniformity, and transparency: the street grid, the "glittering glass of the pavements, the divine parallelepipeds of the transparent houses, the square harmony of the gray-blue ranks" (Zamyatin, *We* 5). Uniformity pervades smaller spaces also; as D-503 says, if he were to go to R-13's apartment, "everything would seem to be exactly the same as mine: the Table, the glass chairs, the closet, the bed" (41).

With its emphasis on order and limitation, One State appears to have conquered individuality and freedom almost entirely. The multiplication table provides an example of truth, utility, and unfreedom; it "never errs. And there are no happier figures than those which live according to the harmonious, eternal laws of the multiplication table. No hesitations, no delusions. There is only one truth, and only one true way; this truth is two times two, and the true way—four" (Zamyatin, *We* 67). Freedom leads to error, criminality, and unhappiness. One State provides the truth and the way, "the beneficent yoke of reason" (1).

One State extends that "beneficent yoke" to solve human problems that have led in the past to dissatisfaction and revolt. In the face of hunger, people created synthetic petroleum-based food, small cubes of nourishment to be chewed fifty times in unison at the "long glass tables" (Zamyatin, *We* 102). One State seeks to conquer love, another cause of social disorder and unpredictability, of individual suffering, pain, envy, and "innumerable stupid tragedies"; and so love is transformed into sex, a "harmonious, pleasant, and useful function . . . like sleep, physical labor, the consumption of food, defecation, and so on" (22). Moreover, sex is commodified, and one's body is not one's own: "Each number has a right to any other number, as to a sexual commodity" (21).

In One State, two "Personal Hours" per day remain, during which individuals can lower their shades and engage in sex with whoever has acquired a pink coupon for sex with them for the hour, walk "with measured tread" (presumably, no skipping), or work (Zamyatin, *We* 12). D-503 is confident that soon these Personal Hours will become systematized to eliminate any differences in behavior. Even so, the numbers can "taste the heights of bliss in the shining palace of the One State" (21).

D-503: A True Believer in One State's Perfection

D-503 sees One State as a realized, perfect utopia because he has internalized and believes in it. He is a good example of the hegemonic power of One State—its ability to instill its principles into the minds of its citizens and discipline their thinking so that they see One State's practices as the obvious, indeed the only, embodiment of rational social and political principles. Zamyatin allows D-503's acculturated personality to shine through in his diary.

Like One State, D-503 is organized; his diary has headings, and he rigidly stays inside those headings, at least at the beginning. Especially in the first few entries, he writes in a most mechanical fashion. His early narratives in his diary are flat and emotionless: "My pen, accustomed to figures, does not know how to create the music of assonances and rhymes" (Zamyatin, *We* 2). He is so deferential to the authorities, or so modest about his own writing, that instead of summarizing it or putting it in his own words, he copies verbatim "the proclamation that appeared today in the *One State Gazette*" (1). D-503 plans to "merely attempt to record what I see and think, or, to be more exact, what we think" (2).

D-503 so fully integrates "what we think" that he cannot comprehend alternatives. For instance, because he so believes in the beneficial effects of the Table of Hours, he literally cannot comprehend what life must have been like before the Table, "when people still lived in a free, i.e., unorganized, savage condition" (Zamyatin, *We* 13). His turns of phrase are equally determined; his statements frequently begin with "it is clear," because to the mathematical logic of the reasoning mind, everything should be clear. When he first talks of love, he seeks to place it within the cause-and-effect reasoning of modern science and technology: "love because" (26). When he explores the meaning of happiness, he immediately describes it as a fraction: "Is it not clear . . . that bliss and envy are the numerator and denominator of the fraction called happiness?" (21). D-503 has faith in Taylor—the Benefactor, "unquestionably the greatest genius of the ancients" (33), who maintains "the imperishable fortress of our happiness" (137)—and indeed all the principles and practices of One State, "the greatest and most rational civilization in history" (229).

We as Dystopia: The Struggle in the Mind of D-503

In *We*, much of the tension in the dystopian fiction takes place in the mind of the protagonist. Zamyatin uses the diary form to allow the reader to see D-503's internal struggles as he faces experiences that do not conform to his rational self-understanding as a committed number in One State.

From the beginning of his diary, D-503 indicates some unease in One State. Dedicated to mathematics as providing certainty and utility, D-503 finds infinity perplexing: there is no final number and thus no closure, no wall, no finality, and numbers can sprawl on indefinitely, without order or limits. Nor can he integrate $\sqrt{-1}$, which is even more troubling, perhaps because it signals irrationality in the midst of the rational system.

D-503's hairy hands embarrass him, an atavism connecting him to mankind's primitive past (Zamyatin, *We* 7, 163). He also feels a closeness to O-90 and R-13, using the word "mine" to describe his relation to O-90 (5) and "family" to characterize the threesome (44). Despite his desiccated prose, when he begins to write his diary, his "cheeks are burning" and he feels similar to a woman who, having felt the pulse of her fetus, knows she must "nourish it" and then "tear it painfully" into the world (2). For D-503 to have a sense of creativity, of natality, of bringing something new into the world—all these are organic, not mechanical, images; all suggest a nonmathematical relation to the world; and all suggest not One State's perfected completion but the possibility of change.

D-503 undergoes further internal struggles because of his relations with I-330. He finds himself drawn to her, reflecting his fascination with and repulsion by $\sqrt{-1}$, with the irrational, with the challenge of fitting her mysteriousness into his rationalistic way of understanding the world. The challenge tests him beyond measure. He changes. He starts to dream, and in a cornucopia of colors—dangerous, because One State knows that "dreams are a serious psychic disease" (Zamyatin, *We* 32). The mathematically strong triangle of D-503, O-90, and R-13 is broken (64). No longer does D-503 insist on instrumental reason, certain mathematical knowledge, and clearly delimited action. With I-330, he does not ask where they are going; "the only thing that mattered was to walk, to walk, to ripen, to fill up more and more firmly" (72). His faith in his mathematics is broken: "Knowledge, absolutely sure of its infallibility, is faith. I had had firm faith in myself; I had believed that I knew everything within myself. And now . . ." (59, ellipsis in orig.).

So he questions. He asks, "Who am I, what am I like?" (Zamyatin, *We* 64). After passionate love, in which the state, time, and space are transcended, D-503 discovers that he cannot fit his behavior into a "logical formula" (75); his passions and emotions are bringing him closer to another human being, and indeed to being human, than the disciplined, compulsory conformity of One State. He discovers: "I have a soul. . . . Incurable" (98; ellipsis in orig.). With I-330, he breaks rules, acts as he has never acted with anyone before, and feels his own being acutely: "I want one thing—I-330. I want her with me every minute, any minute, always—only with me," he writes (138). Finally, D-503 becomes aware that "I was I, a separate entity, a world. I had ceased to be a component, as I had been, and become a unit" (157). Then he jumps up and proclaims, "Yes, yes, madness! And everyone must lose his mind, everyone must! The sooner the better! It is essential—I know it" (158).

At the end of the novel, D-503 submits to the Benefactor's operation, the excision of the imagination, and then cannot recognize as his what he has written in his diary; he returns to being the disciplined, structured, rational result of the hegemonic ideals and practices of One State. But his life shows that education and life experiences, even in a totalistic state, can generate questions about the perfection and finality of a rational social order.

We as Dystopia: Shortcomings of One State

Despite D-503's praise of One State's rational perfection, Zamyatin's prose allows a critical reader to see from the beginning that One State disciplines rather than develops. Its rationality is monochromatic and limited, debilitating when applied as the total model for human life. All that D-503 has learned as a faithful and disciplined number does not help him when he confronts the mystery, emotions, passions, sexuality, and feelings engendered by I-330; his rational, efficient, and utilitarian model breaks down in response to her.

But he is not alone in finding One State unsatisfactory. O-90 finds it too restrictive when she wishes to have a child, illegal in One State because it is inefficient. R-13 finds his duties as a state poet too narrowing, limited, and boring; as an artist, he wishes to express himself rather than be yet another cog in the efficiency machine. Although D-503 is too blind to see it, other numbers feel friendship for him and try to help him (Zamyatin, *We* 161, 208–11). Indeed, dissatisfaction seems widespread; when the revolution occurs, numbers break out of their discipline. They eat without chewing in unison, they walk with freedom, and they copulate shamelessly, "without coupons" and without pulling the shades (217–19).

The Mephi, a group beyond the Green Wall opposed to One State ever since its founding, has all along rejected its rationality and efficiency in favor of nature and natural diversity, energy and "tormentingly endless movement," and a Mephistophelian opposition to authority (Zamyatin, *We* 164–65). The Mephi wish to destroy all walls, "to let the green wind blow free from end to end—across the earth" (157); it is they who ignite the revolution against One State.

Limited and destructive as it is, One State's irrational rationality yokes everyone together; Zamyatin depicts well how Taylorism, efficiency, and technical rationality require extensive state power in order to exist.[1] The Benefactor rules with an iron fist. Employing widespread surveillance, he is ruthless when numbers oppose him, destroying them in his Machine; as he says, "the inevitable mark of truth is—its cruelty"

(Zamyatin, *We* 213). His goal is to so limit the numbers' desires and imagination, pity and love, that they become "obedient slaves" (215). No exuberance, no passion, no pity; no concern with good and evil, only with obedience; all brought about and enforced by the Benefactor's power.

The revolution against the Benefactor and his One State meets with some success, as the Green Wall is smashed and social order upset. D-503's last entry notes that in parts of the city, "there is still chaos, roaring, corpses, beasts, and—unfortunately—a considerable group of numbers" still in revolt, to which the Benefactor's forces are responding (Zamyatin, *We* 232). Who will win in One State remains in doubt.

Conclusion

Zamyatin's *We* is at heart a description, distillation, and critique of the defects of modern Western rational, industrial society, with its mathematics, science, technology, and Taylorism (scientific management aiming at efficiency). Such a social order needs to restrict what the citizen might wish, so that citizens' wishes stay within what the social order can provide; it needs to be able to enforce the rules of logic and society against doubters or deviants; and it needs to be able to punish or otherwise deal with them. So it needs a ruler, a Benefactor, some kind of powerful authority who can manufacture consent; establish the ideological hegemony of that particular form of rationality; maintain order by surveillance, discipline, policing, and punishment; and assure a univocal and totalistic system. That totalistic system, like the Crystal Palace, presents a kind of static, crystalline perfection, the attainment of the most efficient and rational society imaginable, the final accomplishment of human progress.

The value of One State for its inhabitants is that they are happy. They have no fear for the morrow, because they know that they will be fed, clothed, and housed well. They have no anxiety about choices, because they have almost no choices to make. As long as they follow the rules, they have no problems with the authorities. Innocent of an understanding of why anyone would do anything wrong, D-503 at the beginning of the book is like Adam in paradise; and as the story unfolds, D-503 comes to see that the Benefactor, like the Grand Inquisitor, can give him order, stability, and intellectual and psychological security in anxious times. Like the inhabitants of the arcadian Garden of Eden and those ruled by the Grand Inquisitor, the people in One State are happy because they are not free (and so cannot err) and their desires are satisfied.

But that happiness comes at a great cost. In addition to enforcing coercive rule, surveillance, and discipline, One State narrows the human being. Because efficiency is such a central goal, for instance, any act of imagination, whimsy, or feeling is rejected as contrary to efficiency and therefore not worthy of the modern, efficient human being. Love is replaced by sex, and indeed sex as a commodity; food, by a petroleum product shaped like a small cube. Human relations are limited to the utilitarian and beneficial, and human desires are limited to what the society can satisfy. Morality has nothing to do with good and evil or universal principles and everything to do with what suits Taylorite efficiency. Moreover, individuals' perceptions are limited by what the society makes available to see, touch, hear, and feel. One State's narrowness becomes apparent in D-503's inability to respond to O-90's and U's feelings for him, his incapacity to see in sweet-smelling flowers anything more than the abstraction of "smell" (Zamyatin, *We* 36), and his confusion at the hands of I-330. One State is monochromatic, rectilinear, and transparent, a world of "psychological entropy" (175).

So *We* is a critique of modern Western industrial Taylorite organization: its principles, its practices, its characterization of progress, and its vision of utopia or the good society. By unfolding the shortcomings of One State and its inhabitants and by showing D-503's difficulties, Zamyatin calls into question the promise of attaining material happiness through the technological domination of nature, the vision of order and stability through the imposition of rational rules and coercive authority, and the manipulation and disciplining of human beings necessary to generate that order and stability. A utopia of material happiness, crystalline order, static well-being, and efficient coercion is a flawed vision.

Zamyatin presents two contemporary societies in *We*: One State and the Mephi's world beyond the Green Wall. The Mephi's world of nature may seem like the opposite of One State's urban, civilized, rational, ordered life, but Zamyatin recognizes overlaps and complementarities. Nature still exists in One State, in D-503's hairy hands, R-13's lisp, and the numbers' shameless copulations when the revolution breaks out. Equally, the Mephi use instrumental reason, the great tool of One State, to plan to entice D-503 and seize the *Integral*. I-330 is nothing if not instrumental, manipulative, cunning, and very smart.

Zamyatin has D-503 at one point wonder about "the half we have lost," speculating about how H_2 and O need each other (*We* 163). Zamyatin also has I-330 realize that the Mephi may well make the same mistake as One State, namely the assumption that their way of life is the best, the final, the last stage in human progression: "We [Mephi] know for the time being that there is no final number. We may forget it. No, we are even sure to forget it when we get old—as everything inevitably gets old. And then we, too, shall drop—like leaves in autumn from the tree" (175–76). In short, Zamyatin breaks down or blurs binary oppositions.

Because Zamyatin breaks down dichotomies rather than endorsing them, neither society presented in *We* is likely to be his vision of the good society, and the reader needs to actively look for hints and think about what a good society would be. One State does suggest a set of characteristics that the good society should not seek: static perfection, monochromaticity in any dimension of life, the suppression of human desires and capabilities in order to satisfy the demands of rationality or social order. A good society will include change and constant revolution, seek to rediscover and restore whatever "half we have lost," and be open to mystery as much as to rationality.

Most importantly, perhaps, the good society should not seek happiness as material well-being; the Garden of Eden, the Grand Inquisitor's society, and One State all show the limits of such happiness and of seeking it at the expense of freedom. But modern utopian thought—modern thought that, like Zamyatin's, aims for a better society—cannot ignore the Grand Inquisitor and his claims that human beings want material happiness and well-being most of all; modern utopian thought must come to terms with the parable.

Ursula K. Le Guin, a utopian writer, quotes utopian scholar Robert Elliott: "If the word [utopia] is to be redeemed, it will have to be by someone who has followed utopia into the abyss which yawns behind the Grand Inquisitor's vision, and who then has clambered out on the other side" (Le Guin 100). How far Zamyatin has clambered out on the other side is not explicit in *We*. But he has confronted the abyss, entered it, refused to accept the Grand Inquisitor's dichotomies (and the Grand Inquisitor's interpretation of happiness), and set the stage for his readers to clamber out. Zamyatin has shown that material well-being and happiness may not be the principal goals for human beings; people may also seek other kinds of well-being, such as diverse intellectual development, an active relation to nature, and the free time in which to act in ways that are not solely efficient, and they may seek political influence that allows them to have a say in the way they are governed.

There is no final revolution, no perfected final state of mankind; "revolutions are infinite" (Zamyatin, *We* 174). "The finite, fixed world . . . is a convention, an abstraction, an unreality. And therefore Realism—be it 'socialist' or 'bourgeois'—is unreal" (Zamyatin, "On Literature" 112). There is always a need for change and, given that the practices if not the ideals of the good society will always be limited, always an impetus for change by inhabitants of the good society. Happiness cannot be the limitation and disciplining of desires and capabilities; that is the route to entropy and immobility, the end of action and of imagination. Nor can happiness be a childlike innocence, a world without psychological pain or anxiety; the innocent Eve and

Adam could not effectively confront the serpent any more than D-503, an innocent and a naïf, could understand I-330 or his reactions to her, because Eve, Adam, and D-503 all lacked the diversity of experiences, sufferings, and joys that would have enabled them to be wise inhabitants of a world replete with good and evil.

Like innocence, walls serve to limit and to narrow, to wall in as well as wall out. Zamyatin seems to wish to break down walls, and he wishes his readers to think with D-503 about the "half we have lost" in any paradisiacal, Grand Inquisitor, or One State definition of happiness: where are imagination, love, passionate emotions, curiosity, color, diversity, privacy, individuality, the soul? Where and how can human beings come to grips with the problem of good and evil, the Kantian problem of how to act in the world, not for material well-being or order or security alone, but for good and not for ill? At the end of *We*, Zamyatin raises the stakes. Technological societies like One State can obliterate the imagination, so preventing or stymieing technological societies like One State is essential. But equally important are the questions, raised and reraised by the humanist tradition symbolized by D-503's mentions of Kant, about how human beings should lead their lives. One State's answer impoverishes human beings and their societies; to find possibilities, interpretations, and directions for action, human beings need to revisit and extend the humanist tradition. As I-330 says, when D-503 blurts out that "I talk such nonsense, so foolishly": "And why do you think that foolishness is bad? If human foolishness had been as carefully nurtured and cultivated as intelligence has been for centuries, perhaps it would have turned into something extremely precious" (Zamyatin, *We* 132). Foolishness, noninstrumental reason, the education of desire, the acceptance of suffering, the embracing of change, the expanding of what it means to be human and to engage in human action in the world—Zamyatin's story points toward possible ways of clambering out of the Grand Inquisitor's abyss.

Notes

1. Like Huxley in *Brave New World*, for whom Henry Ford's assembly line symbolizes modernity's powerful organizing of human beings, Zamyatin does not distinguish, as some contemporary Americans might wish to, between a free-enterprise system and a centralized government. Both Ford and Taylor are American phenomena who organized, mobilized, disciplined, and controlled workers, transforming them into unthinking cogs in an industrial productive machine. And both Ford and Taylor required hierarchy, authority, and, if necessary, the coercive power of the state to keep workers in line. Neither was a democrat; neither suggested freedom for the worker as he worked on the assembly line; and Ford also encouraged a high mass-consumption society, with happiness as material well-being. "Free" enterprise can be as Taylorite—as disciplinary, restrictive, and coercive—as a centralized economy.

Works Cited

Elliot, Robert C. *The Shape of Utopia: Studies in a Literary Genre*. Chicago: U of Chicago P, 1970.

Le Guin, Ursula K. *Dancing at the Edge of the World: Thoughts on Words, Women, Places*. New York: Harper, 1989.

Taylor, Frederick Winslow. *The Principles of Scientific Management*. Mineola, NY: Dover, 1997.

Zamyatin, Yevgeny. "H. G. Wells." *A Soviet Heretic*. Ed. and trans. Mirra Ginsburg. London: Quartet, 1991. 259–90.

_____. "On Literature, Revolution, Entropy, and Other Matters." *A Soviet Heretic*. Ed. and trans. Mirra Ginsburg. London: Quartet, 1991. 107–12.

_____. *We*. Trans. Mirra Ginsburg. New York: Bantam, 1972.

The Meaning of "I" in Ayn Rand's *Anthem*

Aaron Weinacht

Introduction

In her dystopian novella *Anthem* (1938), Ayn Rand portrays a culturally and technologically primitive society that is governed by shadowy "Councils." The Councils are convinced that the individual as such is an evil, and that people must be trained to think of themselves only as members of a society and as subordinate to the needs of that society. Even the word "I" is banned; individuals must always refer to themselves as "we" and "us."

By contrast, Rand herself was committed to the proposition that humans are beings whose purpose in life is to think and reason, activities that Rand believed to be the sole province of individuals. The governing state in *Anthem* denies this, using its power to coerce the individual to bow to what it sees as the wisdom of the collective will. To Rand's mind, then, a world ruled by such a state would be a true dystopia; a government of the sort depicted in *Anthem* would be a kind of social surgeon, bent on removal of that which makes us human beings.

The following analysis will have a dual focus. First, it will consider Rand's time in Russia before she immigrated to the United States, focusing on those aspects of her Russian experience that are directly relevant to the dystopian world she created in *Anthem*. Second, this essay will consider the fictional world of *Anthem* in light of this historical context, with an eye to identifying exactly what Rand thought was so horrific about a world in which the needs and development of the individual are irrelevant in the face of the requirements of the group.

The Russian Context

Rand seems to have come to her view of human nature through a combination of abstract philosophical commitments and her responses to, and later memories of, the practical implementation of Soviet communism in her native Russia. The year 1905, when Rand was born in Saint Petersburg, Russia, was a turbulent time for the tsarist autocracy that governed Russia prior to the Russian Revolution of 1917. For example, in 1904–5, Russia fought a war with Japan and was defeated. This loss diminished Russian military prestige both internationally and domestically, and as the Russian government was about to experience a serious domestic insurrection, it needed all the respect it could get.

In January 1905, there occurred an infamous event known as Bloody Sunday. A crowd of workers marched to petition the tsar for help, but instead of a hearing, they received the gunfire of state police. As the tsar's image was supposed to be that of a protector of the people, this massacre did not improve Tsar Nicholas II's public face. Bloody Sunday was a key part of the broader revolution of 1905, which forced the tsar to grant Russians a measure of representative government and the rule of law. Nicholas II immediately set about abrogating as many of the gains of the 1905 revolution as possible. The year of Rand's birth was not an auspicious one for the stability of the Russian state, or for the chances that the tsarist government might be replaced by a government with more respect for individual freedoms.

In 1914, like much of the rest of Europe, Russia became embroiled in the First World War. For present purposes, this war is significant in the sense that it was one of the key causes of the tsarist government's final collapse, ushering in the era of Bolshevik power, which in turn had a very significant effect on the development of Rand's thought. In October 1917, the Bolshevik Party, drawing on the ideas of Karl Marx, among others, and led by V. I. Lenin, assumed control of the Russian state. The Bolsheviks began an effort to create a communist utopia in Russia, but Lenin's utopia proved to be Rand's dystopia, and much of her philosophical interpretation of her experience of Soviet Russia is recast in dystopian terms in *Anthem*.

Rand regarded capitalism, one pillar of which is the inviolability of private property, as the economic philosophy most conducive to human flourishing. Drawing on the ideas of Marx and others, Russian Communists took exactly the opposite view; to them, private property was a key root of unjust inequality between social classes. Broadly, this meant that all private property in Russia should be eliminated. Narrowly, this meant that in 1917, Rand's father's business was nationalized, and that her class origins as the child of a property owner would always make her suspect in the eyes of the state. After 1917, she and her family traveled south to the Crimea, where she graduated from high school. Returning to Saint Petersburg in 1921, Rand went to university and took up the study of history and philosophy. In 1926, she left Russia for good. As something of a film aficionado, Rand had watched many Russian and American movies—some 433 films between 1922 and 1929, according to her movie diary (Rand, movie diary). She went to America filled with dreams of a movie career and deeply imbued with the sense that the United States was a land of creative opportunity where the creative individual could stand or fall on his or her own merits.

In contrast to this idealized version of her destination, Rand saw her former homeland as a dystopian land of ruin, backwardness, and darkness where individual creativity was quashed, justice was ignored, and all existence was beholden to the power of the state, which rested not on reason but on force. In her fiction, Rand comments most directly on the Soviet scene in her 1936 novel *We the Living*, published only a year prior to her writing *Anthem*. Literature scholar Zina Gimpelevich has done a useful comparison of Rand's work and that of the well-known Russian writer and critic of Soviet communism Yevgeny Zamyatin, finding that both Rand's "romantic realist" *We the Living* and her dystopian *Anthem* are closely related to Zamyatin's *We* (1924) in particular (see Gimpelevich).

Rand's general view, however, was that the point of literature was to envision the ideal: what could and should be. So while her fiction often has easily identifiable historical contexts, Rand still regarded fiction as the best medium through which to communicate her ideas because fiction could leave the realm of the factual, of what is, and help humans identify what should be instead. As Rand herself said, "The motive and purpose of my writing is *the projection of an ideal man*" (*Romantic* 127; italics in orig.). Rand saw fiction as a way to narrow the divide between our "is" and our "should," and so in her 1961 book *For the New Intellectual*, largely comprising excerpts from her fiction, she argues that the speech of a fictional character in her work *Atlas Shrugged* (1957) is the "briefest summary" of her ideas and that her "full [philosophical] system is implicit in these excerpts" (vii–viii).

To summarize, then, one might say that Rand saw the real, historical world as a sort of proving ground for the relative worth of ideas. So although *Anthem* is very abstract, even quasi-mythological at times, and seemingly set in no specific time or place, it is useful to examine the Soviet context for Rand's life in further detail. Rand sometimes considered herself to be a historian; she once listed her profession as "historian" on a Russian questionnaire ("*Oprosnyi list*"), even though she was not at the time employed as such. Rightly or wrongly, for Rand, Russia tended to stand as a reservoir of evidence as to what happens when individuals lose, by defeat or by forfeit, their right or power to determine their own individual destinies. In her view of the Soviet state—which was sometimes exaggerated, due to her deep involvement in the ideological front of the Cold War—Russian Communism stood as a model version of the kind of antihuman exercise in naked power seeking that, left unopposed, might well destroy the world and result in an *Anthem*-like scenario.

So what were specific Soviet ideologies and policies that find specific analogues in Rand's dystopia? First and most broadly, Rand rejected what she took to be the Marxist position that history is marching toward some final end, operating on some inexorable logic that transcends the wills of particular individuals. The political language employed by Russian Marxists such as Lenin was full of terminology such as *class struggle, the working class, enemies of the people, the revolution, the counterrevolution*, and the like. Rand rejected the notion that we can talk about social classes, for example, as though they were "things" with their own desires, wills, or logics. She believed that only individuals possess these things, and that group designations, if useful at all, serve only as shorthand for groups of discrete individuals who lose none of their individuality for having a place in a group. According to Rand's view, group affiliations describe what is; they do not prescribe what should be. For Russian Marxists, history was the scene of struggle between peasants and aristocrats, workers and factory owners; for Rand, it was the site of the individual's struggle to succeed against the irrational forces of groupthink, so to speak. There is no reconciling these two disparate visions.

Second, Russian Marxists took the view that *freedom* was a meaningless term if not accompanied by a measure of economic equality. Put another way, they asked, what good is freedom if people are starving? One can see this emphasis in the Bolshevik slogan "Peace, Land, and Bread," two-thirds of which is devoted to economic and physical sustenance. In the Russian Marxist view, an equality of economic outcomes far outweighed in importance any unprogressive attachments to private property rights, for example. An additional window into the Bolshevik willingness to circumscribe individual freedom is provided by a quote from Lenin himself: "A revolution is the most authoritarian thing imaginable" (qtd. in Riasanovsky and Steinberg 63). Here, Lenin was arguing that there was a broader social good to be served by using authoritarian political power to implement communism, and that freedom needed to take a backseat to revolutionary necessity for the time being. For her part, Rand categorically rejected this sort of thinking, arguing that "I" is always more important than "we." By contrasting the stultifying authority of the Councils in *Anthem* with the revolutionary genius of the book's hero, who reinvents electric lighting, Rand further suggests that even if we reverse the proper order of "I" and "we," what we get is the opposite of progress in any sense of the word.

By having Equality 7-2521 rediscover the uses of electricity, Rand may also have been poking fun at Lenin in particular. Lenin saw electric lighting as a sign of progress, and "Electrification plus Soviet power equals communism" became one of the catchphrases of the

Soviet effort to nationalize industry and achieve dramatic technological progress (Riasanovsky and Steinberg 485). In *Anthem*, the members of the "World Council of Scholars" (and the Russian word for "council" is *soviet*) hold their deliberations under a mural depicting the group of men who invented the candle. While she is not generally renowned for her sense of humor, this is probably Rand's way of lampooning the view that expropriation of the property of individuals, including her father's, is one step to technological progress. For Rand, when "progress" is in the hands of the state, what results is a group of impotent old men celebrating the candle. When progress is left to the creative vision of the individual, however, the result is the vibrant and virile hero of *Anthem*, who reinvents electric lighting.

A third aspect of Rand's dystopia arose from the fact that she lived through a great deal of economic chaos in Russia. Among the causes of this chaos were the First World War, the revolutionary political climate, the harsh winter of 1918–19, and the fact that during the initial phase of the revolution of October 1917, "nothing changed for the better," in the phrase of historian William Rosenberg. On the contrary, Rosenberg notes, by early 1918, economic activities in major Russian cities were grinding to a halt, and the flow of goods and services into Petrograd, for example, had "dropped catastrophically" (639). This crisis did nothing to ameliorate the broad reality that prior to the 1917 revolution, "everyday life at all levels of Russian society was beset with anxiety and tension" (638). This sense of imminent collapse is evident in *Anthem*, whose world is primitive in economic terms. Rand witnessed the collapsing monetary value and economic turmoil in Petrograd, and she witnessed the early militant phases of the revolution, when ideological opponents of the revolution were executed or exiled. (For a good look at Russian conditions in light of the texts of *Atlas Shrugged* and *The Fountainhead*, see Rosenthal.)

The Communist response to this economic collapse was to embark on a crash economic program to dramatically increase productivity in both industry and agriculture. The industry campaign was fairly successful, particularly in heavy industrial production, while the campaign for agriculture was much less so. Both programs began with the nationalization of individual property in the late 1910s and early 1920s, then reached a zenith with the advent of the First Five-Year Plan in the late 1920s, shortly after Rand's departure for America. (See Riasanovsky and Steinberg 484–89 for a good summary of the First Five-Year Plan and Suny 218–31 for an excellent section on the origins, process, and results of agricultural collectivization. In addition, Stephen Kotkin's *Magnetic Mountain: Stalinism as a Civilization*, 1995, is among the best historical works covering industrialization in the First Five-Year Plan.)

Here, it is possible to see the Soviet logic that economic progress is only possible if "we" reject individual desire and subordinate ourselves to the wisdom of the state. Good examples of this are the phenomena of shock work and Stakhanovism, both of which were movements to help build a new socialist state through total work commitment to the Soviet project. Not content to merely return the economy to its prewar levels, Russia sought to scale previously unheard-of heights of industrial and agricultural productivity, leading the world into a new socialist land of plenty. With this utopian goal in mind, there arose a movement to sacrifice one's time, energy, and even health, if necessary, to serve the state and advance industrial productivity through fulfillment or overfulfillment of work quotas. Shock workers and Stakhanovites were also expected to attend classes in literacy, technical skills, and Marxist-Leninist ideology (see Riasanovsky and Steinberg 484–94; see also Siegelbaum for further information on Soviet industrialization in its cultural dimension). One thinks here of Rand's "Ancient Ones," servants of the state worn out at forty-five years of age, who now inhabit the "Home of the Useless" (*Anthem* 25).[1] As Riasanovsky and Steinberg have pointed out, this industrialization often took the form of the workers serving the state, rather than the other way around, and some were even killed in industrial accidents due to the frenetic pace of production (493).

Parallels with *Anthem* are readily apparent. Note that in Rand's novella, it is not the individual but the state that determines one's career path. This would indicate that man exists to serve the state, not the reverse. Historian Bernice Rosenthal has noted that in the late 1910s, food rationing was defined along the lines of social class, where those the Communists deemed privileged under the tsars got the least. By contrast, workers and "[Communist] Party members and persons they favored got higher rations. They were the new privileged class, the beginning of what Rand called 'an aristocracy of pull'" (Rosenthal 198). Here it is evident that the Russian state rewarded those it deemed loyal servants and punished those it deemed unreliable. In the same way, in *Anthem*, the state exists for its own sake, and man to serve it. The state does not exist to better the lives of its inhabitants; if it did, Equality 7-2521's invention would have been adopted, even if the Council still rejected its individual origins. Likewise, agriculture in *Anthem* appears to operate on a fairly primitive footing, far less mechanized than one would expect, and so state control again matters more than progress for agricultural workers, for instance. Overall, then, Rand's view was that the state, to the extent that it needs to exist, exists to serve man, and she saw the Soviet Union as a world in which man existed only to serve the state.

Life in post-1917 Russia often bore out this conviction, as dissenters both real and imagined were executed, imprisoned in Siberian camps, or exiled from the country. At least eight million individuals were arrested during the Great Purge of the 1930s (see Halfin for a convincing view of what the purges were attempting to achieve). One commentator explains these astounding events as follows: "The vast resources of the NKVD [the secret police] were concentrated on one objective—to document the existence of a huge conspiracy to undermine Soviet power" (qtd. in Riasanovsky and Steinberg 496). The Great Purge was in full swing in 1938, the year of *Anthem*'s publication, and provides a shining example of the notion that man exists to serve the state, a notion Rand roundly rejected with the bedtime prayer uttered by the child inhabitants of her dystopia: "We are nothing. Mankind is all. By the grace of our brothers are we allowed our lives. We exist through, by and for our brothers who are the State. Amen" (*Anthem* 16).

Equality 7-2521 escapes the fate of real-life victims of the Soviet purges—in Rand's parlance, the "Palace of Corrective Detention" (*Anthem* 14) or being "lashed to death" (32)—and instead flees to the woods, where he can begin life anew. Rand, too, saw her exile as a necessity, and while her fictional hero dreams, at the end of *Anthem*, of returning to his former home and enlightening the people there with the fire of Prometheus, Rand herself remained to the end of her life an ardent critic of Communism, serving as a friendly witness at a hearing of the infamous House Committee on Un-American Activities and writing her *Screen Guide for Americans*, in which she advised the moviegoing public on how to tell if a film was worthy of attention or was merely Communist "propaganda." It is this dark vision of her former home, then, that provides much of the backdrop for her fictional dystopia in *Anthem*, where one sees many of the same themes.

What Does It Mean to Be Human?

In nearly all of Rand's writings, her starting point is a simple question: what does it mean to be human? In *Anthem*, as in her later work, Rand's answer is that we are discrete, distinctive individuals who reason, who think. If reasoning and thinking is who we are at the core, then for Rand, every negative state of affairs is the result of a bad idea or bad thinking, and every positive state of affairs is the result of a good idea or good thinking. Thus, in the very beginning of *Anthem*, Rand has her hero state that in his world, "there is no transgression blacker than to do or think alone" (11), while lamenting his natural tendency to have unacceptable thoughts, a "curse" that "has always driven us to thoughts which are forbidden" (13). With this formulation, Rand suggests that the behavior of her hero, Equality 7-2521, is the result of his ideas, not the other way around. Further, Rand's hero seems unable to stop himself from his terrible tendency toward uniqueness.

In just these two brief sentences, then, Rand makes the claims that (1) human beings are not infinitely malleable, but have inescapable hard wiring (see Stites for an excellent historical treatment of the Russian revolutionary effort to remake individuals and society wholesale); (2) this hard wiring requires that humans always act on the basis of some idea, be it rational or irrational; and (3) since the point of living is to use one's reason, which Equality 7-2521 is trying to do, the problem is not with himself but with those who deem his thoughts forbidden.

One of Equality 7-2521's fellow street sweepers breaks out in un-explained fits of crying, and another, Solidarity 9-6347, incessantly screams "Help us!" in the night (Rand, *Anthem* 48). The "doctors," whose methods include bleeding the patients (19), have no answer for Solidarity 9-6347's mysterious ailment. In an early draft of *Anthem*, Rand even included a section where an unexplainable "disease" over-takes "Madmen"; this was intended to illustrate the oppressiveness and irrationality of the environment involuntarily manifesting itself as madness in its inhabitants (*Anthem*, draft 50). The rulers in *Anthem*'s fictional setting may possess the power to decree, but for Rand, it is a classic case of the emperor's new clothes; no amount of coercion of the Equality 7-2521s of the world will make them see clothes where none exist, and those who try to see clothes on the emperor are either mentally handicapped, like Union 5-3992 (*Anthem* 17), or destined to succumb eventually to madness and despair.

Given her linkage of humanity with reason, one wonders if Rand thought that human beings who cannot or will not exercise their reason also forfeit their humanity. Certainly she evinces not a jot of sympa-thy for whatever catastrophe prompted the creation of the oppressive regime in *Anthem*. In 1963, commenting on the Soviet Union, Rand wrote that "any free nation . . . has the *right* to invade Soviet Russia . . . or any other slave pen," since the only rights that matter are those of free individuals; for Rand, collective bodies have no "rights," properly speaking (*Virtue* 103–4, italics in orig.). With this stringent comment in mind, Rand's total and sometimes unsettling lack of interest in the unenlightened characters of *Anthem* becomes clearer.

Upon his rediscovery of electric lighting, Equality 7-2521 takes his invention to the World Council of Scholars. Sitting under their mural of the "twenty illustrious men who had invented the candle" (Rand, *Anthem* 76), the "scholarly" council rejects the light bulb as progress and rejects Equality 7-2521 for having the temerity to disregard his appointed station as a street sweeper and do something on his own. As the World Council of Scholars damns Rand's hero, so Rand damns the scholars, having Equality 7-2521 shout as he makes his hasty exit, "You fools! You thrice-damned fools!" (83). Worthy of note here is that the World Council of Scholars does not reject Equality 7-2521 because of any particular abhorrence of electric lighting as such, but rather because his invention was conceived alone, and "what is not thought by all men cannot be true"; "what is not done collectively cannot be good" (81). The World Council of Scholars rejects Equality 7-2521 for having "flawed" ideas about the proper relationship between the individual and the group, giving Rand the opportunity to excoriate them in turn, not only for having committed the same sin, but also for having and exercising the power to compel others to pretend they have not.

After striking out into the great unknown, accompanied (through her own choice) by his beloved "Golden One," Liberty 5-3000, Equality is free to live as he pleases. His choice, as it turns out, is to build a "fort," from which he, his offspring, and like-minded escapees from the "city of the damned" can evangelize the world according to the logic of the word he carves above the door of his new enclave: "EGO" (Rand, *Anthem* 121–23). In short, the revolution will be a revolution of ideas, not of guns (which are only the results of ideas), and Equality 7-2521 is confident, as is Rand, that the councils that rejected him "will be impotent against me" (122). In short, Rand argues in *Anthem* that the only force that can oppose reason as the basic fact of existence is naked power, and in the long run, like the emperor, naked power can pretend it is clothed only for so long.

To Be Human Is to Reason, So What Next?

If Rand wants the reader to conclude that *Anthem*'s dystopian scenario is first and foremost the result of bad philosophy, what does she want us to do with this information? Rand provides a clear answer to this question as well. Note that the final scenes of *Anthem* have Equality 7-2521 rediscovering his "I," his ego. In contrast to the dreary do-what-you-are-told-because-the-collective-wills-it dystopianism of most of the book, Rand's hero's final vision has a distinctly utopian flavor, communicating that once one discovers one's individuality and feels no need to apologize for the fact, the rational possibilities are limitless.

Here, again, it is worth considering the Russian context for Rand's views. That *Anthem* is a dystopia does not make Rand an anti-utopian thinker. On the contrary, it may be useful to see Rand as promoting a third installment in a series of Russian cultural utopian visions. Leaving aside the beliefs of specific individuals, prerevolutionary Russia was, culturally speaking, a thoroughly Christian country, and Christianity in its Russian variant, as in other forms, contrasts the injustices and violences of the "now" with the "not yet" of a heaven in which the lion will lie down with the lamb, so to speak. For the Marxists who replaced the quasi-theocratic tsars, by contrast, religion was the "opiate of the masses," obscuring humans' true class interests; Russian Marxists therefore rejected Christian eschatology, replacing it with the "now" of class warfare and economic injustice that precedes the "not yet" of the Communist "kingdom of freedom," to borrow a line from Russian and Polish historian Andrzej Walicki. Rand rejected both Christian and Marxist utopianism, regarding the concept of God as an insult to man and the concept of class struggle as an excuse for those with power and guns to expropriate the wealth of those without (for further on this point, see Weinacht 154–72; Rand, *For the New* 9–58). To put the point another way, Russian Marxists rejected God and offered men as a replacement; Rand rejected both God and men and replaced them with the singular "man," who, in effect, becomes God—or at least, as in *Anthem*, the new Adam or Prometheus, bringing light to a world fresh, clean, and new. Reading the final scenes of *Anthem*, one is struck by how inevitable the utopian future feels once Equality 7-2521 has rejected his past. There is no doubt that he will triumph in his upcoming struggle for knowledge, self-discovery, and intellectual mastery over his former oppressors. To return to the question at the beginning of this section, then, Rand wants the reader to replace her dystopia with a new utopia; and in her view, understanding the flaws in anti-individualist systems such as the Soviet Union is an important first step toward that end.

More narrowly, Rand wants the reader to identify his or her individual passions and desires and pursue them. Equality 7-2521 envisions his enclave as the future "capital of a world where each man will be free to exist for his own sake" (Rand, *Anthem* 122), which is a rather sweeping vision of the future possibilities. Equality 7-2521 had been assigned to be a street sweeper, but he wanted to be a scholar—knowledge was his passion (18–20). Rand's other fiction is populated with positive characters who are variously musicians, architects, inventors, engineers, industrialists, philosophers, playwrights, and farmers; her idea is not that everyone should like the same things but that each of us should do what we are passionate about, because we desire to, not because someone else wills it so. In other words: be an individual.

Equality 7-2521 is not just an original thinker; he is physically distinctive as well. He happens to be taller than average. His social superiors lament this but, of course, cannot do anything about it. Rand's point is not just that some persons are head and shoulders above the rest but that individuality is a fact of human hard wiring that can be neither hidden nor denied, just like one's height. The path to Equality 7-2521's redemption, at the end of *Anthem*, lies in his recognition that he can leave his city, overcome his fear of the unknown, and strike out on his own. His change in behavior results from his change in reasoning: he recognizes that his worth as an individual does not depend on the approval of the laughable World Council of Scholars, with their candles.

The creed of the mysterious rulers in *Anthem* reads as follows:

> *We are one in all and all in one.*
> *There are no men but only the great WE,*
> *One, indivisible and forever.* (14)

For Rand, we can repeat this creed all we want, but repetition will not make it so. As her hero notes, "We repeat this to ourselves, but it helps us not" (14).

At *Anthem*'s close, Equality 7-2521 rediscovers the word "I." With this rediscovery, he reverses the creed of the rulers of his dystopia and thereby brings his understanding of reality back into line—with an almost audible sigh of relief—with Rand's view of human hard wiring. Twenty years after *Anthem*, in *Atlas Shrugged* (1957), Rand composed a new positive credo diametrically opposed to the credo of "we," transforming the individual discovery of "I" by Equality 7-2521 into a maxim for living when she has hero John Galt state, "I swear—by my life and my love of it—that I will never live for the sake of another man, nor ask another man to live for mine" (*Atlas Shrugged* 983; see also 680).

Written during a series of Soviet show trials of supposed "enemies of the people" in the 1930s, *Anthem* is a ringing rejection of the idea that the individual exists to serve the state. During these trials, the accused confessed to fantastic crimes against the state—crimes that were certainly fabricated and confessions extracted under torture. In some cases, the accused seemed to actually believe in their guilt, and in any event, the fact that the Marxist kingdom of freedom had not yet been reached implied the objective existence of counterrevolutionary activity: where there is a crime, there must be a criminal. This resulted in a perverse scenario in which it mattered not whether the defendant had actually committed a crime; what did matter was that someone confessed to the crimes that the state prosecution had determined must objectively exist, thus showing the public the fantastic depravity and duplicity of those who opposed the state (for further, see Halfin).

The show trials, then, illustrate an extreme case in which the credos of Equality 7-2521 and John Galt are reversed. While Rand believed that no one should be made to live for the sake of another, the show trials were predicated upon the logic that if the state required a person's guilt, that person must therefore be guilty. With the publication of *Anthem*, Rand roundly rejected this logic; and with her hero who applies his individual talents for the sake of his own satisfaction, she made a good start on the formulation of the maxim around which, twenty years later, she would build her most important book.

Conclusion

Commentators such as Zina Gimpelevich, Bernice Rosenthal, Chris Sciabarra, and myself have previously noted that understanding the Russian context is critical to understanding the writings and ideas of Ayn Rand. *Anthem* is no exception to this, and a look at Rand's interpretation of the Russian Revolution and its aftermath sheds a great deal of light on the nature of her dystopian scenario. The ruling councils in *Anthem* reject individual creativity, accomplishment, and intelligence as inimical to human flourishing, but the world that results is bereft of enjoyment, beauty, and technological progress. In Rand's view, this was exactly where Russia was headed, and what she saw in real life was what she tried to reject in her fiction.

Whether Rand was successful in this is a matter of sometimes-heated dispute. Rand's extreme individualism provides grounds, particularly in her novels *The Fountainhead* (1943) and *Atlas Shrugged*, for an argument that her ideas, if carried to their logical conclusions, would be at least as inhumane as any of Stalin's transgressions against Russian citizens. (What will happen to people who refuse to give up "we" in favor of "I"? See Rand, *Atlas Shrugged* 1066 for a possible answer.) In *Anthem*, however, Rand is still thinking very much in the abstract, and as such, the novel emphasizes the priority of ideas in life and the practical implications of adopting bad ones, with her experience of the Soviet Union serving as a kind of laboratory for what she deemed to be bad philosophy. These were themes to which she would return again and again until her death in 1981, an individualist to the end.

Notes

1. All citations of Rand's *Anthem* refer to the published Signet edition and not the typescript draft unless otherwise stated.

Works Cited

Gimpelevich, Zina. "'We' and 'I' in Zamyatin's *We* and Ayn Rand's *Anthem*." *Germano-Slavica* 10.1 (1997): 13–23.

Halfin, Igal. *Stalinist Confessions: Messianism and Terror at the Leningrad Communist University*. Pittsburgh: U of Pittsburgh P, 2009.

Rand, Ayn. *Anthem*. New York: Signet, 1946.

_____. *Anthem*, draft. 30 Sept. 1937. TS. Ayn Rand Inst., Irvine, CA.

_____. *Atlas Shrugged*. New York: Signet, 1985.

_____. *For the New Intellectual: The Philosophy of Ayn Rand*. New York: Signet, 1961.

_____. Movie diary. 1922–29. MS. Ayn Rand Inst., Irvine, CA.

_____. "*Oprosnyi list* [Questionnaire]." 1924. MS. Ayn Rand Inst., Irvine, CA.

_____. *The Romantic Manifesto: A Philosophy of Literature*. New York: Signet, 1971.

_____. *Screen Guide for Americans*. Beverly Hills, CA: Motion Picture Alliance for the Preservation of Amer. Ideals, 1947. *Online Books Page* [U of Pennsylvania]. Web. 25 Apr. 2012.

_____. *The Virtue of Selfishness: A New Concept of Egoism*. New York: New Amer. Lib., 1964.

Riasanovsky, Nicholas V., and Mark D. Steinberg. *A History of Russia*. 7th ed. New York: Oxford UP, 2005.

Rosenberg, William G. "Problems of Social Welfare and Everyday Life." *Critical Companion to the Russian Revolution, 1914–1921*. Ed. Edward Acton, Vladimir Iu. Cherniaev, and William G. Rosenberg. Bloomington: Indiana UP, 1997. 633–44.

Rosenthal, Bernice Glatzer. "The Russian Subtext of *Atlas Shrugged* and *The Fountainhead*." *Journal of Ayn Rand Studies* 6.1 (2004): 195–225.

Sciabarra, Chris Matthew. *Ayn Rand: The Russian Radical*. University Park: Pennsylvania State UP, 1995.

Siegelbaum, Lewis. *Stakhanovism and the Politics of Productivity in the USSR, 1935–1941*. Cambridge: Cambridge UP, 1988.

Stites, Richard. *Revolutionary Dreams: Utopian Vision and Experimental Life in the Russian Revolution*. New York: Oxford UP, 1989.

Suny, Ronald Grigor. *The Soviet Experiment: Russia, the USSR, and the Successor States*. New York: Oxford UP, 1998.

Walicki, Andrzej. *Marxism and the Leap to the Kingdom of Freedom: The Rise and Fall of the Communist Utopia*. Stanford, CA: Stanford UP, 1995.

Weinacht, Aaron. "What Would Bazarov and John Galt Do? Ayn Rand as a Latter Day Russian Nihilist." Diss. U of Kentucky, 2009.

Frontierism and Dystopian Representations of Home in F. Pohl and C. M. Kornbluth's *The Space Merchants*_____

Enrica Picarelli

April 12, 2011, was the fiftieth anniversary of the first manned exploration of space, accomplished in 1961 by the Soviet pilot Yuri Gagarin. The memory of that mission, which initiated the so-called race to the stars between the United States and the USSR, prompted many nostalgic evocations of the pioneering spirit of the 1960s space program. The search engine Google created a special doodle showing an astronaut and a rocket station, drawn in the fashion of postwar comic-book illustrations; a statue was erected in London to mark Gagarin's achievement; footage of the moon landing was broadcast on television and shared via social networks. Such nostalgic journeys to the past returned the contemporary audience to the days when the colonization of space was seen as the enterprise that could restore, in John F. Kennedy's words, America's lost "sense of historic purpose" (Kennedy). The president's romantic vision stemmed from an ideological reading that reinterpreted America's mythology of expansion and moral right to power for the age of the atomic bomb. The aim of this essay is to revisit the cultural atmosphere that preceded the launch of the space program by foregrounding the satirical look that Frederik Pohl and Cyril M. Kornbluth cast at space exploration in the 1950s. The essay contends that the novel's dystopian approach to the frontier imaginary reveals the presence of an internal frontier running through the affluent postwar society.

Weeping for New Worlds to Conquer: *The Space Merchants* as a Dystopian Narrative

Frederik Pohl and Cyril M. Kornbluth's *The Space Merchants* (1953) provides an ironic representation of the future of American society, describing a world where giant conglomerations looking to extend their power fight to launch the first human exploration of Venus. Originally published in 1952 as "Gravy Planet" in the magazine *Galaxy*, *The Space Merchants* is regarded as "a founding text of science fiction satire" (Booker and Thomas 207), weaving a dystopian reading of the frontier mythology into a narrative about the threats of rampant capitalist expansion. The novel's ironic tone describes the months that prepare Mitchell Courtenay, its main character, for a journey in outer space, giving a bleak vision of life in a hyper-consumeristic society.

Although the prospect of interplanetary colonization kick-starts the narrative and remains essential to the plot's unfolding, the novel takes place mainly in the United States and Costa Rica, where Fowler Schocken Associates is one the world's most powerful advertising agencies. The events concerning the Venus mission are set in an unspecified future and narrated in the first person by Courtenay, who works as a young executive at Fowler Schocken. Having obtained the rights to explore a new planet, the firm commissions him for a campaign to promote interplanetary colonization. The enterprise is immensely lucrative, promising to guarantee Fowler Schocken absolute control of market management and commodity circulation in an unspoiled market.

The first chapters of *The Space Merchants* introduce the context of the narrated events, depicting the world of advertising as a degenerated version of the professional-managerial system that was employing Americans in growing numbers at the onset of the 1950s. Bolstered by the expansion of the private sector and an economy of luxury goods, postwar American society was being reshaped by upward social mobility and the conformism bred of abundance. The middle class, employed to fill administrative and executive positions, represented the rise of a new "affluent society" (Galbraith) where complacency and social acceptance were the norm.

The Space Merchants relates to the anxieties raised by social transformations and materialism. Fowler Schocken provides the intellectual or mental occupations that American sociologists relate to the shift to a post-Fordism system of production. Like Tom Rath, the protagonist of one of the most representative texts about postwar culture, Sloan Wilson's *The Man in the Gray Flannel Suit* (1955), Mitchell Courtenay is a copywriter in the pay of a system that profits from selling immaterial goods—that is, desires and dreams.

Courtenay happily embraces his workplace and the prosperous lifestyle that his job provides him. He professes loyalty to the god of sales like the members of the complacent society that Mordecai Roshwald condemned in 1958 in his article "Quo Vadis, America?" (Seed 226–27). He initially seems comfortable with a workplace swarming with "stamped-out-of-tin assistants" (Pohl and Kornbluth 30) who produce impressions, subsonics, "semantic cue words" (4), and other subtle forms of audiovisual stimulation to motivate a global population of "consumers" to pursue the goods advertised by Fowler Schocken.

The Space Merchants takes place in a world where corporations exterminate one another by way of feuds and nations like Costa Rica spend their annual budgets on the taxes due to industrial conglomerates. Courtenay learns that commercial controversies are regulated by a code that considers killing in a feud "a misdemeanour" that must be accompanied by a "Notification" (Pohl and Kornbluth 38), and power lies in the hands of those who know how to "make people happy" (39) to live in a hyper-consumeristic society.

The novel's vision of the future, then, is not unlike that of 1952 America, where advertising agencies were reshaping collective life standards. Commenting on postwar dystopian fiction, David Seed points out that *The Space Merchants* "successfully dramatize[s] the political power of business combines" (231) by revisiting the Cold War culture through a commercial grid. The representation of the corporate world, which benefits from Pohl's brief work experience as an adman in the 1940s, is essential to the book's critique of consumerism and social alienation. Indeed, in spite of its futuristic frame and hyperbolic unfolding, *The Space Merchants* invites the reader to interpret the narrated events in light of present concerns and as a response to real-life anxieties.

Taking place in the corporate universe, the novel has at its core the business maneuvers relating to the opportunity to control commercial revenues on Venus. Fowler Schocken III, Courtenay's boss, describes the pleasant prospect of having a "whole planet to *sell*" (Pohl and Kornbluth 7; italics in orig.) and plunder as an enterprise of primary value. The firm's aim is to integrate Venus's future economy into its circuit of commodity distribution:

> What we wanted was the year-after-year reliability of a major industrial complex; what we wanted was the colonists, and their children, added to our complex of accounts. Fowler, of course, hoped to repeat on an enormously magnified scale our smashing success with Indiastries. His Boards and he had organized all of India into a single giant cartel, with every last woven basket and iridium ingot and caddy of opium it produced sold through Fowler Schocken advertising. Now he could do the same with Venus. Potentially this was worth as much as every dollar of value in existence put together! A whole new planet, the size of Earth, in prospect as rich as Earth—and every micron, every milligram of it ours. (16–17)

Underlying Schocken's fantasy of absolute power is a plan to branch out and expand that is motivated by the exhaustion of exploitable markets on Earth. Indeed, centuries of strategic placement, psychological manipulation, spherical trusts, and mergers have brought capitalism to the verge of implosion.

The need to avert a collapse and reboot the system thus surfaces as a top priority in Courtenay's world. Schocken, knowing how important the conquest of Venus would be for the survival of capitalism, describes it in terms that compare advertising to the colonial adventures of the past:

> "There's an old saying, men. 'The world is our oyster.' We've made it come true. But we've eaten that oyster." He crushed out his cigarette carefully. "We've eaten it," he repeated. "We've actually and literally conquered the

world. Like Alexander, we weep for new worlds to conquer. And *there*—"
he waved at the screen behind him [showing images of Venus] "—*there*
you have just seen the first of those worlds." (Pohl and Kornbluth 7; italics in orig.)

Appointing himself as conqueror and visionary mind, Schocken explicitly connects space exploration with capitalist expansion. The comparison of Earth to an empty shell that must be cast aside by capitalism's ravenous search for ripe resources exposes the profit motive that
underlies the frontier imaginary represented in *The Space Merchants*.

In addition, the use of the oyster metaphor and the reference to
Alexander the Great express the voraciousness of the consumerist system in a way that sets the feverish speed at which the narrative unfolds,
jumping from Washington to Costa Rica, from the moon to Venus. Indeed, Pohl and Kornbluth's novel is not about an interplanetary journey so much as it is about the ideology of space exploration and how
it operates to sustain a hierarchical structure of power. At the end of
The Space Merchants, a rocket leaves for Venus, but it does not carry
Schocken's capitalist pioneers. In their stead is Courtenay, who, in one
of many narrative twists, has ended up joining the underground organization of Conservationists, or "Consies," to leave on a utopian mission
and save Venus from exploitation.

In spite of its seemingly naive ending, *The Space Merchants* effectively critiques the conditions of production and reception of cultural
works in the capitalist system. More extensively, one can argue, as Tom
Moylan does, that the novel "isolates and examines the disciplinary
tendencies of consumerism . . . as they tighten the grip of hegemonic
power on the newly affluent society" (169). Like many other science-
fiction works published at a time of epochal transformations, Pohl and
Kornbluth's narrative is markedly self-reflexive, incorporating some
essential elements of dystopian writing.

As a literary genre that offers a dark vision of power and control,
dystopia comments on the present by showing a character's growing

disaffection with the society in which he or she lives. In *The Space Merchants*, alienation is relayed by a "characterological action" (Moylan 148) that focuses on Courtenay's adventures. The action produces a coming-of-age narration in which the totalizing mechanism of power that engulfs the protagonist is exposed and its similarities with postwar American society are made clear.

Often in dystopian fictions the characterological action is expressed by a first-person narrative that conveys the character's disillusionment with his world in intimist tones. According to Moylan and Raffaella Baccolini, the emphasis on the character's fate serves to generate a "didactic account in the critical encounter that ensues when the [character] confronts, or is confronted by, the contradictions of the society that is present on the very first page" (Baccolini and Moylan 6). Through Courtenay's movement from promoter to antagonist of the capitalist system, *The Space Merchants* proceeds dialectically, developing a narrative about hegemony and a counter-narrative of resistance that is also found in novels by other science-fiction authors from the 1950s. As Seed notes, like Kurt Vonnegut's *Player Piano* (1952) or Yevgeny Zamyatin's *We* (1924), *The Space Merchants* uses "the dissatisfaction of one individual to reflect on the general inadequacies of a regime perceived as in some sense totalitarian" (235).

In Pohl and Kornbluth's narrative, the critique of capitalism derives from Courtenay's progressive estrangement from the corporate world and his final rejection of consumerism. During a trip to Antarctica, where he means to unmask a colleague's double deal, the protagonist is knocked unconscious and wakes up on a freighter to Costa Rica under the identity of a "lower-class consumer" (67) named William George Groby. Abruptly removed from his everyday reality, Courtenay finds himself among a mass of desperate individuals that corporations like Fowler Schocken hire for manual labor. His progressive disillusionment with the fantasy of unending affluence that inspires the "American dream" first begins to form as he comes into contact with this anonymous mass.

Courtenay's experience in Central America forces him to acknowledge the existence of a fracture that shatters the capitalist fantasy of mass prosperity. On the plantation, the heroic pioneers envisioned by Schocken morph into misfits who project inward the frontier myth of progress and materialism, distorting it into a nightmarish vision of exploitation and violence.

A Mediated Knowledge: Manufacturing the Fantasy of the Interplanetary Frontier

The Space Merchants's critique of consumerism finds its way into the narrative via Courtenay's insight into the profit motive behind interplanetary travel. The prospect of colonizing Venus provides the occasion to reflect on the political implications underlying the American frontier mythology.

The frontier has always been a motif through which Americans define their identity. David Mogen observes that "the frontier, as history, prophecy, or metaphor, is still a place where Americans seek imaginatively to define their character, their relationship to their culture" (38). A structural component of this process of self-definition is the right to independence, which produces an individualistic vision of conquest and supremacy. The latter, in turn, inspires an ideological reading that associates frontiersmanship with progress and human evolution.

Since the frontier myth is an embodiment of cultural identity, cultural works that redefine its form and function contribute to shifts in collective perceptions of the self. From nineteenth-century landscape painting to postwar television shows, representations of frontier life in popular culture have portrayed the American impulse to conquer in a positive way. Indeed, encouraging tales of frontier life have typically spun the fantasy of the American imperial myth, or manifest destiny. Underlying such tales is a discourse on domination that is essential to hegemonic politics of expansion, since it correlates the violent subjugation of new lands and peoples with the promise of a better life.

Science fiction is one of the genres that deals most extensively with the frontier mythology (Westfahl). Like the Western, it combines images of unknown outer realms with an emphasis on technological power, foregrounding the symbolic correlation between physical wilderness and human determination. Many traditional themes associated with the frontier discourse recur in postwar American science-fiction literature, sometimes becoming the object of social criticism that finds its most effective manifestation in the dystopian novel.

The Space Merchants unfolds when direct contact with Venus is foreclosed and preparations for colonization are under way. Courtenay's retrospective on the months preceding his launch takes the form of an ethical journey from embedded adman to disillusioned consumer to outspoken antagonist of capitalism. As the events relating to the mission are told in the first person, Schocken's vision of capitalist pioneerism undergoes a mediation, becoming the object of a secondhand knowledge and of Courtenay's progressive alienation from his corporate self.

Schocken's reference to Alexander places the Venus mission in the longer history of colonization that has served to justify American imperialism since the nineteenth century. The interests of the firm root space exploration, with its undiscovered frontiers and territories, in the terrestrial context of industrial development: "Never forget," says Schocken, "that Venus is there for us to exploit, and don't ever get it turned around" (Pohl and Kornbluth 162). Indeed, Schocken's vision does not contemplate the geophysical reality of Venus. The executive describes the planet in entirely fictional terms to make it more appealing for his audience. Courtenay's first contact with Venus is thus mediated by his boss's words, which, unsurprisingly, turn into a successful experiment in advertising that moves his board to believe in the righteousness of the project.

Viewing the commercial that introduces the colonization program to the executive team, Courtenay recounts his audiovisual experience in epiphanic terms. The planet comes to life on the screen in a burst of celebrations of technological advancement, pioneerism, and virgin lands. Courtenay is fascinated by the ease with which the picture slips into the realm of the mythical/fictional and enthusiastically reviews the way it fabricates a brand-new Venus for the audience. Showing the spaceship that will transport humans across space, the commercial represents it as a symbol of technological evolution and progress: "a thousand-foot monster" (Pohl and Kornbluth 5), "the ship that a modern Columbus will drive through the void . . . an ark for eighteen hundred men and women, and everything to make a new world for their home" (6). The blurb then moves to a domestic interior where a family of future pioneers discusses the benefits of the mission, envisioning for the second time a dreamlike Venus covered in "verdant valleys, crystal lakes, brilliant mountain vistas" (6).

Courtenay's experience of the commercial, along with his report of Schocken's plans for colonization, operates dystopically to expose the constructed nature of the colonial discourse. To the protagonist, the reality of the planet is secondary; rather, he focuses on the work done by the copywriters and "the organ-toned commentators in Aural Effects" (Pohl and Kornbluth 5–6) to subtly lavish positive connotations upon an unwelcoming planet and a dangerous mission, recalling the manipulation of perceptions of reality that is crucial to the work of dystopian regimes such as that in George Orwell's *Nineteen Eighty-Four* (1949). Courtenay praises the picture's romantic vision that artfully molds a dangerous mission into a revitalized version of the American dream, glossing over "the decades of hydroponics and life in hermetically sealed cabins that the pioneers would have to endure while working on Venus's unbreathable atmosphere and waterless chemistry" (6).

Courtenay is immersed in, and makes explicit for the reader, the strategic use of affective solicitation that underlies the commercial as it packages a nightmare in the cheerful colors of a colonizer's dream. This passage is central to *The Space Merchants* because it effectively lays bare the work of advertising as an interpretive mechanism that relies on subliminal cues to shape public opinion. As M. Keith Booker argues, the marketing tactics that Schocken uses to sell Venus were also in use by American advertisers in the 1950s, who employed subtle forms of subliminal suggestion to influence consumer choice (40). Such strategies included the association of success with sexual activity and the assertion of manhood as a source of attractiveness and power. In *The Space Merchants*, masculinist overtones mark Schocken's brief. By comparing the corporate domination of interplanetary markets to an act of hedonistic pleasure such as eating an oyster, the executive conjures up a sensual imaginary that is clouded by the shadow of frustration, as an act of sexual performance can be. The conquest of a world that bears the name, surely not by chance, of the Roman goddess of love is fraught with implied meanings relating symbolic and material acquisition to courtship and enthrallment. Venus, the object of desire of a reborn Alexander, is the trope around which a fight against impotence is waged, and connections may be drawn between consumerism and sexual desire. The image of the conqueror's tears expresses a frustrated urge that can be satisfied through the enticement of a feminized land.

As Mogen observes, one aspect of the lure of the frontier that exposes *The Space Merchants*'s continuities with colonial narratives is "the opportunity to demonstrate *machismo*" (63; italics in orig.). Referring to the ad copy for the campaign that compares Venus to "a mean lady" (Pohl and Kornbluth 166) to tame, Mogen observes that it expresses a "subliminal appeal to the desire to demonstrate virility" and "insinuate[s] a message latent in much fantasy about the effects of frontier environments" (63). Indeed, Courtenay describes the only man who has ever been to Venus on a mission, the midget pilot Jack O'Shea, as a sexual fiend and interprets his success with women in spite of his appearance as an effect of the notion that "Venus environment increase[s] male potency" (Pohl and Kornbluth 94).[1]

By weaving together capitalist expansion, space colonization, and sexual appetite into a tale of outer-space frontiersmanship, Pohl and Kornbluth represent interplanetary travel as part of a self-reproducing mechanism of desire that operates, symbolically and materially, to stave off the threat of capitalism's collapse, represented by Alexander's tears of impotence. In Courtenay's world, capitalism's thirst for pleasure must perpetuate itself by never ceasing to desire. In the passage where Schocken introduces the mission, the screen that broadcasts the fantasy of a fertile Venus stands as the frontier where the present meets the future and the history of accumulation that has made Fowler Schocken the most powerful advertising agency in the world fades into the future of the pioneer's courtship of the planet that Courtenay must perform. The protagonist's precarious situation between fact and fabrication is the core of the novel's critique of frontiersmanship and imperialism.

"I Knew about It, but I Had Never Seen It": Courtenay as Pioneer

Frontier mythology represents unknown wilderness as a source of wonder, profit, and scientific knowledge. In classical literature, the encounter with alien territory inspires an ideology-driven narrative in which a man's approach to geographical space is essential to produce a tale of heroism. According to Joseph Campbell, heroic frontier narratives are informed by the themes of initiation and social responsibility; they traditionally represent the hero as a social servant who restores life and redeems community by taking upon himself the task of taming wilderness. Campbell's paradigm involves a hero who "ventures forth from the world of common day into a region of supernatural wonder: fabulous forces are there encountered and a decisive victory is won: the hero comes back from this mysterious adventure with the power to bestow boons on his fellow man" (23).

A tale of individual salvation is found in *The Space Merchants*, replete with adventurous incursions into mysterious realms, presenting Courtenay as the leader of a revolutionary anticapitalist movement. His adventures recall those of a pioneer who, by redeeming himself, finally redeems humanity. The novel foregrounds the opposition between corporate interest in Venus and the symbolic value of the planet for those who imagine it as a world of infinite opportunities. Courtenay stands on the border where fantasy and reality meet, and his task is to make sure that they merge in a successful enterprise. As in other dystopian narratives, the dystopian effect is relayed by the character who, navigating his way through opposite registers and moral positions, becomes alienated from both.

Courtenay's dilemma, and the core of his experience as a frontiersman, lies in his growing uneasiness with maintaining the balance between fabrication and fact. If he embraces corporatism, he cannot deny the grave risk at which he is putting future pioneers. O'Shea's reports describe Venus as an entropic realm that hardly submits to Fowler Schocken's plans of domestication. Venus, which would be the first of a series of "assembly-line planets owned and operated by . . . the enterprising American business men who had made civilization great" (Pohl and Kornbluth 176), is a lifeless and deadly world that would most likely kill the colonizers. Contrary to traditional literary approaches that describe the frontier as merely a wild, anarchic realm, *The Space Merchants* represents Venus as a lethal planet. Its inhospitable surface hardly conforms to the imaginary of a tamable terra nullius that informs colonial literature, and, more interestingly, its geophysical features are never foregrounded in the plot. Rather, the novel relates the protagonist's growing estrangement from Earth and his everyday reality, which becomes increasingly unfamiliar to him.

As Courtenay puts a larger physical gulf between himself and Fowler Schocken's headquarters, he comes to experience his world as a hostile environment that harbors unknown dangers and is populated by outsiders. Once he leaves the protective walls of the workplace and is unwillingly forced to wander the world, he encounters a tough and violent reality that the glossy worlds pictured by advertising have never acknowledged. As he runs from Los Angeles to Antarctica to Costa Rica to the desert of the American Southwest, ending up first on the moon and finally on a spaceship leaving for Venus, Courtenay's estrangement escalates until his native world appears alien to him and his peers are revealed to be not what he thought they were.

Courtenay's journey takes place across inhospitable locations that he often describes in hallucinatory terms. These spaces, which seemingly float between fantasy and reality, are thresholds that the former adman crosses as he gets closer to the heart of the capitalist pyramid. Traversing them, Courtenay comes into contact with a humanity that, living on the margin, has itself become marginal (if not expendable) to the system.

The most significant border adventures take place during Courtenay's stay in Costa Rica. Waking up on the labor freighter (appropriately named *Thomas R. Malthus*), he cannot contain his shock at the surrounding "red-lit darkness." In terms that evoke the anarchic caravan environment of the Western pioneers, he writes, "I fell asleep on a mountain of ice; I woke up in a throbbing, strumming inferno, complete with red fire and brutish-looking attendant devils" (Pohl and Kornbluth 67). The freighter stinks with the body odors of hundreds of "cargo slobs" (68) who bear their class marks on their forearms as long streams of tattooed social security numbers and spend their time fighting, vomiting, and getting high on drugs.

Compared with the airy, lined corridors of Fowler Schocken and the quietness of his own apartment, the freighter appears to Courtenay as a hellish heterotopia—the social space that, according to Michel Foucault, lies between reality and illusion, a site of isolation that serves a purpose of social disciplining. As Courtenay understands when he finally gets to his destination, the heterotopic space of the freighter is the antechamber of another zone of marginality and alienation—the protein plantation whose marketing campaign Courtenay himself has devised: "From the sun-drenched plantations of Costa Rica, tended by the deft hands of independent farmers with pride in their work, comes the juicyripe goodness of Chlorella Proteins" (Pohl and Kornbluth 73–74). As he recalls these hypnotic words, Courtenay's former life comes alive in a dystopian experience that conveys the first instantiation of an ongoing identity. Working among hundreds of manual laborers who skim nutrients and feed a protein-like organism called Chicken Little that is sliced and marketed by Fowler Schocken, Courtenay acknowledges the hypocrisy of his own words and of the system they stand for. Surrounded by "blinding tropical sunlight" and "plain hell" (73), Courtenay sees the American motto of material prosperity and unending progress reverberate as a distorted melody. On the frontier of the underworld of industrial exploitation, Courtenay loses faith in the words that "tickle people" and make them "hopeful about what they might be" (39), until he realizes that he is becoming alienated from his old self.

Since the life cycle on the plantation is dictated by shifts that are almost deadly in the tropical heat, Courtenay spends his leisure time attending to his basic needs and soon finds himself hooked on cigarettes, coffee, and other Fowler Schocken goods. His dependence, which leads him into debt, prompts him to reflect on the effects that advertising has on men:

> I'd been paid again, and my debt had increased by eight dollars. . . . I came off shift dehydrated, as they wanted me to be. I got a squirt of Popsie from the fountain by punching my combination—twenty-five cents checked off my pay-roll. The squirt wasn't quite enough so I had another—fifty cents. Dinner was drab as usual. . . . Later I was hungry and there was the canteen where I got Crunchies on easy credit. The Crunchies kicked off withdrawal symptoms that could be quelled only by another two squirts of Popsie from the fountain. And Popsie kicked off withdrawal symptoms that could only be quelled by smoking Starr cigarettes, which made you hungry for Crunchies . . . Had Fowler Schocken thought of it in these terms when he organized Starrzelius Verily, the first spherical trust? (Pohl and Kornbluth 84–85; 3rd ellipsis in orig.)

Dependence prompts Courtenay to question the righteousness of corporate capitalism that subjects consumers to the psychological and material pressures to conform to a predefined life standard. From his dislocated and estranged position, he develops a bleak vision of the invisible mechanism that allows executives to live a pampered life in North America.

Becoming more alienated from the corporate world, he comes into contact with the Conservationists, an underground organization of environmentalists who fight the system by violent means. By approaching the organization and then becoming a member, Courtenay once again crosses a border. The membership, which he initially accepts as a means to gather the information necessary to denounce the Consies, instead brings him to the deepest layer of the system and to a new understanding of it. Thanks to his public-relations abilities, Courtenay moves quickly up the group's hierarchy and finally gains access to the organization's headquarters in New York. This experience, which makes him dive into the heart of the Consie movement, marks his definite shift from passive object of exploitation to active subject of the resistance.

Significantly, the meeting that confirms his position in the top ranks of the organization takes place in a secret room inside the Metropolitan Museum of Art, amid statues and exhibitions that triumphantly celebrate the history of advertising. Courtenay's journey of estrangement has finally returned him to the heart of the system from which he is now totally detached. Meandering through the museum's corridors, he scans the darkness, detecting the invisible geometry of composition and decomposition that Consie members, passing for visitors and security, put into action. Before him, the transparent, homogeneous surface of the museum's social landscape discloses the presence of hidden layers, swarming with the activity of anonymous consumers-turned-terrorists. The corporate world suddenly appears to him as a crippled body, uncomfortably harboring the agents of its own destruction: "I could have passed any of them in the street without a second glance. Yet—this was New York, and Bowen had spoken of it as though the Consies I'd meet here were pretty high up in the scale" (Pohl and Kornbluth 110).

However, Courtenay's epiphanic vision of a layered society is destined to remain just a vision. Pohl and Kornbluth describe his parable of disillusionment as a flight away from the capitalist system, not as an invitation to struggle. In a matter of weeks, Courtenay will leave for

Venus to begin a new life on the planet with his wife, Kathy. Looking out of the spaceship's port, he sees "white night. Brilliant stars shining against a background of star particles scattered over a dust of stars. There wasn't a breadth of space the size of my thumbnail where there was blackness; it was all light, all fiery pastels" (Pohl and Kornbluth 184). Although this time he is not envisioning a universe of wealth, his representation of a bright universe retains a quasi-mythical aspect. It connects the interplanetary realm with the promise of a new beginning, resuming the fantasy of the frontier as a blank space open to appropriation. Such a romantic epilogue makes it difficult not to note, as David Mogen argues, that although *The Space Merchants* criticizes the colonial imaginary, it nevertheless "finds its resolution in the tried and true American solution to social and personal problems: escape to the frontier" (66).

Conclusion

The most interesting aspect of *The Space Merchants* is its ability to reflect on the existence of an unacknowledged fracture running through the postwar affluent society. The recourse to the frontier motif helps to highlight the fact that the border is not just an external, spatialized reality but also an internal notion, one related to an experience of alienation, adjustment, and conquest. The desire to conquer new lands thus signals a realization of the dystopian nature of life in the here and now, despite the attempts of advertisers and others to sell contemporary capitalist society as an ideal space. Courtenay's character provides just such a complexified representation of life on the border as he dwells at the juncture of multiple worlds, moving between the sanitized spaces of the corporation and the agoraphobic heterotopia of the labor colony, traveling from the surface to the depths of the Earth and back again, at the same time experiencing belongingness and alienation in relation to the consumerist society of Washington and the underground resistance movement of the Consies.

Notes

1. O'Shea is appointed to the mission due to his small build, which facilitates operations associated with spending three months immobilized in a space capsule, such as feeding and disposal of bodily fluids. His looks and personal history of alienation make him a dystopian version of the outcast pioneer who populates classical frontier literature. As in those narratives, O'Shea's responsibility is to tame the wilderness and make it ready for plowing and other forms of human exploitation.

Works Cited

Baccolini, Raffaella, and Tom Moylan. "Introduction: Dystopia and Histories." *Dark Horizons: Science Fiction and the Dystopian Imagination*. Ed. Raffaella Baccolini and Tom Moylan. London: Routledge, 2003. 1–12.

Booker, M. Keith. *Monsters, Mushroom Clouds, and the Cold War: American Science Fiction and the Roots of Postmodernism, 1946–1964*. Westport, CT: Greenwood, 2001.

Booker, M. Keith, and Anne-Marie Thomas. *The Science Fiction Handbook*. Malden, MA: Wiley, 2009.

Campbell, Joseph. *The Hero with a Thousand Faces*. Novato, CA: New World Lib., 2008.

Foucault, Michel, and Jay Miskowiec. "Of Other Spaces." *Diacritics* 16.1 (1986): 22–27.

Galbraith, John Kenneth. *The Affluent Society*. New York: Houghton, 1958.

Kennedy, John F. "Address of Senator John F. Kennedy Accepting the Democratic Party Nomination for the Presidency of the United States, July 15, 1960." *John F. Kennedy Presidential Library and Museum*. JFK Presidential Lib. and Museum, n.d. Web. 20 Apr. 2012.

Mogen, David. *Wilderness Visions: The Western Theme in Science Fiction Literature*. 2nd ed. San Bernardino, CA: Borgo, 1993.

Moylan, Tom. *Scraps of the Untainted Sky: Science Fiction, Utopia, Dystopia*. Boulder, CO: Westview, 2000.

Pohl, Frederik, and Cyril M. Kornbluth. *The Space Merchants*. London: Gollancz, 2003.

Seed, David. "The Flight from the Good Life: *Fahrenheit 451* in the Context of Postwar American Dystopias." *Journal of American Studies* 28.2 (1994): 225–40.

Westfahl, Gary, ed. *Space and Beyond: The Frontier Theme in Science Fiction*. Westport, CT: Greenwood, 2000.

A *Nineteen Eighty-Four* for the Twenty-First Century: John Twelve Hawks's Fourth Realm Trilogy as Critical Dystopia

Alexander Charles Oliver Hall

The first thing listeners hear in the audiobook edition of John Twelve Hawks's *The Traveler* (2005), the first novel in the Fourth Realm trilogy, is the scrambled voice of the author behind the John Twelve Hawks pen name. The voice is scrambled because, as Twelve Hawks later explains in an interview with the audiobook's executive producer Brian Smith, he "tr[ies] to live a private life," a "simple act" that he says "these days can be very difficult" (Twelve Hawks, interview). However, Twelve Hawks has taken the idea of a private life to an extreme that has been characterized as reclusive by many media outlets, edging out Thomas Pynchon as the recluse par excellence in contemporary fiction writing. As the author says in his interview with Smith, "I've never met my editor Jason Kaufman or any of the staff at Doubleday. I talk to them using a [satellite telephone] or we communicate through the internet." Just as, perhaps, for Pynchon, Twelve Hawks's "decision to live off the grid," as he terms it, is "relevant to the publication" of his work in that he "want[s] people to focus on the book itself—not on its author." This is because, he says, "the typical . . . slant of most media arts coverage trivializes the power of ideas, and I've deliberately put a great many provocative ideas in this novel" (interview).

In fact, his ideas are so provocative that the entire Fourth Realm trilogy, in which these ideas are carried out even further, might just be a *Nineteen Eighty-Four* (1949) for the twenty-first century, except that the despair that comes at the end of George Orwell's novel is positioned as a premise of Twelve Hawks's series—that is, the damage has already been done. The trilogy is informed by our contemporary world and takes as its focus the surveillance under which we find ourselves each day. In this way, as well as in terms of its bleak tone, the trilogy is quite comparable to Orwell's *Nineteen Eighty-Four*, which sought to warn readers of what the world might look like if action were not taken in the reader's empirical world to keep its evils from coming to pass. In Twelve Hawks's series, we find that many of these evils have come to pass. The novels seek to wake readers from their complacency, but they do so in a different way than Orwell's novel; the series is not so much cautionary as reactionary, and its characters do not all meet bad ends. The inclusion of hope within the narrative situates the series as a critical dystopia rather than a classical dystopia. In addition to producing an effective sort of cognitive estrangement that allows its readers to see the problems with their empirical world more clearly, a critical dystopia also gives readers the sense that there is hope yet to improve that world. This hope can promote social action and quell the tendency to wallow in cynicism or apathy.

Nineteen Eighty-Four, perhaps the best-known dystopian text, falls under the category of the classical dystopia, and thus its literary form, according to Tom Moylan, is "epic" or "open" and contains a "militant pessimism" (*Scraps* 157) that is inherent in the novel's "narrative and political closure" (160) and embodied in Winston Smith's "utter defeat" (161). In effect, as Moylan puts it, "there is no meaningful possibility of movement or resistance, much less radical change, embedded in any of the iconic elements of the text" (162). This is not the case in Twelve Hawks's Fourth Realm trilogy, which includes *The Traveler*, *The Dark River* (2007), and *The Golden City* (2009).

Indeed, the Fourth Realm trilogy is more accurately described as a critical dystopia; that is, a version of the dystopia that Raffaella Baccolini and Moylan define broadly as dystopian "texts that maintain a utopian impulse," thereby "allow[ing] both readers and protagonists to hope by resisting closure: the ambiguous, open endings of these novels maintain the utopian impulse *within* the work" (7; italics in orig.). Twelve Hawks's series adheres to the generic attributes of the critical dystopia in several ways, among them its rejection of what Baccolini and Moylan describe as "the traditional subjugation of the individual at the end of the novel." In so doing, the trilogy achieves the goal of the critical dystopia in general, which, according to Baccolini and Moylan, is to "[open] a space of contestation and opposition for those collective 'ex-centric' subjects whose class, gender, race, sexuality, and other positions are not empowered by hegemonic rule" (7). Nevertheless, there is a more overt political significance to the critical dystopia's development.

For Moylan, the rise of neoliberalism that was ushered in by the Reagan administration in the United States (and by others elsewhere in the world) during the 1980s facilitated the development of the critical dystopia,[1] and I would argue that the events of September 11, 2001, and their aftermath have intensified the cultural fears that manifested then and continue today. The Fourth Realm trilogy seems to be a reaction to, if not a product of, these fears. The timeline of the series' publication alone makes a good case that it is informed by the culture of the post–September 11 world, and it is precisely this world on which the Fourth Realm trilogy's critique zeroes in.

The narrative deals with a war being fought between an ancient order of fighters known as the Harlequins and an international consortium of conspirators who call themselves the Brethren, known to their enemies as the Tabula.[2] The Tabula are concerned with establishing ubiquitous surveillance—inspired specifically, the narrator explains, by the British philosopher Jeremy Bentham's panopticon prison design, which allowed all prisoners to be monitored at all times without knowing if they were being monitored at any specific time and which, incidentally, was used metaphorically by Michel Foucault to describe modern society in his *Discipline and Punish* in 1977—and they employ a variety of surveillance technologies toward this end. However, there are a few people known as Travelers who have the ability to move between parallel dimensions, or realms, thereby undermining the Tabula's control, both by being able to escape that control and by spreading the possibility of its alternatives to a largely docile and naive public. The Harlequins are charged with the task of protecting these Travelers from the Tabula, and the conflict has been going on for a very long time; it is even suggested that Jesus Christ was a Traveler, and his apostle Peter a Harlequin.

As *The Traveler* begins, readers meet a Harlequin named Maya, who, on a visit to Prague, is asked by her father, a now-wheelchair-bound Harlequin named Thorn, to go to the United States and find two potential Travelers, Gabriel and Michael Corrigan. They are the sons of a Traveler named Matthew who has long since disappeared, leaving many with no hope that any Travelers remain. Maya at first refuses the task, but she has unknowingly led the Tabula directly to her father, allowing them to murder him. As a result, Maya decides to embark on the journey after all; she will try to find the brothers and bring them to a Pathfinder, who can show them how to discover their potential to visit other realms. The Tabula, however, are also looking for the brothers, as they intend to use a Traveler to visit the other realms and try to gain control there too, or at least obtain the scientific knowledge they need in order to establish the virtual panopticon in their own realm once and for all. Both Maya and the Tabula have difficulty finding the brothers because they have lived "off the Grid" (Twelve Hawks, *Traveler* 45) their entire lives, using fake names and never opening bank accounts or using credit cards. However, the elder brother, Michael, has begun to use his real name, allowing the Tabula and the Harlequins to close in. Though Michael falls into Tabula hands, Maya manages to rescue Gabriel, and thus the brothers travel down considerably different paths, one with help from the Tabula and the other with help from the Harlequins.

Aside from the narrative frame, the world that Twelve Hawks introduces readers to is in some ways quite familiar. As he writes at the beginning of *The Dark River*, we can see the trilogy as "a work of fiction inspired by the real world" (vii). In his introduction to the audiobook edition of *The Traveler*, Twelve Hawks says that he wrote the novel "in an attempt to understand our contemporary world"; in other words, he says, "I'm not describing the future or some Hollywood fantasy; this is our life right now" (*Traveler* CD). Nowhere are these sentiments more evident than in what the novels describe as "the Vast Machine" or "the

Grid." The Grid is described early in *The Traveler*, when readers first meet Gabriel:

> In the dictionary, a grid was defined as a network of evenly spaced horizontal and vertical lines that could be used for locating a particular object or point. If you looked at modern civilization in a certain way, it seemed like every commercial enterprise or government program was part of an enormous grid. The different lines and squares could track you down and fix your location; they could find out almost everything about you. (45)

Essentially the same concept with another name, the Vast Machine is described by Maya, also in *The Traveler*, as "the worldwide system of computers that monitors and controls our society" (203). This ubiquitous surveillance network pervades the narrative—just as, Twelve Hawks might say, it does our own world. As an example, the author points specifically to a real-life e-mail surveillance software program known as Carnivore that was developed by the FBI as early as 1997 but abandoned by 2005, when better programs used for the same types of operations became available commercially. In *The Traveler*, Maya explains that Carnivore is "an Internet surveillance program developed by [the] FBI," adding,

> The National Security Agency has developed even more powerful tools, but my father and his Harlequin friends kept using the word "Carnivore." The old name reminded them to be careful when using the Internet. Carnivore is a packet sniffer program that looks at everything that comes through a particular network. It's aimed at specific Web sites and e-mail addresses, but it also detects certain trigger words and phrases. . . . [The Tabula] have unauthorized access through their Internet monitoring operation. (169)

Twelve Hawks also mentions the existence of malware "spy worm[s]" (*Dark* 221), one of which allows the Tabula to locate the dormant body of Gabriel and Michael's realm-traveling father on a remote island off

---

the coast of Ireland called Skellig Columba (probably a fictionalized version of the real-life island Skellig Michael) when the daughter of an aging boat captain sends a seemingly harmless e-mail that mentions "exotic" visitors to the island. These visitors include Matthew Corrigan; his Harlequin protector, a character called Mother Blessing; and, more recently, Gabriel, Maya, and others for whom the Tabula are searching. According to the narrator, "hidden within the computer was a spy worm that had infected millions of computers throughout the world. The worm waited like a tropical snake at the bottom of a dark lagoon. When certain words and names appeared, the program detected the new information, copied it, and then slithered off through the Internet to find its master" (221).

In addition to the Carnivore program and spy worms, Twelve Hawks points to the surveillance cameras that are increasing in number every day in real life. *The Traveler*'s narrator uses Great Britain as an example, reporting that the country has "four million closed-circuit television cameras . . . , about one camera for every fifteen people," and adding that "under the shield of new antiterrorism laws, every industrial country was following the British example" (73). The implications of this are compounded by the availability of "facial-scanning programs" (73), which reduce "the nodal points" of a person's face to "a string of numbers" (78) that can be matched against an algorithm for the purposes of identification. Using these and other existing technologies, the Tabula can easily find anyone living on the Grid, so it would seem that they have nearly completed the virtual panopticon.

One example of the Vast Machine's power as a Tabula resource comes in *The Traveler*, when a Harlequin spy who has been discovered inside the Tabula organization is located via helicopter in New York City, driving a Tabula car. The car is equipped with an in-vehicle security system, not unlike General Motors' OnStar, which allows the Tabula to lock the doors with the spy inside and sound the vehicle's alarm to help his pursuers find the car. The spy, still bent on escaping, breaks one of the vehicle's windows and attempts to get away on foot but is photographed by several surveillance cameras along the way, allowing the facial-recognition technology to continue monitoring his general location. He jumps into a taxicab just as the Tabula helicopter lands on the street to drop off an agent, who chases the spy into a building and kills him.

The Vast Machine gives the Tabula an almost limitless power— a power that, due to its expansion, has nearly solidified their victory against the Harlequins and Travelers. The danger, of course, is that the Tabula want to "control the entire world," and with the Vast Machine, they "finally ha[ve] the means to track down and destroy their enemies" (Twelve Hawks, *Traveler* 95), which would help them achieve their goal of total control. As Maya attempts to thwart this plan by helping Gabriel to realize his potential to become a Traveler, she must constantly take measures to avoid the Vast Machine, such as injecting herself with "facer" drugs to change her appearance enough to not be recognized by facial-recognition programs and using careful language when communicating via the internet or satellite phones. These technologies and others depicted in the Fourth Realm trilogy give the series an Orwellian quality that cannot be overlooked.

Even though, as Moylan puts it, the "paranoid society" depicted in Orwell's *Nineteen Eighty-Four* is "the quintessence of the bad place in our time," still "a structural counter-narrative suggests itself in the story of Winston and Julia." Nevertheless, Moylan notes that "the dominant narrative of their utter defeat . . . is so total that no possibility for resistance exists by the end of the plot" (*Scraps* 161). This lack of any possibility of resistance has a powerful effect on readers. In fact, despite the decades that have passed since *Nineteen Eighty-Four*'s publication, not to mention the time since the calendar year of 1984,[3] the novel still resonates with readers as a frighteningly dystopian cautionary tale. Moylan writes that "Orwell sought to counter the utopia-gone-wrong that embodied the central plan and the authoritarian mind" with a story that "could possibly make people conscious of what might happen and therefore work to avert it" (162). Like Orwell's novel, other classical dystopias such as Yevgeny Zamyatin's *We* (1924), Aldous Huxley's *Brave New World* (1932), and Katharine Burdekin's *Swastika Night* (1937) are also set in the future, and these works can be considered cautionary dystopias in the same way that *Nineteen Eighty-Four* can, since they too "could possibly make people conscious of what might happen and therefore work to avert it."

This cautionary narrative device maintains a hope for the present that is not granted in the Fourth Realm trilogy. Whereas readers of the classical dystopias can find hope in the fact that action in the present could help avoid the futures depicted, Twelve Hawks's trilogy takes place in the present day, and the damage seems to have already been done. Modern readers of *Nineteen Eighty-Four* can see a progression of events since the novel's publication that suggests the partial realization of some of its horrors, but we still seem, at least on the surface, to be a long way from the installation of a two-way telescreen in every home. The description of the Vast Machine in the Fourth Realm trilogy, however, contains a sobering truth about the extent to which we are actually monitored, and the empirical truth behind the ubiquity of the Vast Machine brings the bleak nature of the worlds of the classical dystopias to the forefront of the reader's imagination. This provides a considerable sense of immediacy that has an effect similar to the sense of hopelessness readers experience at the end of Orwell's dystopia.

Despite the continued effectiveness of Orwell's novel, the Fourth Realm trilogy is a bit more timely for modern readers, producing a cognitive estrangement that is perhaps more powerful because of the familiarity of the trilogy's world and the reality of its evils. Readers need not look far to see parallels in their own world; as Twelve Hawks puts it, "the aspects of the Vast Machine described in the [trilogy] are . . . real or under development" (*Dark* vii). In fact, readers are positioned as what the Harlequins call "citizens" or "drones." Citizens, Maya says, "are people who think they understand what's going on in the world," even though "the facts [they] know are mostly an illusion" to hide "the real struggle of history . . . going on beneath the surface"—that is, the struggle between the Harlequins and the Tabula. Drones, meanwhile, "are people who are so overwhelmed by the challenge of surviving that they're unaware of anything outside of their day-to-day lives" (*Traveler* 9). The trilogy can help awaken the citizens and drones from their complacency, but in doing so, it leaves readers with little hope, because so much of what they learn is actually going on around them seems out of their control. From this initial despair, Twelve Hawks will attempt to cultivate hope, but not without first reinforcing the despair via the defeat of several characters. Regardless, the inclusion of hope within the pages of the trilogy disqualifies it as a classical dystopia and positions it instead as a critical dystopia.

At the close of the Fourth Realm trilogy, the Tabula are exposed as the conspirators they are thanks to Gabriel Corrigan, whose brother, Michael, has been acting as the leader of the Tabula. When Gabriel attempts to apprehend Michael with help from a Harlequin named Priest, Michael exits his body to enter another realm, and Gabriel follows suit in order to chase after him. Priest arrives to find the bodies of the two brothers lying dormant as they travel. The brothers meet in the fire barrier—a barrier between realms that is forever burning down and reappearing—and seem to transcend their own consciousnesses when Gabriel decides to protect Michael from burning to death, leaving them both unable to return to their bodies. In the end, Maya, who is now carrying Gabriel's child, finds herself living in Rome with Priest, a friend of her father's named Simon Lumbroso, and a child named Alice Chen—the lone survivor of an anti-surveillance community wiped out by the Tabula in *The Dark River*. Readers are left with Maya's belief that the child she is carrying will be a Traveler and the assumption that Alice, who is already receiving training from Priest and Maya, will become the child's Harlequin protector.

This assumption, of course, lends little to a reading of the Fourth Realm trilogy as a critical dystopia, for, as we have seen above, Moylan and Baccolini see the critical dystopias as works that "maintain the utopian impulse *within* the work," and this assumption is an extrapolation.

We cannot even be sure that Maya's knowing "with a subtle, quiet certainty" (Twelve Hawks, *Golden* 358) that her child will be a Traveler means that this will in fact come to pass. Still, the series does contain hope within its pages, and it is motivated, as Moylan says of the critical utopia, by "the Enlightenment sense of *critique*—that is expressions of oppositional thought, unveiling, debunking, of both the genre itself and the historical situation" in addition to a desire for "the *critical mass* required to make the necessary explosive reaction" (*Demand* 10; italics in orig.). Furthermore, the multiple-protagonist narrative style of the trilogy makes it difficult for any kind of Winston Smith–style "utter defeat" to take place, even if some protagonists are defeated.

One way in which hope is included within Twelve Hawks's narrative is its implicit presence in the continuation of the struggle against the Tabula. When Maya is initially asked by her father to go and find the Corrigan brothers before the Tabula can, it is because he believes that they may be the last Travelers and that the cultivation of their abilities in the service of the struggle may help to keep the Fourth Realm—that is, our world—from becoming "a cold, sterile place where everyone is watched and controlled" (Twelve Hawks, *Traveler* 24). Even though Maya believes that "it's that way already," she is eventually convinced that she must do her part and become what her father wanted her to be, a Harlequin. In so doing, she contributes to the continuation of the "important cause," thereby negating her earlier assertion that it "doesn't exist anymore" (24) and maintaining some hope in what is otherwise a considerably hopeless world. Gabriel, too, provides hope within the narrative, as he goes from being practically a "citizen" to a central actant in the struggle against the Tabula.

The very existence of a Traveler lends some hope to the narrative as well. Gabriel's brother Michael learns to cross over to other realms before Gabriel can, doing so with the help of a drug that acts as a quick Pathfinder. As Michael is brainwashed to agree with the ideology of the Tabula and use his abilities to help them, Gabriel's realization of his powers comes more slowly, and there is no guarantee that he even possesses the power to cross over. When he finally discovers that he does possess the power, thanks to a human Pathfinder, new hope is injected into the narrative. As the trilogy continues, Gabriel will become a prophet of sorts, reassuring his followers that the fight against the Tabula can have a positive outcome. When Gabriel follows Michael into the fire barrier, he sacrifices himself to ensure that Michael will not do any more damage as the leader of the Tabula, and this after exposing a plot by the Tabula to use fear tactics to intensify the virtual panopticon in the Fourth Realm. As a result, the Tabula's influence over the drones and citizens is partly undone, and even if Gabriel does conclude that "this is just one battle. The conflict will never end" (Twelve Hawks, *Golden* 345), hope is present in this turn of events.

Apart from the inclusion of hope, another interesting departure from the classical dystopia that helps situate the Fourth Realm trilogy as a critical dystopia is the way in which the Vast Machine is harnessed by the resistant enclave to call attention to its evils. Winston Smith does not even have the freedom to use the telescreen or speakwrite against Big Brother, but with the help of a computer hacker, Gabriel is able to create a computer worm to send a message to the citizens and drones of his dystopian world, one that might help to bring down the Tabula from within and convince people to oppose the expansion of the Vast Machine. Since the Vast Machine is perhaps the Tabula's most significant tool for exerting its power over the Fourth Realm, harnessing that power for subversive purposes also results in the inclusion of hope within the narrative.

The role of the Vast Machine in the narrative suggests the critical mass Twelve Hawks hopes to achieve in the trilogy. Peter Marks notes that the surveillance at work in the trilogy is viewed by the masses of its world as "benign"—or, worse, it goes "largely unrecognised"—and is accepted "as the price of security, convenience and stability." Still, "readers quickly recognise that social proclamations of security, convenience and stability need to be treated sceptically," and while "this thumbnail guide to panopticism remains just that, a gloss on something far more complex," it serves "for the wider public who might not have heard of Bentham, Foucault (who does not rate a mention) or panopticism" to introduce "some emerging surveillance technologies, practices and theories" (234). Since the description of the Vast Machine is one of the most important aspects of the series, it might be fair to say that it alone helps the novel achieve the critical mass that is sought by the critical dystopia.[4] In fact, the very mention of the series in Marks's paper, an academic paper dealing with surveillance theory, supports this claim, but so too does the fact that the first novel in the series became a *New York Times* best seller and the entire series has been optioned for film adaptation by 20th Century Fox. Still, while critical mass would seem to have been achieved by the series, the resonance of the Vast Machine with both readers and critics may not be solely responsible, for the critical dystopia is generally motivated by the problems of its historical situation.

Moylan sees twentieth-century utopian literature as having undergone significant changes in the 1970s and 1980s. In the 1970s, the uprising against the war in Vietnam and the civil-rights struggle, among other causes, produced a hopeful attitude in culture that manifested in literature as the new critical utopia,[5] but with the election of Ronald Reagan in 1980 came the rise of neoliberalism in the United States, which would equal the undoing of the progress that had been made to promote social justice in the 1960s and 1970s. This turn of events produced an attitude of hopelessness, apathy, cynicism, and depression in the cultural production of the era, which brought about a new version of the dystopia: the critical dystopia. Reagan would go on to serve two full terms, followed by his vice president, George H. W. Bush, who was defeated by the Democrat Bill Clinton after a single term in office. Under Clinton, Moylan writes, "the logic of economic growth and governmental abdication of social responsibilities was not only not stopped but actually intensified in a more efficient and seemingly responsible manner" (*Scraps* 184). In 2000, George W. Bush was able to win the presidency, but his "compassionate conservatism"

---

platform was quickly overshadowed by the September 11 attacks in 2001, which produced an outpouring of support for the very technologies that comprise the Vast Machine as a means to help prevent any such attacks from ever happening again. The technology of the real-life Vast Machine does, as Marks says, "need to be treated sceptically," in part because the deployment of surveillance tactics since September 11 "is pushing the pendulum from care to control" (Lyon 11). Twelve Hawks seems to be directly influenced by this mentality, for it is fear that the Tabula use to move the pieces of the virtual panopticon into place. Late in the series, after Michael Corrigan has taken over as the leader of the Tabula, he hires a man he knows to be a murderer of children to begin kidnapping children in California. Once several children have gone missing and a sufficient level of panic has been achieved, Michael addresses the Los Angeles Press Club to suggest that parents begin having tracking devices placed under their children's skin so that they can be located if they ever go missing. Parents begin doing so in droves, and the Tabula see their dream of a virtual panopticon becoming a reality, until Gabriel intervenes. Still, the parallel to September 11 is clear enough; after the attacks, the fear so many felt made the choice between security and freedom easier to make, and the citizens and drones of our world largely chose security, if the USA PATRIOT Act is any indication. Unfortunately, Twelve Hawks's narrative has not been paralleled in the reader's empirical world in terms of the cathartic exposure of the more dubious aspects of the surveillance situation post–September 11. Thus, we await a real-life Gabriel Corrigan to wake us from our nightmare, even if so many of us are unaware that we are living in a nightmare in the first place.

Notes

1. See Moylan, *Scraps* 186–94.
2. In *The Traveler*, a character named Thomas Walks the Ground explains the Brethren's other name, the Tabula, like this: "Tabula comes from the Latin phrase tabula rasa—which means 'a blank slate.' The Tabula think the human

mind is a blank slate when you're born. That means the men in power can fill up your brain with selected information. If you do this to large numbers of people you can control most of the world's population. The Tabula hate anyone who can show that there's a different reality" (156).

3. It is worth noting that there is a certain level of ambiguity surrounding the year in which the novel takes place, in spite of the title. After writing the date in his journal (a punishable act itself in Oceania), Winston begins to feel helpless, in part because "he did not know with any certainty that this *was* 1984. It must be round about that date, since he was fairly sure that his age was thirty-nine, and he believed that he had been born in 1944 or 1945; but it was never possible nowadays to pin down any date within a year or two" (Orwell 10; italics in orig.).

4. Still, the inclusion of the fantastic Traveler motif, specifically the existence of the parallel worlds or "realms," not only drives the plot but also suggests the possible existence of a world qualitatively different from our own, which is also a hugely important maneuver of the text.

5. See Moylan, *Demand*.

Works Cited

Baccolini, Raffaella, and Tom Moylan. "Introduction: Dystopia and Histories." *Dark Horizons: Science Fiction and the Dystopian Imagination*. Ed. Raffaella Baccolini and Tom Moylan. New York: Routledge, 2003. 1–12.

Lyon, David. *Surveillance after September 11*. Cambridge: Polity, 2003.

Marks, Peter. "Imagining Surveillance: Utopian Visions and Surveillance Studies." *Surveillance & Society* 3.2/3 (2005): 222–39.

Moylan, Tom. *Demand the Impossible: Science Fiction and the Utopian Imagination*. New York: Methuen, 1986.

_____. *Scraps of the Untainted Sky: Science Fiction, Utopia, Dystopia*. Boulder, CO: Westview, 2000.

Orwell, George. *Nineteen Eighty-Four*. New York: Signet, 1950.

Twelve Hawks, John. *The Dark River*. New York: Doubleday, 2007.

_____. *The Golden City*. New York: Vintage, 2009.

_____. Interview by Brian Smith. Twelve Hawks, *Traveler* CD.

_____. *The Traveler*. New York: Vintage, 2005.

_____. *The Traveler*. 2005. Narr. Scott Brick. Random, 2005. CD.

This Edged Hymn: China Miéville within and against Dystopia

Sandy Rankin

> Then, from time to time, like a diseased eyeball in which disturbing flashes of light are perceived or like those baroque sunbursts in which rays from another world suddenly break into this one, we are reminded that Utopia exists and that other systems, other spaces, are still possible.
>
> (Fredric Jameson, *Valences of the Dialectic*)

> [The Ariekei] could be mythologers now: they'd never had monsters, but now the world was all chimeras, each metaphor a splicing. The city's a heart, I said, and in that a heart and a city were sutured into a third thing, a heartish city, and cities are heart-stained, and hearts are city-stained too.
>
> No wonder it made them sick. . . . They were in a new world. It was the world we live in.
>
> (China Miéville, *Embassytown*)

A dystopian vein pulses on the surface of China Miéville's science-fiction horror-surrealist-phantasmagoric fantasies, which means they seem to have a great deal in common with key dystopian novels, more or less canonized and referred to as science-fiction classics: Yevgeny Zamyatin's *We* (1924), Aldous Huxley's *Brave New World* (1932), George Orwell's *Nineteen Eighty-Four* (1949), Anthony Burgess's *A Clockwork Orange* (1962), and Margaret Atwood's *The Handmaid's Tale* (1985), among others. Indeed, Miéville says, "Weird fiction . . . is about an aesthetic of the fantastic; you alienate and shock the reader. That's what I really like" ("Interview"). Consolatory fantasy and imaginary wish fulfillment do not alienate and shock readers; nightmare fictions and nightmare realities do. As M. Keith Booker and Anne-Marie Thomas say, "If a utopia is an imaginary ideal society that dreams of a world in which the social, political, and economic problems of the real present have been solved (or at least in which effective mechanisms for the solutions to these problems are in place), then a dystopia is an imagined world in which the dream has become a nightmare" (65).

Tom Moylan suggests the catch phrase "scrappy utopian pessimism" (160) for dystopian novelists and "deeply negative" (197) but "informed and empowered by a utopian horizon" (196) for critical dystopian novelists (bleak, but distinct from dystopian). This latter category includes writers such as Ursula K. Le Guin, with her novels *The Dispossessed* (1974) and *The Word for World Is Forest* (1976), among others; Samuel R. Delany with *Dhalgren* (1975), *Trouble on Triton* (1976), and so on; Octavia Butler with her Xenogenesis trilogy (1987, 1988, 1989; later renamed Lilith's Brood) and her Parable series (1993, 1998); Marge Piercy with *Woman on the Edge of Time* (1976) and *He, She and It* (1991); and Kim Stanley Robinson with his Three Californias trilogy (1984, 1988, 1990). We may very well, in the manner of a double-voiced or paradoxical narrative within and against narrative, apply "deeply negative" but "informed by a utopian horizon" to Miéville's fiction. Clearly, Miéville, as Moylan says of Robinson, "searches for Utopia by way of a dystopian pessimism that turns the wisdom of history and the commitment of daily struggle against the anti-utopian fear and loathing of radical political interrogation and transformation" (221).

Indeed, in a carte-blanche pseudo-dismissal (or very real but probably contingent dismissal) of the utopian value of utopianism, Miéville, who earned a PhD in international relations from the London School of Economics, equates *capitalist* utopianism with delusion, failure of the worst kind, and protection of the nightmare capitalist status quo:

> The attempt to replace war and inequality with law is not merely utopian—it is precisely self-defeating. A world structured around international law cannot but be one of imperialist violence.
>
> The chaotic and bloody world around us *is the rule of law*. (*Between* 319; italics in orig.)

Miéville seems to agree with Moylan that a language, a literature, and an ongoing history of dissidence should and will "expose the horror of the present moment" (Moylan 196).

However, Miéville's published works, which include numerous novels, short stories, and comics, as well as scholarship about science fiction, fantasy, horror, weird fiction, surrealism, and international law, un-neatly contain (or rather fail to contain, in the sense of restraining) an ecstatic visionary excess, an indefatigable if chimerical utopian impulse, in a manner that constellates more utopian energy for dystopian fiction than has, perhaps, previously been recognized, and in ways stronger than "deeply negative" but "informed by a utopian horizon" suggests for the critical dystopias. Miéville's aesthetic, never consolatory and rarely ironic, is always motivated by his love affair with chimerical monsters and chimerical language, and by the irrepressible revolutionary wish, not as allegory but as literalized metaphor. Each metaphor is a splicing of two into a third thing, and all things are chimeras when we are immersed in metaphor, in language, where we can stain language, stain metaphor, twist it, reshape it.

Chimera can mean many things: fantasy; daydream; vision; hermaphrodite; "an organism, organ, or part consisting of two or more tissues of different genetic composition, produced as a result of organ transplant, grafting, or genetic engineering"; "an imaginary monster made up of grotesquely disparate parts" ("Chimera"). However, after speaking of chimera as social dreaming or vision, now is the time to say that in Miéville's view, we need chimeras—he says "fantasy"—"to think the world, and to change it" ("Editorial" 48). Miéville's dystopian vein and utopian impulse within that vein fulfill Marxist cultural critic and science-fiction scholar Fredric Jameson's invocation of "a diseased eyeball in which disturbing flashes of light are perceived," or "baroque sunbursts in which rays from another world suddenly break into this one, [reminding us] that Utopia exists and that other systems, other spaces, are still possible" (612), without the reversed triumph of the dystopian nightmare.

To be fair, perhaps critical dystopias are the best—the most theoretically credible, most theoretically revolutionary—that we can do (read, study, and write) when it comes to representing the utopian impulse within dystopia. According to Lyman Tower Sargent, the critical dystopia is "a non-existent society described in considerable detail and normally located in time and space that the author intended a contemporaneous reader to view as worse than contemporary society but that normally includes at least one eutopian enclave or holds out hope that the dystopia can be overcome and replaced with a eutopia" (222). The spelling of eutopia suggests "good place" rather than "no place." Raffaella Baccolini and Tom Moylan argue that critical dystopias, though bleak, "maintain" within them "a utopian impulse" ("Introduction" 7) against the negation of utopian thought, which was a symptom of the conservative turn in America in the 1980s as well as the Thatcherite proclamation that "there is no alternative" to capitalism.

Baccolini points out, however, that in the critical dystopia, "even in the presence of utopian hope there is not much room for happiness. Rather, a sense of regret and of missed opportunity accompanies the awareness and knowledge that the protagonists have attained. Instead of an easily compensatory and comforting happy ending, the critical dystopia's open ending leaves its protagonist dealing with his or her choices and responsibilities" ("Useful Knowledge" 130). For Baccolini, "a constant awareness of a 'slight suffering,'" a notion she borrows from feminist science-fiction writer Joanna Russ, "is the necessary condition of Utopia." She argues that "one of the things that make memory and possibly nostalgia relevant for Utopia is that we must keep feeling uncomfortable" ("Finding Utopia" 162). Her "slight suffering" and "feeling uncomfortable" probably equate with Miéville's conception of "weird fiction" that "alienate[s] and shock[s] the reader."

Yet Miéville's fictions do include room for happiness, as if agreeing with George Orwell, who wrote, "Certainly we ought to be discontented, we ought not simply to find out ways of making the best of a bad job, and yet if we kill all pleasure in the actual process of life, what sort of future are we preparing for ourselves? If a man cannot enjoy the return of spring, why should he be happy in a labour-saving Utopia? What will he do with the leisure that the machine will give him?" ("Some Thoughts"). Neither Orwell nor Miéville is as dystopian as the dystopian vein in their fictions suggests; and, as this essay argues, Miéville's utopian impulse out-pulses his dystopian vein. The latter appears as Jameson's diseased eyeball, showing disturbing flashes of light, while the utopian impulse appears as baroque sunbursts; thus, in Miéville's fictions, other utopian spaces are present—with utopia conceived as a process, as permanent revolution.

Nightmare images of dystopian grotesquerie from the minor to the major, which may discomfort, alienate, and shock readers, abound in Miéville's fictions, much as they do in Atwood's *The Handmaid's Tale*, in Huxley's *Brave New World*, in Burgess's *A Clockwork Orange*, in Orwell's *Nineteen Eighty-Four*, and so on. Here are a few points of mutual dystopian contact, present in image and language, beginning with three of the aforementioned novels (for the sake of brevity) and concluding with where Miéville apparently draws from a similar dystopian vein in order to expose the horror of our present moment. With the images and language of horror, we may think of the world differently, and when they are infused with the utopian impulse, we can use images and language of horror to help us change the world. From Atwood:

Beside the main gateway there are six more bodies hanging, by the necks, their hands tied in front of them, their heads in white bags tipped sideways onto their shoulders. . . . What they are hanging from is hooks. . . . It's the bags over the heads that are the worst, worse than the faces themselves would be. It makes the men like dolls on which faces have not yet been painted; like scarecrows, which in a way is what they are, since they are meant to scare. . . . The heads are zeros. (32)

From Huxley:

"Kill it, kill it, kill it . . ." The Savage went on shouting. . . .

The door of the lighthouse was ajar. They pushed it open and walked into a shuttered twilight. Through an archway on the further side of the room they could see the bottom of the staircase that led up to the higher floors. Just under the crown of the arch dangled a pair of feet.

"Mr. Savage!"

Slowly, very slowly, like two unhurried compass needles, the feet turned towards the right; north, north-east, east, south-east, south, south-south-west; then paused, and, after a few seconds, turned as unhurriedly back towards the left. South-south-west, south, south-east, east. . . . (259; first and third ellipses in orig.)

And Orwell has O'Brien, the triumphant antagonist of *Nineteen Eighty-Four*, say to the utterly defeated protagonist Winston Smith, "Always, at every moment, there will be the thrill of victory, the sensation of trampling on an enemy who is helpless. If you want a picture of the future, imagine a boot stamping on a human face—forever" (267).

Minor dystopian/grotesque imagery from Miéville's *Perdido Street Station* (2001) looks like this: in Bas-Lag, the alternative world of multiple sentient species in which Miéville also set his next two novels, New Crobuzonian human Isaac is lying in bed one morning when his "arse itche[s]." Isaac—whose lover Lin is a female khepri, a sentient insect being—"scratched under the blanket, rooting as shameless as a dog. Something burst under his nail, and he withdrew his hand to examine it. A tiny half-crushed grub waved helplessly on the end of his finger. It was a refflick, a harmless little khepri parasite. *The thing must have been rather bewildered by my juices*, Isaac thought, and flicked his finger clean." He tells Lin, "Bath time" (9).

Moving from minor grotesquerie to violent major grotesquerie, we find, reminiscent of Atwood, Huxley, and Orwell, a boot stamping on a human face, or on the face of a sentient being. For example, in *Iron Council* (2004):

Breaking the soil like the first shoots of a grotesque harvest were bones. They were abrupt and blacked by fire, fibrous like dense wood. . . .

Planted scarecrow in the middle was a degraded corpse. A human man. He was naked, slumped, upheld by spikes that pinned him to a tree. Javelins pierced him. One emerged point-first from his sternum. It had been forced up his anus and through him. His scrotum was torn off. There was a scab of blood on his throat. He was leathered by sun and insects worked on him. (33)

In *King Rat* (2000):

The Piper leapt up, pulled his legs up hard and stamped down with all his strength.

Bones crunched and split in Anansi's head. (293)

In Miéville's *Embassytown* (2011), the Ariekei, known as Hosts— indigenous to the planet Arieka, "stuck out in the middle of nowhere" (50)—are hoofed, horselike, and winged like insects. They are sentient beings with two mouths who speak a double-voiced language that is incomprehensible to most humans, except for the empathic human biorigged doppelgangers known as Ambassadors. Each Ambassador consists of two humans biorigged together for the double-mouthed effect. Some of the Ariekei, withdrawing from an addiction to their own language when spoken by a new human biorigged doppelganger (one of whom commits suicide, thus ending the doppelganger's ability to speak Ariekei) and wishing to end domination by and codependence on the human colonizers, tear off their own fanwings, equivalent to ears, then tear off the fanwings of other Ariekei. The tormentors think they are liberating similarly afflicted Ariekei. Avice Benner Cho, the human narrator, an immerser in "immer" and "the out" and an inhabitant of Embassytown in the center of Arieka, describes seeing one such incident: "The fanwing wrenched free: roots of gristle and muscle part-ed and with a burst of blood came finally away, pulling fibres out of the quivering back, trailing them." Fanwings, Avice tells us, "are at least as sensitive as human eyes. The traumatised Ariekes opened its mouths and fell, stupefied with pain. It was dragged away. The deafener held up its grotesque dripping bouquet. It made a loud wordless noise. Triumph or rage" (270–71).

Baccolini and Moylan point out that the dystopian text "usually begins directly in the terrible new world" and "the focus is frequently on a character who questions the dystopian society," which is to say that a "counter-narrative develops," in triumph or rage, "as the dystopian citizen moves from apparent contentment into an experience of alienation and resistance. This structural strategy of narrative and counter-narrative most often plays out by way of the social, and antisocial, use of language. Throughout the history of dystopian fiction, the conflict of the text turns on the control of language." Indeed, "language is a key weapon for the reigning dystopian power structure" ("Introduction" 5–6). But as any of Miéville's fictions and nonfictions indicate, language is also a key weapon, along with educated, planned, and spontaneous collective action, for those who struggle within and against power structures—in reality as well as in dystopian (in which protagonists typically fail), critical dystopian (bleak, but with weak hints of success), ambiguously utopian, and ambiguously heterotopian fictions. In Miéville's fiction, wordlessness—languagelessness, muteness—spells the end of the utopian impulse, the end of the possibility of potential collective praxis (theory and practice combined).

Embassytown is the only one of Miéville's novels that we can say with near certainty is set in our future, and in which we can, from there, evaluate whether the boot should be imagined, via Miéville (or, for that matter, via Orwell as opposed to O'Brien), in this future—forever or not. It is also the one novel of Miéville's that is most overtly about language as a key weapon, both of oppression and of resistance to oppression. Indeed, Orwell's "doublethink," when thought of as lying via metaphor, becomes, in Miéville's representations, part and parcel of the utopian impulse, which should compel us to rethink Orwell's apparent anti-utopian dystopian vein as perhaps more utopian, more hopeful, than previously generally acknowledged. We can say the same of Atwood's *The Handmaid's Tale*, particularly since Atwood takes the structure of her ending straight from *Nineteen Eighty-Four*: an appendix seemingly written after the demise of the dystopian regime of the main narrative. If, looking backward with Miéville as our contemporary guide, we can recognize *Nineteen Eighty-Four* and *The Handmaid's Tale* as containing an ecstatic-visionary unrestrained excess, whether despite or because of their apparent foreclosing bleakness, then we can envision other dystopian and critical dystopian novels similarly, despite or because of the chimerical nature of images and language—which shape us, but which we can also reshape in turn.

Embassytown is written in the form of a journal or letter, its unnamed addressee an anticipated future audience, much like in the dystopian novels *We*, *A Clockwork Orange*, and *The Handmaid's Tale*. In *Embassytown*, Avice, the keeper of the journal or the writer of the letter, appears to signal that we are in a dystopian world, or at least in a dystopian vein. She begins the narrative in contentment. She questions very little about the possible machinations of either Bremen, the planet from which the human colonizers travel to Arieka, or the Ariekei, who cannot lie because of the nature of their literalized language. For that matter, she also fails to question the possible machinations of her husband, Scile, who ultimately betrays and even tries to kill her. Scile thinks the Ariekei language and people should remain as they are, something like prelapsarian. However, we could not call them utopians in utopia, and neither would Scile. Ariekei are not pacifists. They are sometimes at war with one another. They are no more or less utopian than the colonists from Bremen, or even than we are, but they are also no more or less dystopian than Bremen or we are.

As a protagonist in a dystopian novel or in a critical dystopian novel—if the novel can be called either, or one but not the other—Avice begins to question the world as she has known it after an Ariekei assassinates another Ariekei attempting to lie, to metamorphose in a performance, and Scile subsequently disappears. At one point, reminiscent of Offred in *The Handmaid's Tale*, Avice says, as if speaking to us, addressees of a letter or addressees in a journal: "I admit defeat. I've been trying to present these events with a structure. I simply don't know how everything happened. Perhaps because I didn't pay proper attention, perhaps because it wasn't a narrative, but for whatever reasons, it doesn't want to be what I want to make it" (Miéville, *Embassytown* 145). Similarly, Atwood's Offred, inhabitant of Gilead, a near-future totalitarian theocracy in which women are thoroughly subjugated, addresses a future anticipated audience. She says, "I wish this story were different. I wish it were more civilized. I wish it showed me in a better light, if not happier, then at least more active, less hesitant, less distracted by trivia." But more importantly, prefiguring a point of contact with Miéville's Avice, Offred says, "I wish it had more shape. I wish it were about love, or about sudden realizations important to one's life, or even about sunsets, birds, rainstorms, or snow." She says, "I'm sorry there is so much pain in this story. I'm sorry it's in fragments, like a body caught in crossfire or pulled apart by force. But there is nothing I can do to change it." However, she also acknowledges (dialectically? a hint of baroque sunburst?), "I've tried to put some of the good things in as well. Flowers, for instance, because where would we be without them?" (Atwood 267).

Furthermore, via the journal or letter form, Atwood and Miéville are, with the novel's narrator, addressing an imagined future audience, establishing a point of contact with Burgess's *A Clockwork Orange* and Zamyatin's *We*. In *A Clockwork Orange*, whether we mean the British ending that Burgess intended or the American ending foisted on him by American publishers, we have a narrator who celebrates violence, who revels in dystopia. In the British ending, sociopathic Alex, a murderer and a rapist, says that "[t]omorrow is all like sweet flowers." He says he is "on his oddy knocky seeking like a mate. And all that cal. A terribly grahzny vonny world, really. . . . But you, O my brothers, remember sometimes thy little Alex that was. Amen. And all that cal" (Burgess 212). The American version, one chapter shorter, ends with, "Oh, it was gorgeosity and yumyumyum. When it came to the Scherzo I could viddy myself very clear running and running on like very light and mysterious nogas, carving the whole litso of the creeching world with my cut-throat britva. And there was the slow movement and the lovely last singing movement still to come. I was cured all right" (199). In *We*, Zamyatin's D-503, cipher-inhabitant of the One State—utopian in theory, rationalized and instrumentalized nightmare in reality—writes:

> . . . Strange: I was writing today about the highest of heights in human history and all the while breathing the cleanest mountain air of thought, but, meanwhile, there were clouds and cobwebs and a cross, some kind of four-pawed X, inside me. Maybe it was my own paws, since they were in front of me on the table all this time—my shaggy paws. I don't like talking about them and I don't like them: they are evidence of the savage epoch. Could there actually be, within me—
>
> I wanted to cross out that last part because it goes beyond the bounds of my preselected keywords for this record. But then I decided: I won't cross anything out. Let my records—like the most sensitive seismograph—produce the crooked line of even the most insignificant brain oscillations. Sometimes it is exactly these oscillations that serve as a forewarning of . . .
>
> Okay, this is really absurd, this really actually should be crossed out: we have channeled all the forces of nature—there cannot be any future catastrophes. (22; ellipses in orig.)

The critical dystopia genre (but supposedly not the dystopian) typically features an open or inconclusive ending. Ursula K. Le Guin, for example, ends *The Dispossessed* when "things are . . . a little broken loose, on Anarres" (309; ellipsis in orig.). The protagonist, Shevek, who is a scientist from Anarres, says, "So, you see, nobody is quite sure what happens next" (309). Shevek, ready to disembark from a rocket ship on his home planet, Anarres, says he has nothing to pack and laughs "a laugh of clear, unmixed happiness" (311). He says that tonight he will lie down beside his wife, Takver. He says, "I wish I'd brought the picture, the baby sheep, to give to Pilun," his child. The narrator says, "But he had not brought anything. His hands were empty, as they had always been" (311). Miéville concludes *The Scar* (2002) similarly. The protagonist, Bellis Coldwine, is on a ship heading for her home city of New Crobuzon in Bas-Lag. Whip-scarred, she says that

> everything has changed. . . . What I do now, I do for me. And I feel, for all that has happened, as if it is *now*, only now in *these* days, that *my* journey is beginning. I feel as if this—even all this—has been a prologue. . . .
>
> I am coming home. I will amass much more to tell you on the return journey, which will be long, but *will end*. I do not need this letter delivered. Whoever I decide you are, dear friend, I will give it to you myself.
>
> I will deliver it by hand. (Miéville, *Scar* 638; italics in orig.)

Language as a weapon, language delivered by hand, is the subject of *Embassytown*. The titular town is a settlement of humans on the planet Arieka, which itself is at the outer edge of what is called *machmal* (German for "sometimes"), or known space. Or perhaps Embassytown is at the edge of known *immer* ("always"), a psychic inner and physical outer hyperspace, similar to the space negotiated by the warp drive in *Star Trek*, similar to language itself where words fail and language defies symbolization—neither dystopian nor utopian, but also potentially dystopian and potentially utopian, as an alternative space to machmal and to our space. About all we know about immer is that it is filled with "renegades and refugees," as Avice, an immerser, tells us when she shows "a changing display of the pharos that marks the edge of the known always: here, right beside Arieka." She "show[s] it through various filters, culminating in the tropeware that ma[kes] it a lighthouse, a beacon in murk" (Miéville, *Embassytown* 154). Embassytown's human inhabitants are aliens to the indigenous Ariekei, called Hosts, who apparently do not yet know what it means to be colonized by an imperialist nation. Or they know very well but do not yet know how to say "colonized" or "imperialist," and for the Ariekei, what they cannot say is not real—yet.

Despite their stark differences in appearance, the Hosts differ most significantly from the humans in that they cannot lie. The Hosts consider language to be reality and can only describe what is. They are unable to speak figuratively until the figurative is tangibly concrete, an event. They can imagine the existence of a needed trope, an imagining that Miéville, via Avice's husband Scile, calls a "pre-ghost in their heads" (*Embassytown* 56), but can speak a trope only once it refers to a real event. As a child, Avice became part of their language, a simile, when she acted out the part of "the girl who was hurt in darkness and ate what was given to her"—a traumatic experience for her, though she is told that it is an honor to be selected by the Ariekei to perform a simile. There are other humans who are similes for the Ariekei, including "the man who swims weekly with fish" (336) and "the boy who was opened up and closed again" (100). Indeed, Avice's existence as a simile anticipates (as if the Ariekei are precognitive) her talent as an immerser: her ability to "go into the out" (23) without being debilitated by alienation and shock, but rather finding joy in it.

Due to their open endings, critical dystopias, unlike classic dystopias, tend not to function as cautionary tales. Instead, they allow for a certain degree of hopefulness, though supposedly not happiness, notwithstanding Le Guin's Shevek. Shevek's companion on the rocket ship, Ketho, who is of a race other than human and whose home is not Anarres, looks at Shevek (after Shevek laughs) "gravely, as if he was not sure what happiness was, and yet recognized or perhaps remembered it from afar. He stood beside Shevek as if there was something he wanted to ask him. But he did not ask it" (311). As utopian philosopher Ernst Bloch says of all works of art:

The solution to the question of aesthetic truth lies in this direction: *art is a laboratory and also a feast of accomplished possibilities* plus the experienced alternatives within it while the performance as well as the result take place in the manner of the substantiated illusion, i.e., of the worldly completed anticipatory illumination. . . . Whether, of course, the call for perfection—we could call it the godless prayer of poetry—becomes practical to some degree and not only remains within aesthetic anticipatory illumination is not for poetry to decide but for society. (147–48; italics in orig.)

It may be that, given Shevek's happiness despite his empty hands, Le Guin's *The Dispossessed* consists of scrappy utopian optimism, rather than scrappy utopian pessimism or dystopian pessimism; and it may be that instead of critical dystopianism, *The Dispossessed* illustrates immanent utopianism, which we may decide to grasp and bring forth—or not. Indeed, Le Guin's novel has been identified, by Jameson and others, as a major contribution to utopian literature.

As for *Embassytown*, its conclusion is open ended and double voiced, and also rather happy, though it is ambiguous as well. Are the Ariekei "better" now that they can lie, now that they can speak what is not but can potentially be without an event to allow them to do so? It seems so, but of course it would seem so via Avice, the narrator. Yet Avice says, "It would be foolish to pretend we know what'll happen. We'll have to see how Embassytown gets shaped" (Miéville, *Embassytown* 345). However, Avice, preparing to immerse into immer, where the Ariekei can now go as well, also says:

"Ready," I'll say, and set the helm beyond *void cognita*. I'll push the levers that set us out. Or perhaps the gracious thing will be to allow my first lieutenant to do it. We don't know how the passage will affect such crew: I've warned them that. They're still insistent.

So perhaps it'll be Lieutenant Spanish Dancer [an Ariekes] who'll instigate that indescribable motion from everyday space through the always. We'll immerse, into the immer, and into the out. (345; italics in orig.)

The Ariekei, too, seem rather happy, recovering from their "new world" sickness. Because of Miéville's diseased eyeball, Miéville's baroque sunbursts, Miéville's ecstatic-visionary excess and immanent utopian impulse, Spanish Dancer says: "Before the humans came . . . [w]e were like hunters. We were like plants eating light. The humans made their town in our town like a star in a circle. They made their place like a filament in a flower. We spoke the name of their place, but we know it had another name, sitting in the city like an organ in a body, like a tongue in a mouth." He says, "Before the humans came we didn't speak . . . we were mute, we only dropped the stones we mentioned out of our mouths, opened our mouths and had the birds we described fly out, we were vectors, we were the birds eating in mindlessness, we were the girl in darkness, only knowing it when we weren't any more" (335–36).

Perhaps "beyond *void cognita*" is how we should, in moments of our awareness of our own utopian impulses, read Winston, thinking of *Nineteen Eighty-Four* as representative of scrappy utopian optimism rather than utopian pessimism or something "deeply negative" though "informed by a utopian horizon." Kenneth M. Roemer points out that twentieth-century Americans "had been disappointed (New Deal, War on Poverty), frightened (Soviet communism), and repulsed (Nazism and Stalinism) by well-known and sometimes well-intentioned attempts to realize utopian ideals" and that "powerful dystopias by Yevgeny Zamyatin, Huxley, and Orwell had merged the images of totalitarian regimes and Utopia in the popular mind" (148). In the twenty-first century, with Miéville in mind—"we were the girl in darkness, only knowing it when we weren't any more"—we can read *Nineteen Eighty-Four* and Winston differently. Winston is supposedly utterly defeated, and in effect he is. He is "troubled by false memories occasionally" (Orwell, *Nineteen Eighty-Four* 307), though they are not really false but true, and usually of happy past moments. "They did not matter so long as one knew them for what they were." We do know them for what they are—intratextual baroque sunbursts—even if

Winston does not know. Winston "turned back to the chessboard and picked up the white knight again. Almost in the same instant it dropped onto the board with a clatter. He had started as though a pin had run into him" (307). The possible new world in his head—attempting to emerge from the past, attempting to disrupt the present, reshape it and thereby reshape the future—makes him sick. And perhaps we will now notice, even emphasize, that in Zamyatin's *We*, besides D-503's defeat, besides I-330's murder by the One State (for I-330's stubborn refusal to recant, more of a victory than a defeat), there is "still chaos, howling, corpses, wild beasts, and"— though D-503 says "unfortunately," we say *fortunately*—"a significant amount of ciphers betraying reason in the western quarters" (203).

Writers of scrappy utopian optimism, though concerned with exposing the horrors of the present moment, are doubly concerned with exposing what and how happiness, fulfillment, feels like, can be like— which one cannot know or imagine unless one has been "there," even if temporarily and chimerically (via language, via image, via metaphor, via dream logic), even if edged. Which is why, in the otherwise horrifying world of *The Handmaid's Tale*, Atwood concludes with the open-endedness of two endings. Offred says, "And so I step up, into the darkness within; or else the light" (295). But in an alternative ending, which occurs long after Offred has died and totalitarian, theocratic Gilead is no more, an anthropologist says, "Are there any questions?" (311)—or, as scrappy utopian Frantz Fanon says in a moment of ecstatic-visionary excess, "My final prayer: O my body, make of me always a man who questions!" (218). Scrappy utopianism, ecstatic-visionary excess is also why Miéville's giant Dada-esque cosmic world-spinning, word-spinning spider, known as the Weaver (a fervent and lovable grotesquerie, a visionary), sings in *Perdido Street Station*:

FLESHSCAPE INTO THE FOLDING INTO FLESHSCAPE TO SPEAK A GREETING IN THIS THE SCISSORED REALM I WILL RECEIVE AND BE RECEIVED. . . . AGAIN AGAIN AND AGAIN DO NOT

WITHHOLD THIS BLADED SUMMONS THIS EDGED HYMN I AC-
CEPT I AGREE YOU SLICE SO NICE AND NICELY YOU LITTLE
ENDOSKELETAL FIGURINES YOU SNIP AND SHAVE AND SLIV-
ER THE CORDS OF THE WOVEN WEB AND SHAPE IT WITH AN
UNCOUTH GRACE . . . (330)

Miéville says of early modern religious visionaries and contemporary
secular visionaries, "The God in the everyday *is* the everyday. The oppressive uncanny, and the transcendence we so want—it's us. It's this"
("Limits" 6–7; italics in orig.). We will reconfigure Miéville's words as
"The chimerical in the everyday, the baroque sunbursts in the everyday, *are* the everyday. The oppressive diseased eyeball, and the transcendence or the edged hymn we so want—it's us. It's this." Thus,
we are reminded that utopia, although and because it is heart stained,
exists and that other systems, other spaces, besides dystopian are still
possible, particularly if our living, embodied prayer is to always question, to shape questions and contingent answers with uncouth grace
But, with Miéville, we will add this caveat: "Transcendence is necessary, and it is (im)possible, and it is all around us . . . and it leads back
here" (6): reality with the future in it; no boot stamping on the human
face—forever.

Works Cited

Atwood, Margaret. *The Handmaid's Tale*. New York: Random, 1998.
Baccolini, Raffaella. "Finding Utopia in Dystopia: Feminism, Memory, Nostalgia,
    and Hope." Moylan and Baccolini 159–89.
_____. " 'A Useful Knowledge of the Present Is Rooted in the Past': Memory and
    Historical Reconciliation in Ursula K. Le Guin's *The Telling*." Baccolini and
    Moylan, *Dark Horizons* 113–34.
Baccolini, Raffaella, and Tom Moylan, eds. *Dark Horizons: Science Fiction and the
    Dystopian Imagination*. New York: Routledge, 2003.
_____. "Introduction: Dystopia and Histories." Baccolini and Moylan, *Dark Hori-
    zons* 1–12.
Bloch, Ernst. "Art and Utopia." *The Utopian Function of Art and Literature: Selected
    Essays*. Trans. Jack Zipes and Frank Mecklenburg. Cambridge, MA: MIT P, 1989.
    78–155.

Booker, M. Keith, and Anne-Marie Thomas. *The Science Fiction Handbook.* Chichester: Wiley, 2009.

Burgess, Anthony. *A Clockwork Orange.* New York: Norton, 1986.

"Chimera." *The American Heritage Dictionary of the English Language.* Houghton, 2011. Web. 1 May 2012.

Fanon, Frantz. *Black Skin, White Masks.* New York: Grove, 1994.

Huxley, Aldous. *Brave New World.* New York: Harper, 2006.

Jameson, Fredric. *Valences of the Dialectic.* London: Verso, 2010.

LeGuin, Ursula K. *The Dispossed.* New York: Hearst, 1974.

Miéville, China. *Between Equal Rights: A Marxist Theory of International Law.* Chicago: Haymarket, 2006.

_____. "Editorial Introduction." *Historical Materialism* 10.4 (2002): 39–49.

_____. *Embassytown.* New York: Del Rey, 2011.

_____. "Interview: China Miéville." By Cheryl Morgan. *Strange Horizons.* Strange Horizons, 1 Oct. 2001. Web. 19 Apr. 2012.

_____. *Iron Council.* New York: Del Rey, 2004.

_____. *King Rat.* New York: Doherty, 1998.

_____. "The Limits of Vision(aries); or, M. John Harrison Returns to London, and It Is Spring." Introduction. *Things That Never Happen.* By M. John Harrison. San Francisco: Night Shade, 2003. 1–9.

_____. *Perdido Street Station.* New York: Del Rey, 2001.

_____. *The Scar.* New York: Del Rey, 2002.

Moylan, Tom. *Scraps of the Untainted Sky: Science Fiction, Utopia, Dystopia.* Boulder, CO: Westview, 2000.

Moylan, Tom, and Raffaella Baccolini, eds. *Utopia Method Vision: The Use Value of Social Dreaming.* Bern: Lang, 2007.

Orwell, George. *Nineteen Eighty-Four.* New York: Penguin, 2003.

_____. "Some Thoughts on the Common Toad." *Orwell.ru.* O. Dag, 12 Feb. 2000. Web. 19 Apr. 2012.

Roemer, Kenneth M. "More Aliens Transforming Utopia: The Futures of Reader Response and Utopian Studies." Moylan and Baccolini 131–58.

Sargent, Lyman Tower. "US Eutopias in the 1980s and 1990s: Self-Fashioning in a World of Multiple Identities." *Utopianism/Literary Utopias and National Cultural Identities: A Comparative Perspective.* Ed. Paola Spinozzi. Bologna: Cotepra/U of Bologna, 2001. 221–32.

Zamyatin, Yevgeny. *We.* Trans. Natasha S. Randall. New York: Random, 2006.

1983: Cory Doctorow's *Little Brother*_____

Susan L. Stewart

Casually sprinkled in with the quotidian—descriptions of unpleasantly cold weather, the smell of food cooking, a broken elevator—are the clues that something is amiss in Winston Smith's world as described in the first few pages of George Orwell's *Nineteen Eighty-Four* (1949). The clocks chime thirteen times. Hate week is just around the corner in Oceania, Winston's home. Posters with the now-infamous words "BIG BROTHER IS WATCHING YOU" dominate the landscape (1). As the narrative continues, the quotidian quickly gives way to a quagmire of repression: Thought Police, the Ministry of Truth, Newspeak. The narrator never offers detailed explanations of how the world became this way; Winston, whom political theorist Judith N. Shklar characterizes as the "hero" (345) of the book, remembers some historical incidents, but he can never be certain of what he knows, for history is a series of constructions and reconstructions. He suspects that at one time, history was to some degree fixed and stable, but it is best to ignore history and pretend the world has always been the way it is now. To do otherwise only leads to torture, as Winston soon enough discovers.

Winston lives in what Tom Moylan describes as a "social 'elsewhere'" or "the terrible place" of dystopian narratives (xiii). Oceania's past is constantly erased and replaced, thus reducing history to a terrible fiction in which the past consists of "whatever the records and the memories agree upon" (Orwell 263), as "the Party has been able—and may, for all we know, continue to be able for thousands of years—to arrest the course of history" (265). Even if reliable accounts of past events were to be provided, they would be rendered useless, and perhaps even dangerous. Indeed, many dystopias can be characterized as places without a past, because the past is only mentioned in passing. Such is not the case in Cory Doctorow's *Little Brother* (2008),[1] at least not yet, for it has a past we know quite well: our present or very near future. Unfortunately, a similar future to Winston's looms on the horizon for Marcus Yallow, the protagonist, who is also known online as w1n5t0n or Winston. Brian K. Vaughn, author of *Y: The Last Man* (2002–8), makes the intertextual link when he describes *Little Brother* as "a worthy younger sibling to Orwell's *1984*" (qtd. in Doctorow, *Little Brother* online). The books are related, as are the protagonists, making Marcus Winston Smith's metaphorical younger teenage brother.

Considering the connections to Orwell's narrative, it should not be surprising that what follows relies a great deal on what Orwell describes in *Nineteen Eighty-Four*, but under different circumstances. *Nineteen Eighty-Four* represents Orwell's response to Hitler and Stalin—albeit not a prophetic response, according to Shklar, in the way that many dystopias are. Rather, Shklar writes, "Orwell meant it to draw out the logical implications of the thinking of his fellow intellectuals who were blind to the character of Stalin's and Hitler's regimes. . . . It was not a prediction, but a savage satirical malediction on his contemporaries" (341). However, Shklar's either-or characterization is far too limiting and ultimately inaccurate, for *Nineteen Eighty-Four* is both a prediction and a critique. It is also a terrible, if not obvious, reminder of what a full-blown fascist government looks like. *Little Brother* does not offer the same view of fascist or authoritarian government; instead, as a pre-dystopian novel, it identifies the symptoms, the beginning fever and rash, of a fascist government in its infancy. Worse still, the novel conveys how easy it is to ignore and forget the nearness of the symptoms. In fact, while reminders of Big Brother—or Homeland Security, a consequence of September 11—occasionally surface in the news, the majority of Americans probably seldom think of those entities. Instead, we live quotidian lives, forgetting that the slouch toward fascism is possibly already under way, even though the movement is less evident than it was in the few years following September 11, 2001, a time when choices were frequently reduced to either-or propositions (patriotic or unpatriotic, for instance). One probably would not expect a similar response from a novel that so thoroughly embraces a democratic model. However, as I will argue, *Little Brother* does ask us to think in either-or terms: we can either be safe or we can maintain our civil liberties; we can live in a democracy or we can live under an authoritarian regime. In this way, the novel offers an unfortunate model.

The second part of my argument is very specific to *Little Brother* as a young adult (YA) novel. One of the concerns regarding YA literature is the relationship between the adult writer and the young-adult reader. "Critics of young adult fiction," writes Mike Cadden, "have good reason to dwell on the nature of narrative authority in the young adult novel, especially the authority claimed through the consciousness of young characters" (146). The good reason? Ethics, or an "ethical theory of irony" through the use of "double-voiced discourse," as identified by Bakhtin (qtd. in Cadden 147). That is, as Cadden explains, "when an adult writer speaks through a young adult's consciousness to a young adult audience, he or she is involved in a top-down (or vertical) power relationship. It becomes important, then, that there be equal (or horizontal) power relations between the major characters within the text so that the young adult reader has the power to see the opposing ideologies at play" (146). Unfortunately, *Little Brother* offers little in the way of opposing ideologies. Instead, any form of dialogic discourse becomes diminished due to the nature of those who offer opposition, which, considering the political nature of the novel and what it attempts to accomplish, is quite problematic.

With the above in mind, then, I will first offer a definition of what I refer to as a *dystopia becoming*, which is very similar to traditional dystopian novels but with, as I shall explain, an important difference. *Little Brother*, a novel that speaks to fascism, is a dystopia becoming. I will also address some of the characteristics associated with fascism as explained by Henry Giroux. I will not identify all of the characteristics, nor does *Little Brother* actually embody all of Giroux's descriptions, for *Little Brother* has not reached maturation. Nevertheless, it reflects enough elements to give one pause. Embedded in those characteristics is a description of how individual rights and the right to privacy become expedient sacrifices in the name of safety, even if the sense of safety is an illusion. And last, I will discuss the problems associated with the narrative frame of *Little Brother* as a YA novel.

Dystopia Becoming: The Future Has Arrived

Little Brother is a fusion of the present and a possible, even likely, near future, but it is not a traditional dystopian novel. M. Keith Booker writes that "dystopian fictions are typically set in places or times far distant from the author's own, but it is usually clear that the real referents of dystopian fictions are generally quite concrete and near-at-hand" (19). Dystopian novels feel familiar even if they depict a very different future, for they frequently examine the real concerns and anxieties of the author's culture. Dystopian fiction also usually offers a view of "spatially or temporally distant settings" in order to "provide fresh perspectives on problematic social and political practices that might otherwise be taken for granted or considered natural and inevitable" (19). *Little Brother*, though, is much closer to our own reality and feels familiar in terms of its spatial, temporal, and ideological setting. The two most evident realities of *Little Brother* are this: surveillance cameras have become commonplace, and in order to protect citizens, the US government, including the Department of Homeland Security, has taken liberties with the Constitution and with individual rights. Indeed, the only things that mark the novel as not belonging to our present are the technological advances depicted, which are likely brewing somewhere, and the destruction of the Bay Bridge and the BART tunnel between San Francisco and Oakland. *Little Brother* could best be described as a dystopia becoming, a dystopia in process, or a pre-dystopian narrative, for it has not reached the level of a full-blown, temporally distant dystopia. Rather, it uses the years after September 11 to demonstrate how close the United States is to a fascist future. Its spatial and temporal proximity to the present makes it even more disturbing, because it rubs up against the present and thus makes the wall of separation from the future quite thin. Indeed, because of its contemporary setting and close ties to *Nineteen Eighty-Four*, *Little Brother* could be characterized as describing the year(s) leading up to Orwell's *Nineteen Eighty-Four*—the 1983 preceding his 1984.

Even if *Little Brother* does not fit easily into traditional definitions of dystopian fiction—the big brother or father of pre-dystopian fiction—it nevertheless operates in the same way as other dystopian narratives. Dystopian fiction serves as "social criticism," according to Booker (18). Equally important, he believes that "the best dystopian fiction is always highly relevant more or less directly to specific 'real-world' societies and issues" (19). In reality, it is easier to equate *Little Brother* to our "realworld" cultural setting than to a distant one.

Little Brother takes place sometime after September 11, for it is quite clear that the events that transpired on that day and the creation of (or reorganization of previous governmental entities into) the United States Department of Homeland Security (DHS) serve as the backdrop. PATRIOT Act II has been enacted. Surveillance is tighter than it was prior to September 11. Face-recognition cameras and software "covering nearly every public space" (Doctorow 14) at Chavez High School have been replaced by gait-recognition cameras. Apparently the face-recognition software is unconstitutional, which is quite ironic considering other measures Homeland Security will take as the narrative unfolds, and gait recognition does not provide sufficient surveillance by itself; thus, students have been equipped with "School-Books," laptops that track "every keystroke, watching all the network traffic for suspicious keywords, counting every click, keeping track of every fleeting thought you put out over the net" (14). In other words, a series of panopticons, or all-seeing devices, are part of everyday life, as students—citizens—are captured on camera and monitored. A vigilant DHS hovers in the background, waiting for terrorism. Terrorists, according to authorities, do indeed strike, taking out the Bay Bridge and the BART tunnel. Once that occurs, something similar to martial law is put in place. Unfortunately, Marcus and his friends are in the wrong place at the wrong time. The DHS takes them into custody and transports them to Alcatraz, which Marcus will later call "Guantanamo-by-the-Bay" (347). There, Marcus is interrogated by soldiers who tell him they "won't stop at anything in [their] efforts to bring the perpetrators of these heinous crimes to justice" (64). His interrogators shackle and hood him and deprive him of food and bathroom facilities. They humiliate him until he succumbs and gives them the information they want: passwords that will release all of the information on his cell phone. While Marcus has issues with authority, he is not a terrorist, but they treat him that way nonetheless. Marcus is considered "a potential enemy combatant by the government of the United States" who could potentially "vanish" into "very dark deep holes" with the help of the DHS (49). Said bluntly, the DHS could "disappear" him quite easily. This scenario, then, establishes an imaginable setting, one in which a second attack on US soil has occurred and Homeland Security is at hand to find the terrorists with no holds barred.

The future has arrived.

A Contemporary Turn toward Fascism

That *Little Brother* was first published (and to this date remains) online in its entirety, and that the electronic version includes an explicit directive from Doctorow to be vigilant regarding the decrease of privacy and the increase of censorship, speaks to the sociopolitical nature of the text. Marcus never discloses the current president's political party, only that his father had "hated the President since the day he was elected, saying he wasn't any better than the last guy and the last guy had been a complete disaster," but after the attacks, "all he could do was talk about how decisive and dynamic the new guy was" (Doctorow 141). Mr. Yallow tells his wife and son after the police have picked up Marcus for questioning, "The world isn't the same place it was last week" (109). When Marcus asks his dad, "So you wouldn't mind if they pulled *you* over?" his father replies, "I'd consider it my duty. I'd be proud. It would make me feel safer" (124; italics in orig.). Ironically, Marcus's father teaches at Berkeley, which during the 1960s and

1970s was a hotbed of civil-rights activism, protests, and marches. Mr. Yallow, then, has possibly assumed a more conservative stance since his days as a student.

Mr. Yallow's comment that people should surrender to searches even without cause because doing so would provide a sense of security marks a feasible turning point toward a much more restrictive—and authoritarian or fascist—government, which is the path *Little Brother* warns against. Fascism is a notably slippery term, the definition of which is highly contested. Roger Griffin indicates it is "the growing tendency of scholars working on aspects of the role of the extreme right in shaping modern history to define fascism (explicitly or implicitly) as a revolutionary form of ultra-nationalism" (5). A sense of nationalism is not necessarily a bad thing and serves to hold a nation together through its ideals, but ultranationalism is inherently dangerous for those who disagree with its tenets. Thus, the use of the words *authoritarian* or *fascist* in conjunction with the United States might seem a bit dramatic or extreme, but Giroux helps contextualize the terms. Granted, Giroux is known as a liberal political thinker and offers an explicit critique of the Bush-Cheney response to September 11. However, his politics (and clear disapproval of the Bush-Cheney administration) do not mean he should be dismissed, for his comments go directly to the relationship between "freedom to" (read: rights) and "freedom from" (read: safety)—always a precarious balancing act regardless of one's political leanings—that is addressed in *Little Brother*.

Drawing from Umberto Eco's description of what fascism might look like in the future, Giroux writes that "any updated version of fascism will not openly assume the mantle of historical fascism; rather, new forms of authoritarianism will appropriate some of its elements . . . fascism, if it comes to America, will have a different guise, although it will be no less destructive of democracy" (101). Fascism might even wear the guise of our need to be protected. He also explains, "The United States is not simply governed by a center-right party supported by the majority of the populace, it is a country that is moving rapidly towards a form of authoritarianism that undermines any claim to being a liberal democracy" (98). Giroux goes on to say that "fascism is not an ideological apparatus frozen in a particular historical period, but a theoretical and political signpost for understanding how democracy can be subverted, if not destroyed" (101). Questions regarding democracy's subversion or destruction remain the focus throughout *Little Brother.*

Giroux, who incidentally references Orwell's *Nineteen Eighty-Four* in his essay, identifies several characteristics of the future (and possible presence) of fascism in the United States, including an atmosphere or "politics of fear" (126) that contributes to a willing diminution of individual rights. He is also concerned that "the military logic of fear, surveillance, and control is gradually permeating our public schools, universities, streets, media, popular culture, and criminal justice system" (124), which is connected to the way in which "zero-tolerance policies turn public schools into prison-like institutions, as students' rights increasingly diminish under the onslaught of new disciplinary measures" (127). *Little Brother* contemplates both of these concerns.

One of the hallmarks of *Nineteen Eighty-Four* and several other dystopias is Big Brother, who apparently sees all and is thus omnipotent. It does not actually matter whether or not Big Brother sees all, as long as the people being watched believe he is omniscient. Big Brother finds its roots with Jeremy Bentham's (1748–1842) architectural panopticon. As conceived by Bentham, the panopticon was to be used where the need for surveillance existed. Bentham's architectural design, still used in modern prisons, consists of a tower with windows; whoever is in the tower has the ability to "pan" the landscape and remain unseen. As described by French theorist Michel Foucault, the design ensures order:

> If the inmates are convicts, there is no danger of a plot, an attempt at collective escape, the planning of new crimes for the future, bad reciprocal influences; if they are patients, there is no danger of contagion; if they are madmen there is no risk of their committing violence upon one another; *if*

they are schoolchildren, there is no copying, no noise, no chatter, no waste of time; if they are workers, there are no disorders, no theft, no coalitions, none of these distractions that slow down the rate of work, make it less perfect or cause accidents. (201; emphasis added)

Some of the instances above are seemingly benign—avoiding the spread of contagion, a reduction in accidents—but it is quite clear that order and control are the centerpieces of the panopticon, and these are also the centerpieces of fascism. And clearly schoolchildren must be watched at all times, young rebels that they are.

Since Bentham's design, technological advances have made surveillance much easier and more widespread. Technology, an electronic Big Brother or panopticon, provides the ability to maintain power, control, and order, the most important components of a contemporary fascist state. Surveillance and security cameras and the government's ability to track purchases, bank accounts, visited Internet sites, and phone conversations, for instance, make it nearly impossible to remain off the grid. Equally problematic is when citizens believe they have to make either-or decisions: a decrease in individual rights gives way to increased security measures; a decrease in privacy gives way to increased safety—difficult decisions to make, but they are central to *Little Brother.*

One of the most evident either-or decisions comes from Mr. Yallow, Marcus's father. While several people in *Little Brother* take issue with being detained for questioning, as previously indicated, Mr. Yallow is not one of them. In fact, he initially claims that he believes it his duty to do what he can to contribute to everyone's safety, including being detained and questioned if necessary. He also identifies a very positive trade-off, telling Marcus, "They may not have caught any terrorists yet, but they're sure getting a lot of scumbags off the streets. Look at the drug dealers—it says they've put dozens of them away since this all started." Tighter security measures not only protect citizens from terrorists but also get rid of the "scumbags," a bonus in Mr. Yarrow's world. He also falls back on an "if you don't have anything to hide" rationale, a fairly standard response to governmental and police invasions of privacy (Doctorow 123).

Not until later in the novel, when Mr. Yallow is picked up for suspicious travel habits, does he get angry. Mr. Yallow's change of attitude does not last long, however, as he subscribes to what Doctorow characterizes as "a 'neighborly Panopticon'" (qtd. in Fletcher 94). Mr. Yallow reads a newspaper report that the DHS has asked for an enormous budget increase (300 percent, which they will receive) and he has a surprising response: "These guys may be fools, but they're methodical fools. They'll just keep throwing resources at this problem until they solve it. . . . They'll catch the terrorists." When Marcus protests, he replies, "They'll catch every alimony cheat, every dope dealer, every dirtbag and every terrorist. You just wait. This could be the best thing that ever happened to this country" (Doctorow 137). Once again, Mr. Yallow sees several benefits of increased surveillance. A budget increase of 300 percent reduces his fear of terrorism—surely if the government is going to spend that much money on reducing terrorism, the government's efforts will work—and the possibility of a reduced crime rate distracts him from the curtailment of individual rights. It comes down to this for Mr. Yallow: "Would you rather have privacy or terrorists?" To him, the answer is simple. Under the new security measures, he has no complaints and believes it is "time to make some sacrifices to keep our city safe" (138). Quid pro quo.

Considering Marcus's status as a student, the measures taken to "catch the terrorists," and the belief that terrorists could be anywhere, it should come as no surprise that school plays an important role. As already indicated, after September 11 schools are tightly monitored in *Little Brother.* Drawing from Gail R. Chaddock's article "Safe Schools at a Price," Giroux claims that "the new security culture in public schools has turned them into 'learning prisons,' most evident in the ways in which schools are being 'reformed' through the addition of armed guards, barbed-wired security fences, and lock-down drills"

(128). Giroux also reports that "in Biloxi, Mississippi, surveillance cameras have been installed in all of its 500 classrooms" and questions the effect that "constant surveillance" will have on the students (128). While it can easily be argued that school administrators who decide to hire armed guards and install cameras do so to keep students safe from other students who would do them harm, surveillance does not necessarily protect students. The measures that Giroux addresses, including sting operations, are in place to catch students indiscriminately, under the assumption that they will behave badly. The presence of cameras at school, where teens spend so much time, also anesthetizes them to the presence of cameras everywhere else. They come to expect to be under constant surveillance, and with every year that passes, they become more and more accustomed to being under the gaze of Big Brother. In Marcus's United States, the right to privacy is the most efficient sacrifice that can be made to secure safety, and for many citizens, it is an easy choice. After all, once the terrorists are caught, they can supposedly go back to "normal," which will never happen, and which serves as a critical signpost pointing to the road to fascism.

One Voice, One World

Audience, the events that take place, and the way they are conveyed in *Little Brother* all hold specific significance. Perhaps audience should not be a consideration, but when dealing with children, whether they are very young or in their late teens, audience frequently becomes part of the conversation in terms of ethics. While one could argue that *Little Brother* might be "inappropriate" because of the political nature of the narrative, the violence, and a couple of intimate scenes between Marcus and his girlfriend, the *School Library Journal* nevertheless identifies *Little Brother* as recommended for readers grades ten and up—mature readers. Audience, then, does matter. Audience also matters for scholars of literature for young readers, particularly when considering the relationship between text and reader. Cadden, in his discussion of irony, ethics, and YA literature, rightly believes that "Bakhtin's theories on ethical fiction in general necessarily complement any ethical theory of irony" (147). Bakhtin's theories, though, complement a text like *Little Brother* particularly well because a dialogic narrative—a text that includes genuinely multiple voices—offers an opportunity for readers to avoid being "voiceless slaves" and instead be "*free* people, capable of standing alongside their creator, capable of not agreeing with him and even of rebelling against him" (Bakhtin, qtd. in Cadden 147; italics in orig.). Most often, a dialogic narrative will offer competing ideologies in ways that provide readers with multiple perspectives and genuine choices. Monologic texts—texts dominated by a single voice—frequently become "didactic . . . with no representation of a legitimate alternative position" (Cadden 147).

In terms of *Little Brother*, then, two ironies exist: first, the ironic nature of an adult author attempting to sound like an "authentic"—whatever that might mean—teenager through first-person narrative; and second, that a monologic text, for *Little Brother* is monologic, attempts to speak to freedom. *Little Brother* is very much about citizens rebelling against becoming Bakhtin's "voiceless slaves," but in a way that tends to quash a fair exchange of ideas. Any alternatives provided are offered in such a way that it becomes difficult to legitimately consider those positions, mainly as a result of characterization; characters who hold an opposing view to Marcus are portrayed as being short sighted (Mr. Yallow) or simply despicable (Charles, one of Marcus's classmates). Thus, although he is a nice man, Mr. Yallow's stance is untenable because of the way he is characterized. For instance, when Marcus claims that police practices do not result in "catching terrorists" but simply instill fear, his father characterizes him as "paranoid" (Doctorow 123). Readers know about Marcus's first detainment and know he is not being paranoid, but Mr. Yallow does not. Still, Mr. Yallow's description is a harsh indictment. And he conflates fighting terrorism with "getting . . . scumbags off the streets," including "every alimony cheat, every dope dealer, every dirtbag and every terrorist." His logic contains no logic. Ultimately, if readers agree with Marcus, they will find it relatively easy to think Mr. Yellow narrow minded and dismiss his opinions.

One of Marcus's classmates, Charles Walker, a football player who is supposedly "on the juice," also offers an alternative position. However, he is much more problematic than Mr. Yellow. Early on, Marcus describes him as having "anger management problems" and as "a bully who also snitches" (Doctorow 25). He also tends to "prowl the hallways at Chavez, looking for people to fink on" (26). From the beginning, then, readers have every reason to dislike Charles and his point of view. Charles's alternative position is similar to Mr. Yellow's. When Marcus returns to school after his first detainment, his class engages in a discussion of terrorism. Marcus points out, "Isn't the point of terrorism to make us afraid? That's why it's called *terrorism*, right?" (92; italics in orig.). He further proposes that the terrorists "win if we act all afraid and put cameras in the classrooms." Charles counters Marcus's argument with one similar to Mr. Yellow's: "Putting cameras in makes us safe, which makes us less afraid" (93). Marcus, his father, and Charles are all correct, but it is potentially a greater challenge to be receptive to Charles and Mr. Yellow because of their relationships with Marcus. It is sometimes difficult to listen to a message when the bearer of the message is portrayed in a negative light. Characterization in *Little Brother*, then, lends itself to creating a monologic text.

Characterization, though, is not the only component to consider with regard to the nature of *Little Brother*. Plot elements, when combined with characterization, also contribute to a monologic tone, something similar to guilt by association; that is, events and the individuals and entities who carry out those events become one. As a result, it is easy to despise both the act and the actor—for instance, torture and a government that condones and uses torture.

Unquestionably, the most despicable event in the novel, and the one that serves as the best example of guilt by association, occurs during Marcus's second detention, when he is subjected to "enhanced interrogation techniques," a euphemism for torture and a term that continues to be part of the public discourse following September 11. A woman from DHS, whom Marcus refers to as "Severe Haircut," describes what is about to happen to him after they have strapped him head-down to a stretcher: "'Do you know what waterboarding is, M1k3y?' Her voice reeled me in. 'You get strapped down like this, and we pour water over your head, up your nose and down your mouth. You can't suppress the gag reflex. They call it a simulated execution, and from what I can tell from this side of the room, that's a fair assessment. You won't be able to fight the feeling that you're dying'" (Doctorow 344). That Marcus knows his interrogators do not intend to kill him is irrelevant. His mind and body behave precisely as predicted by Severe Haircut, an agent of the government and a zealot who clearly relishes her role in Marcus's interrogation. Her actions and attitude make it easy to abhor her and the government that resorts to these methods. Additionally, if readers have formed any kind of positive relationship with Marcus, that relationship compounds the government's sinister methods of extracting information. Fortunately, Marcus is rescued before Severe Haircut and her colleagues use the technique on him more than once, but one time is far too many. Nevertheless, complexity is removed from the equation, demonstrating a lack of trust in readers.

One more strategy stands out when contemplating the structure of *Little Brother*. In the online version, before the novel even begins, Doctorow offers his own narrative, that of the many ways in which the government has already impinged on the right to privacy and on civil rights in general. He begins two paragraphs with "If you believe": in the right to privacy, in freedom of speech, or that those who govern us must also follow the rules. He also writes, "This book is meant to be part of the conversation about what an information society means: does it mean total control, or unheard-of liberty?" (Doctorow, *Little Brother* online). I am not convinced that this text signifies a conversation, not when it seems to make "obvious" and clear-cut not "if you believe" but "what you should believe." The monologic nature and narrative tone of the text suggest that teens cannot be trusted to come to the "correct"

---

conclusion. Granted, the strident tone of the governmental response following September 11 was monologic and generously littered with either-or propositions—"a rhetorical ploy," according to Giroux—particularly in terms of what constitutes patriotism. Giroux explains that the thinking demonstrated by the administration after September 11 "is deeply distrustful of critical inquiry, mistakes dissent for treason, constructs politics on the moral absolutes of 'us and them,' and views difference and democracy as threats to consensus and national identity" (106). Giroux, of course, is offering his own set of binaries, as am I for that matter, but offering an opposing set of either-or propositions is seldom conducive to discussion or resolution.

Conclusion: Is There No Escape?

Robert P. Fletcher notes that "the tone of Doctorow's writing, both fiction and non-fiction, has become markedly darker and more urgent" (94). It is not difficult to understand why: wiretapping continues to take place, surveillance is ubiquitous, and various governmental entities, including Homeland Security, will do whatever is necessary to avoid another attack. Additionally, Doctorow should be commended for his very earnest and genuine efforts to defeat what could easily become an authoritarian government. Nevertheless, the problems we face require more than either-or propositions.

This essay is not intended as a way to advocate for some kind of middle ground or compromise. Whether true or not, that stance is frequently considered weak and the proponents of such thinking wishy-washy, particularly because we live in a highly competitive culture. Winning, whether in a game, an argument, or a war, is important, especially considering the ideological battles between safety and privacy that have taken place since September 11, 2001. Additionally, some compromises could actually be worse than the original propositions, resulting in nonsolutions.

Rather than advocating for a middle ground, then, this essay is meant to encourage an awareness of how an either-or state of mind suppresses imaginative thinking and creative responses. Unfortunately, under the adversarial and competitive circumstances resulting from September 11 (winning/losing the war on terrorism, for instance), it is far too convenient to resort to binaries such as monologic/dialogic. Identifying a different logic—escaping binaries and the middle ground—is perhaps the only way a democracy such as ours has a chance to endure the future as predicted by Doctorow and the current realities in which we live.

Notes

1. All citations of Doctorow's *Little Brother* refer to the 2008 print edition unless otherwise stated.

Works Cited

Booker, M. Keith. *The Dystopian Impulse in Modern Literature: Fiction as Social Criticism.* Westport, CT: Greenwood, 1994.

Cadden, Mike. "The Irony of Narration in the Young Adult Novel." *Children's Literature Association Quarterly* 25.3 (2000): 146–54.

Doctorow, Cory. *Little Brother. Cory Doctorow's Craphound.com.* Cory Doctorow, 2007. Web. 19 Apr. 2012.

_____. *Little Brother.* New York: Tor, 2008.

Fletcher, Robert P. "The Hacker and the Hawker: Networked Identity in the Science Fiction and Blogging of Cory Doctorow." *Science Fiction Studies* 37.1 (2010): 81–99.

Foucault, Michel. *Discipline and Punish: The Birth of the Prison.* 2nd ed. Trans. Alan Sheridan. New York: Vintage, 1995.

Giroux, Henry A. "The Emerging Authoritarianism in the United States: Political Culture under the Bush/Cheney Administration." *Symplokē* 14.1 (2006): 98–151.

Griffin, Roger. "General Introduction." *Fascism: Critical Concepts in Political Science.* Ed. Roger Griffin and Matthew Feldman. New York: Routledge, 2004. 1–16.

Moylan, Tom. *Scraps of the Untainted Sky: Science Fiction, Utopia, Dystopia.* Boulder, CO: Westview, 2000.

Orwell, George. *Nineteen Eighty-Four.* New York: Penguin, 1983.

Shklar, Judith N. "*Nineteen Eighty-Four*: Should Political Theory Care?" *Political Thought and Political Thinkers.* Ed. Stanley Hoffmann. Chicago: U of Chicago P, 1998. 339–52.

Future Almost Lost:
Dystopian Science-Fiction Film _____

Sean Redmond

> Science fiction in all its guises has never shed the essential characteristic of an air of menace. In some senses the essence of the science and the futures such fiction imagines is pervasive, potential doom. Science fiction, from the outset, has been the narrative of doomsday scenarios.
>
> (Ziauddin Sardar)

Introduction: Future Almost Lost

In this chapter, I will suggest that dystopian science-fiction film is defined through a recurring set of narrative tropes and audiovisualizations that can be found repeated across the (sub)genre's history. However, while such apocalyptic dreams are an ever-present constituent of science-fiction (SF) film, they nonetheless need to be situated or located in terms of dominant cultural concerns at the time of their making. I will therefore not only outline the narrative, generic, and thematic qualities of SF film dystopia but also read them against the ideological grain of history. Moreover, I will note the ways in which, beyond thematic representation, the audiovisual aspects of film can be used to reinforce the feeling of dystopia in the viewer.

I will argue that at a narrative and thematic level, science and technology (in all its hybrid variations and incarnations, including the medical, domestic, and military) is often imagined to have developed to such an extent that it overdetermines social, economic, and political relations. As a consequence of this techno-scientific extremism, the qualities of humanness, including emotion, independent choice, and freedom of association, are very nearly extinguished, as hyperrational societal apparatuses, ubiquitous surveillance regimes, and military-industrial-scientific relationships hold total power and exert infinite control over the unwashed masses. The commercial aspect of this development is often narrativized as future capitalists forcing their products, services, and mandates on a terrified, obedient, or compliant populace, held further in check by cold and calculating scientists, the military machine, and tyrannical politicians in the pay and service of these (post)industrial demigods. Set in 2018, *Rollerball* (1975) imagines a dystopic future where global capitalism has advanced to such an extent that corporations control the consumption practices, behaviors, and pastimes of the entire population. The violent, full-contact game of rollerball is imagined to be circus for the masses, offering the illusion of individualism as opposed to the commodity spectacle it really is. Jonathan, the hero of the film, is asked to retire from rollerball because his individualized success goes against the real aim of the sport, which is to foster conformity and docility in those who watch and thus maintain the global control of food, leisure, and ideas.

The invasion narrative offers an alternative version of dystopic capitalist expansion: the alien menace comes to embody the destructive capacity of expansive capitalism, harvesting, cloning, or annihilating the human race through the deployment of their superior technology and diabolical takeover plans. In these "eve of destruction" narratives (Franklin 21), aliens emerge, arrive, or return furnished with superior technology and weaponry and advanced scientific knowledge, and at first seem unstoppable in their desire to conquer the world before them. In both *War of the Worlds* (2005) and *Independence Day* (1996), the technological and military power of the alien invaders seems omnipotent, and great acts of destruction take place before a common biological virus, or an electronic virus uploaded from an Apple computer, ultimately defeats them.

In either form, these films suggest that this techno-scientific engineered totalitarianism must be resisted, opposed, and challenged by a heroic narrative agent or ensemble who remembers what it is to be human and fights back. While technology and scientific know-how may be required to defeat the totalitarian state or the alien marauders, they are used in the service of democracy and liberty. Dystopian science-fiction film often employs the very technology that it is being critical of, and its deployment in various forms suggests that humans need a degree of technology to be human and free again. In fact, in alien-invasion narratives, it is often the case that the defeat of the aliens is only achieved through military-scientific cooperation and rationalist means, often with the development of new weaponry or a new invention that requires the input of both agencies.

The figure of the cyborg is central here, since in one body a cyborg brings together technology and humanity, circuitry and flesh, either as a pathological manifestation that seeks destruction of the human (the T-100 in *The Terminator*, 1984) or as a searcher of the human spirit it is not certain it materially, metaphysically possesses (Data in *Star Trek: The Next Generation*, 1987–94). In *The Matrix* (1999), Neo's discovery that humankind has been enslaved within a simulacrum begins a process of self-discovery and resistance against the virtual-machine aesthetic. Neo occupies a liminal position between man and machine, using technology to defeat the matrix that in part defines him. The future is almost lost in dystopian science-fiction film, but the humanist flame of resistance refuses to be put out, and by film's end, a new dawn arises—a metaphor expressed quite literally in *THX 1138* (1971), at the end of which THX emerges from the synthetic underground city as the warm sun rises on the first day of the rest of his life.

It is a point of contention whether such narratives are ultimately critical dystopias, taking political aim at the wrongdoings of the present, or whether they serve to reinforce dominant ideology and its practices and processes by effecting resolutions and solutions to the crises faced. Michael Ryan and Douglas Kellner argue that there are two types of dystopian film: those films in which an inhuman, technologically determinist future is set against an emergent natural world, privileging nature over the mechanical and virtual; and those that critically examine the relationship between technology and nature, refusing to opt for binary oppositions that favor one over the other. They contend that *Blade Runner* (1982) best illustrates this complexity: "The film deconstructs the oppositions—human/technology, reason/feeling, culture/nature—that underwrite the conservative fear of technology by refusing to privilege one pole of the dichotomy over another" (52). For Ryan and Kellner, "dystopias, or negative utopias," can be situated in key crisis moments in history (54), such as the post-Nixon era in the United States.

Further, and to develop my own position on this, the affecting, arguably overwhelming qualities of such dystopian happenings have the potential to invite viewers to sense the dark future as if it were present tense, with possible biopolitical and transformative consequences for what I will suggest are non-signifying sensory encounters. When one is affected to the core by the sublime intensity of dystopia realized, one may experience the future-present as carnal appetite and "hunger" for that which cannot be named or understood through language and representation. The sublime intensity of *The Road* (2009) is a striking case in point, with an ashen future landscape that principally expresses itself through the stratified chaos of the logic of sensational social collapse.

Dystopia is not just narrativized, of course, but visualized and sounded out through such elements as clinical and conformist costumes and behavior traits, spectacular dehumanized future city settings, chillingly efficient (modernist, postmodern) architectural iconography, atonal sound effects and disembodied voices, and spatial and temporal relations—such as high versus low, future versus past—that confirm the film's destructive, dead-end future. For example, the entire desaturated, retrofitted mise-en-scène and unseen authoritarian voices of *Nineteen Eighty-Four* (1984) work to sight and sound the apocalyptic terror of the film.

The direct and indirect violence in these films is imagined both symbolically (through allusion and generic register) and directly, since the technology the film implicitly condemns is employed (through the dark alchemy of special effects) to wreak havoc and cause wondrous ruin. As such, the imagery of dystopian science-fiction film, often conjured up through state-of-the-art special effects, rests on a paradox or sleight of hand. The chilling audiovisualization of dystopia is also si-multaneously a source of technological wonder and a by-product of latent (cultural, authorial) technophilia. As the future liquefies and re-crafts itself, one is asked to marvel at the sights being conjured. In *Blade Runner*'s hellhole of a future, for example, the upper levels of the cityscape are often viewed as a glistening, bejeweled metropolis whose neon beauty lights up the eternal darkness of the sky. In those films that self-reflexively refer to the astonishing special effects as they present themselves to the characters (and viewers), such as *The Thing* (1982) and *Sunshine* (2007), the authorial wonder of their creations and the imagined reception of them align in a way that promotes fan-like technophilia or love of the special effect.

Of course, there is a type of dystopian science-fiction film that ini-tially presents itself as utopian (*Logan's Run*, 1976; *Demolition Man*, 1993; *Minority Report*, 2002; *Surrogates*, 2009); however, the imag-ined utopia is very quickly shown to be faulty and incomplete, an Eden that is actually dystopian. These films, then, point to another paradox or inherent tension in dystopian/utopian science-fiction film: they are two sides of the same coin, despair and hope and nightmare and dream entwined. As Linda Ruth Williams argues, dystopia and utopia exist in narrative, thematic, and character parallels. For example, in *Brazil* (1985) and *Nineteen Eighty-Four*, it is the utopian appearance of a woman that counters the bleak dystopian sentiments that drive both films. For Williams, it is precisely the close-up shot of a woman's idealized face that functions as "the utopic image which does 'freeze the flow of the action'" (165). The woman's face offers hope and the promise of transformation in a future that is tyrannical and barren.

As I note above, one must of course historicize these tropes, since, while generic, they are also culturally locatable, responding to and in-forming contemporary fears and anxieties at a specific political juncture. As Annette Kuhn summarizes, "there is the idea that science fiction films relate to the social order through the mediation of *ideologies*, so-ciety's representations of itself in and for itself—that films speak, enact, even produce certain ideologies, which cannot always be read directly off films' surface contents" (10; italics in orig.). Dystopian science-fiction film is heavy with the ideology of its present, drawing into its narrative framework and semiotic register the ache of rapid changes and transformations occurring at the time it was made. Key historical break-through moments or dominant trends such as the machine age (*Metropolis*, 1927), the nuclear age (*Planet of the Apes*, 1968), environmental degradation (*Soylent Green*, 1973), the rise of new elites and cultural intermediaries (*Rollerball*), the rise of the techno-city (*Blade Runner*), genetic engineering and reproduction (*Gattaca*, 1997), and millennial techno-paranoia (*The Matrix*) find their rearticulation and representation in the dark (but light) arteries of dystopian science-fiction film.

Freedom Lost and Won

In what might be termed earth-framed dystopias, a number of narrative and thematic consistencies can be found. Susan Sontag has usefully defined the apocalyptic tendencies of 1950s science-fiction film as "the imagination of disaster." This destructive envisioning, not limited to this historical period, takes at least two forms, the first of which imagines a future where totalitarian regimes control society and the rights of the individual and the free strokes of individuality have been very nearly extinguished. Social control is enacted and embodied through various technological means and mechanisms, including propaganda, idolatry, censorship, surveillance, drugs, medication and medical intervention, consumerism, scarcity, and the threat and use of force by the police and the military. In effect, such dystopian science-fiction films employ the twin means through which Louis Althusser argues that social order is maintained in capitalist states: the alignment between the "Ideological State Apparatus" and the "Repressive State Apparatus," which ensures that the control of ideas in concert with the probability of violence and repression will maintain and sustain consent (96–98).

In *Equilibrium* (2002), the techno-totalitarian city-state of Libria has outlawed all expressions of emotion, blaming it for the end-of-

---

days Third World War and for being the affective force that creates all conflict. Citizens take the emotion-suppressing drug Prozium and are subject to constant surveillance, propaganda, and the routinization of all aspects of everyday life. Warrior-priests and enforcement officers are at hand to quell resistance and to maintain the status quo, while the charismatic oligarch known as Father, whose image and sermons are broadcast on giant video screens throughout the day, rules over Libria. The city of Libria is thus run and organized on two seemingly contradictory systems of control and repression: the first, the scientific management of both leisure and work time so that human behavior is intensely, rationally shaped; and the second, a form of auratic leadership through which an idolatrized figure is worshipped and obeyed. Libria, then, controls its populace through the microscopic techniques of bio-power and the emotional strings of affect. In effect, it controls its citizens through their minds and hearts.

In the second form of destructive envisioning, the imagined future faces a biological, biogenetic, environmental, or technological catastrophe that threatens the survival of human civilization. The bomb has been dropped (*Planet of the Apes*; *The Road*); oceans, rivers, and fields have been polluted and are now toxic and barren (*Waterworld*, 1995); a deadly, mutating virus has created cities of the walking dead (*Resident Evil*, 2002; *28 Days Later*, 2002); or experimentation in genetics or robotics has produced a race of clones or machines that revolt and threaten humans with the extinction of the species (*Westworld*, 1973; *I, Robot*, 2004). In *Soylent Green*, for example, an explosion in the human population, the warming of the earth, and a pervasive sense of systemic corruption have resulted in the breakdown of social relations. Cities overflow with people and refuse, and the usual daily routines, processes, and social activities have almost ground to a halt. People are hungry, the earth is dying, and it is only the miraculous mass-processed food Soylent Green that keeps the populace from starvation. That Soylent Green is made of people, the core revelation of the film, confirms the diabolical nature of science and its relationship to intensive farming practices and their associated commercial viability.

The figure of the scientist is often central to these films, as he or she will have been involved in the experiments and inventions that have led to future Armageddon. These villainous, inhuman scientists are marked by an excess of rationalism, so much so that they become machinelike and their reason spills into madness, resulting in their pursuing their goals at all costs as they strive to grasp a higher (technological) truth. For example, in *The Thing from Another World* (1951), the chief scientist Carrington is driven by logic and a singular motivation to advance human knowledge and understanding, even if human life is threatened in the process. Carrington admires the alien "vegetable" because he sees it as an advanced life form, superior to the human species. There is seemingly no emotion in his findings or deliberations, just hard, factual scientific truth. As he calmly but coldly says to the rest of the personnel at the base, the alien has "no pain or pleasure as we know it. No emotions. No heart. Our superior in every way. . . . If we can only communicate with it, we could learn secrets that have hidden from man since the beginning" (qtd. in Jancovich 35). For Carrington, then, "the alien is the 'ideal' of the system of scientific-technical rationality" (36), but it also confirms a fascistic hierarchy in which there is an evolutionary continuum of the human species, with the alien creature a coda for the übermensch.

Once Carrington recognizes the superior genetic makeup of the alien creature, he becomes its collaborator. He immerses himself in scientific discourse, distances himself from the other crew and personnel, and ultimately aids and abets the creature through creating the conditions that will allow it to reproduce—at the expense of human life. In *The Thing*, reproduction becomes desexed, without desire or feeling. It requires neither a partner nor physical or emotional connection. Reproduction instead involves practical processes that are easily enacted. As I have argued elsewhere, this is why Carrington, himself a sexless and isolated creature, so admires the perfected nature of this reproduction cycle; the scientist recognizes in the alien's reproduction the purity of science itself (Redmond, "Science Fiction").

In *The Thing*, the coming apocalypse is a reproductive one: if Carrington and the alien can create a future in which sex and intimacy are no longer needed, then humanness will be replaced by mechanical exchanges and the future will be born free of feeling and compassion. As much of Hollywood science-fiction film demands, Carrington and the alien have to be proven to be destructive and inhumane, and humanity shown to be a preferential mode of life and living. The compassionate soldiers and the feeling, feminine female scientist become the positive standard with which the viewer is asked to identify. They destroy Carrington and the alien, and in so doing show humanity to be a superior state of being in the world, able to protect itself and love and emote at the same time.

J. P. Telotte has suggested that there is a "doubling" process in science-fiction film in which humankind constantly seeks to replicate, even if replication and duplication threaten existence or undermine what it means to be human. This doubling process rests on a paradox: it involves the search for eternal life, while incorporating post-human elements that will ultimately result in human annihilation. In contemporary science-fiction film, the cyborg is one of the central manifestations of this doubling process, since it embodies this desire for eternal life while simultaneously offering human damnation. The cyborg, so often made of soft (human) tissue on the outside, is all high-tech circuitry and computer chips on the inside. Its flesh is mortal but its circuitry immortal, and its reproduction is a matter of fatal and fetal abjection.

Artificial intelligence can take other forms as well. In *Demon Seed* (1977), the diabolical computer Proteus is a sonorous entity whose calculating voice and electronic impulses echo and reverberate through the various "eyes" or screens that represent his multiplied and omnipotent self. His futuristic soundings, heard in the present/presence of the film, come from very far away, from very close, and from multiple points of origin, so that time and space are torn asunder. The future impacts upon the present as if a visitation has taken place. Proteus is a voice without a mouth; or rather, he is an impossible mouthless creature who can vocalize through any electronic terminal he can connect with. The mouthless mouth is given the quality of the deep space to which it seems tethered. As an omnipotent force, in multiple spaces and across all of time, he fills the film world with dread, a metallic foreshadowing of what is to come if he (technology) is not stopped. When Proteus becomes body near the film's end and rapes a woman to plant his demon seed, his mouthless mouth, alien voice, and phallic projectiles draw upon woman's deepest fears of invasion and penetration by an unwanted, unwarranted masculine source. This "registers on/in/within the body with terrifying propensity" (Redmond, "Sounding").

As I have noted elsewhere, two distinct types of cyborg emerge in science-fiction film. The first type is the *humanist* cyborg, who works alongside and for human companions and who wants more than anything else to possess those emotions and desires that lead to long-lasting, meaningful relationships. They are often individualist but work in team environments, where their role is an important one—a science officer or engineer or scout, for example. The humanist cyborg is often required to respond to melodramatic or crisis moments with either rationalist commentary or emotional empathy, the latter of which is supposedly out of their reach. However, even though the narrative supposedly frames these cyborgs as circuitry beings, the recurring use of the dramatic close-up reveals emotional tics that signify this "hidden" desire to be fully human. In *Star Trek: The Next Generation*, the android Data, played by Brent Spiner, has been given the gift of a modified or limited form of human consciousness so that his decision making will be colored by emotive and memorial qualities, not just scientific logic. However, having this consciousness leaves Data in a state of existential limbo, since while he can think like a human, he cannot feel like one. Data suffers an identity crisis that becomes one of his character's defining qualities; ever in search of being more human, he constantly confirms his distance from such a goal (Wilcox). Data, consequently, is a melancholic character, and it is this melancholy that actually confirms his humanness without his ever realizing it. This, so the series suggests, is the human condition.

Second, and by contrast, the *pathological* cyborg, found in dystopian science-fiction film, despises its part-human origins, considering its flesh either an inconvenience or a necessary ruse to lure people to their termination. They are programmed to destroy humanity so that the technological future they embody can fully come to pass. Nonetheless, the pathological cyborg seems to be possessed by an incarnate evil, or the darkest qualities of human life. Even they cannot escape being framed by an ethical context that writes them as pure evil. The T-100 in *The Terminator* and the various iterations that follow in the franchise are programmed to destroy that which will keep humanity alive, their death instinct given a past/present/future trajectory that teleports this diabolical plan into any sheet of human history.

The cyborg is always marked by representational excess, so that its very existence in the film world destabilizes identity positions. It is both human and machine, flesh and wires, and as such draws attention to the borders that usually define subjectivity. The cyborg is a transgressive figure; it refuses to obey the rules of the flesh and openly registers as an entity that can move across gender, ethnic, and sexual signifiers and, in so doing, can create a space for their deconstruction and resistance to be carried out. The cyborg also stands as a form of future dreaming about the growth of technology and its potential impact on everyday life. This dreaming suggests that continued technological advancement will either negatively impact on everyday life or, in the long term, lead to a future in which the fusion of mind, body, and technology results in a post-human environment where old prejudices are negated and new subjectivities emerge, free of present bodily constraints.

Susan J. Napier examines the ambivalent attitude to technology and the technological body in *mecha* (hard science fiction) anime. This ambivalence, she argues, responds to deep-seated fears about technology in contemporary Japanese society:

While the imagery in mecha anime is strongly technological and is often specifically focused on the machinery of the armoured body, the narratives themselves often focus to a surprising extent on the human inside the machinery. It is this contrast between the vulnerable, emotionally complex and often youthful human being inside the ominously faceless body armour or power suit and the awesome power he/she wields vicariously that makes for the most important tension in many mecha dramas. (205–6)

Of course, it is the audiovisualizations of science-fiction film dystopias that write and paint their doom and dismay, an analysis I would now like to undertake.

The End of the World (the Beginning of Feeling)

Sensorial Visualizations

Science-fiction film is often at its most terrifyingly beautiful when it employs a heightened and sensorial audiovisual language to bring its dystopian nightmares into existence. Very often it is the representation and presentation of the city that encapsulates the full extent of the future loss. The science-fiction city is the embodiment of all that is wrong in the future, even if that future is spectacularly envisioned through a mise-en-scène created with state-of-the-art special effects. These future cities are enormous in size and scale, and they are either heavily regulated or spiraling out of control. Dystopia is represented in the way the city seems to operate like a machine, in the service of machines, or else has become so corporatized and commodified that life has lost its human components. As Vivian Sobchack argues, "the science-fiction film city's spatial articulations provide the literal premises for the possibilities and trajectory of narrative action." The city space is considered to be a "specific power" that can "affect both people and materials—a power that modifies the relations between them" (123–24).

Sensation is central to the way the science-fiction city oppresses people. For example, brutal modernist buildings create a symbolic space for destructive behavior, such as the concrete-jungle setting of the Thamesmead South housing estate and Brunel University in *A Clockwork Orange* (1971), or else they provide a pathetic environment for conformist life, such as the use of Frank Lloyd Wright's Marin Center in *THX 1138* and *Gattaca*. Liquid-like postmodern settings create a series of any-space-whatevers where transient encounters dominate and speeded-up time conditions people into constant movement. Space seems to be constantly occupied and to exist in sheetlike connections rather than simple high/low, in/out coordinates. One can travel anywhere, and with surveillance cameras often found in every environment one encounters, there is no longer a difference between the private and public. Atomized living is promoted, so that one is constantly alone and lonely while being surrounded by people in movement.

In *Blade Runner*, Los Angeles in the year 2019 consists of towering, flaming oil refineries, advertising-clad skyscrapers, and acid rain–soaked lower levels teeming with people constantly in movement and on the move. Giuliana Bruno observes, "The city of *Blade Runner* is not the ultramodern, but the postmodern city. It is not an orderly layout of skyscrapers and ultracomfortable, hypermechanized interiors. Rather, it creates an aesthetic of decay, exposing the dark side of technology, the process of disintegration" (185). The urban disintegration at the core of *Blade Runner*'s dystopia is a confusing mix of contradictions: there is a population crisis, waste and debris litter the lower levels of the city, and numerous buildings seem antiquated and dilapidated; high-tech, bejeweled high-rises dominate the skyline but seem impersonal and removed from normal life; and everyday life seems to be centered on consumption, with few emotional attachments found to exist there. Sobchack writes that from the 1980s onward, the city in science-fiction film has been exhausted, "groundless in both time and place" (140) and "totally resigned to its ruination" (135).

Of course, it is also the ruined city, partly destroyed and emptied of noise, lights, traffic, movement, and people, that confirms the postapocalyptic and helps create or foster a sense of overwhelming dread in the diegetic world. According to Kirsten Moana Thompson, this type of spatial dread is particularly affecting since these "feelings provoked by haunted spaces . . . bear the traces of repressed personal or national traumas" (129). In *28 Days Later*, Jim wakes up from a coma to find the hospital, the streets, and the city empty of people. London is a ghost town, rubbish sweeps across the empty city streets, cars are abandoned, and the intricacies of stillness are captured in everything that should move but does not. These haunted spaces should speak, should move; they should be full of the signs and codes of the modern metropolis that one is used to hearing and seeing. The national trauma here, one perhaps informed by the fear of contagion or the terrorist attacks of September 11, 2001, is nonetheless one that seems to be best expressed through affecting, unbounded structures of feeling. The buildings and spaces of *28 Days Later*, and other films such as *I Am Legend* (2007), communicate their despair through an experiential framework that has carnal or sensorial determinants that overwhelm the narrative—and the ethical viewer who sits before the screen.

Claire Colebrook has argued that when art "bring[s] us to an experience of 'affectuality'—or *of the fact that there is* affect" (199; italics in orig.), it has an ethical dimension. The pain we feel deeply, for example, is experienced as consequential and biopolitical. It arrests us from our (usual, normalized) corporeal embodiment and shocks us morally, and it brings us to an awareness of the power and force of the body and its abuses in the world. In a dystopian science-fiction film, this ethics of pathos, of violent becoming and becoming lost, of nomadic wandering, has its most profound realization or sensationalization in the apocalyptic death and life that rises up in the dystopian image. In *The Road*, the power and force of the uncanny landscape and the burned-out, abandoned homesteads and homes, and the power and force of the bodies that wander and hope and hunt and cannibalize one another, bring one to an experience of the future as painfully intimate, physically present, and overwhelmingly sensational.

The dystopian film world of *The Road* is built on the death-and-life logic of sensation; its materials, vibrations, and colors pull one toward and away from its blend (while blending) of first traumatic experiences, deadly potentials, and ethical rigor mortis. Father/Man and Son/Boy walk the scarred landscape, moving ever closer to the imagined purity of the ocean, so they can die and begin again. In the film's dreadful spaces, life and death wrap around one another, bathed in pathos and the probabilities that pathos brings. To stop or arrest pathos, one needs to die (an old-world death) so that new life can begin in a postapocalyptic world—a world that demands one live off one's senses and feelings, off the fire that burns within. The death of the Father/Man is the exact moment that the Son/Boy can begin again. To move beyond the old life into the chaos of new thoughts requires a death of the image so that one may become what Gilles Deleuze and Félix Guattari call "a body without organs," the self dismantled and pure potential, "made in such a way that it can only be populated by intensities. Only intensities pass and circulate" (153). Son/Boy is born again into/through sensation.

Sounding Dystopia

One of the central ways that the affective and transformative qualities of dystopia enter the film world is through sound, an observation that has rarely been taken up in the study of the genre (see Whittington). For example, the alien invasion intent on the destruction of the human species is vocalized, given a voice character that confirms not only the aliens' deadly intent but also the power they have to carry out these deeds. The double echo in the voice suggests the ability to double or copy itself; the ability to copy or mimic human voices, albeit without tone or inflection, suggests the ability to take over and become the human body; and the electric undercurrent that can ripple through the voice suggests technology that can annihilate human flesh. This terror in and of the alien voice is compounded by the fact that the alien cannot always be seen, entering the film world through a point-of-view shot, a body double, or the reaction shot in response to its presence (often involving a strangulated scream). When there is only a diabolical voice to hear, the body the viewer gives to the alien is all the more abject. In *Invasion of the Body Snatchers* (1978), the strangulated, discordant, amplified scream one hears in the film emerges from a human body that has been taken over, prompted by the sight of a human not yet turned. This alienated scream, captured by a camera that closes in on the mouth, almost entering it, not only confirms the alien presence in the flesh but also attempts to eat the character (and viewer) it is aimed at. Alien vocalization thus becomes embodied alienation (Redmond, "Sounding").

The "grain of the voice" (Barthes 157) is also important because it suggests a creature that is out of this world, the alien vocalization confirming distance and difference/otherness. The voice is often temporalized by frequencies and harmonics that orient it to (and from) a future world. Given that the alien is often without its own mouth or even a body, the free-forming voice is allowed to fracture or reorient time and space, since it is unbounded, unseen, far and near simultaneously. In a very real sense, time and space are contracted and expanded, infinite and proximate; and with such radical, unhinged soundings come profound sensorial and corporeal consequences for the viewer listening. This is a voice that can kill, vaporize, duplicate or replace a body, whisk itself away to planets far away once its heinous acts have been undertaken—and yet it is a voice that is not even present.

As I briefly note above, the alien creature can be initially sounded through a point-of-view shot in which the viewer is aligned with the as-yet-unseen extraterrestrial's vision and hearing. This alignment of seeing and hearing will often involve the alien killing a human being or destroying something sacred or important in the community. One might describe this experience as radically alternative, built upon a corporeal and sensorial communion that is other, is wickedly strange; the viewer gets to become the alien with a mouthless mouth and engage in destructive acts through a body not yet witnessed but granted enormous power. This radical becoming other is supported by a coupling that allows the viewer to move through the film world with the soundings of the alien inside him or her, so to speak. Mechanical sounds, atonal beats, rusty twangs, and high-pitched screeches fill the ordinary world (and the viewer) with extraordinary physicality. But this is seen to be diabolical, since the abjection and violence inherent in the alignment is too destructive, uncomfortable and discomforting, and does not last (the point-of-view shot is replaced by another shot). However, while this alignment lasts, and in the undeniable trace of excess that is left behind after the camera has cut away, the viewer has his or her own sense of corporeal, behavioral, and ethical alienation augmented. In becoming alien, perception and comprehension are changed and transformed, and the body and its senses are experienced as free, newly awakened, and dangerous. One is physically and chaotically transformed into a body without organs that exists in and across sheets of time and space. The symbiotic terror of such intersubjective alignments is particularly acute because the alien's death wish is also yours/ours/theirs.

The dystopian science-fiction film is prophetic and pathetic; its narratives, themes, settings, and feelings are calls to awake the present from its wrongdoings and catastrophic pathways. At an ideological level, these films can be read as critical, counter-hegemonic; or, alternatively, they can be read as mechanisms to assuage the worries of the here and now. Dystopian dreaming can be read within the context of their historical making, a sign of the times. However, they should also be sensed, understood as particular types of affecting and affective experiences that have a profound effect on the body that feels their pathetic, alien, destructive callings.

Works Cited

Althusser, Louis. *Lenin and Philosophy, and Other Essays*. Trans. Ben Brewster. New York: Monthly Rev., 2001.

Barthes, Roland. *Image, Music, Text*. Trans. Stephen Heath. London: Fontana, 1977.

Bruno, Giuliana. "Ramble City: Postmodernism and *Blade Runner*." Kuhn 183–95.

Colebrook, Claire. "The Space of Man: On the Specificity of Affect in Deleuze and Guattari." *Deleuze and Space*. Ed. Ian Buchanan and Gregg Lambert. Edinburgh: Edinburgh UP, 2005. 189–206.

Deleuze, Gilles, and Félix Guattari. *A Thousand Plateaus: Capitalism and Schizophrenia*. Trans. B. Massumi, London: Athlone, 1988.

Franklin, H. Bruce. "Visions of the Future in Science Fiction Films from 1970 to 1982." Kuhn 19–31.

Jancovich, Mark. *Rational Fears: American Horror in the 1950s*. Manchester: Manchester UP, 1996.

Kuhn, Annette, ed. *Alien Zone: Cultural Theory and Contemporary Science Fiction Cinema*. London: Verso, 1990.

Napier, Susan J. "Ghosts and Machines: The Technological Body." Redmond, *Liquid Metal* 205–15.

Redmond, Sean, ed. *Liquid Metal: The Science Fiction Film Reader*. London: Wallflower, 2004.

_____. "The Science Fiction of Whiteness." *Scope* 6 (2006): n. pag. Web. 18 Apr. 2012.

_____. "Sounding Alien, Touching the Future: Beyond the Sonorous Limit in Science Fiction Film." *New Review of Film and Television Studies* 9.1 (2011): 42–56.

Ryan, Michael, and Douglas Kellner. "Technophobia/Dystopia." Redmond, *Liquid Metal* 48–56.

Sardar, Ziauddin. Introduction. *Aliens R Us: The Other in Science Fiction Cinema*. Ed. Ziauddin Sardar and Sean Cubitt. London: Pluto, 2002. 1–17.

Sobchack, Vivian. "Cities on the Edge of Time: The Urban Science-Fiction Film." *Alien Zone II: The Spaces of Science Fiction Cinema*. Ed. Annette Kuhn. London: Verso, 1999. 123–46.

Sontag, Susan. "The Imagination of Disaster." Redmond, *Liquid Metal* 40–47.

Telotte, J. P. "The Doubles of Fantasy and the Space of Desire." Kuhn 152–59.

Thompson, Kirsten Moana. *Apocalyptic Dread: American Film at the Turn of the Millennium*. Albany: State U of New York P, 2007.

Wilcox, Rhonda V. "Dating Data: Miscegenation in *Star Trek: The Next Generation*." *Extrapolation* 34.3 (1993): 265–77.

Williams, Linda Ruth. "Dream Girls and Mechanic Panic: Dystopia and Its Others in *Brazil* and *Nineteen Eighty-Four*." *British Science Fiction Cinema*. Ed. I. Q. Hunter. London: Routledge, 1999. 153–68.

Whittington, William. *Sound Design and Science Fiction*. Austin: U of Texas P, 2007.

RESOURCES

Additional Works on Dystopia

Drama

Gas I and *Gas II* by Georg Kaiser, 1918 and 1920.
R.U.R. by Karel Čapek, 1920.
They by Stanislaw Ignacy Witkiewicz, 1920.
The Bedbug by Vladimir Mayakovsky, 1929.
The Bathhouse by Vladimir Mayakovsky, 1930.
Roundheads and Peakheads by Bertolt Brecht, 1936.
Rhinoceros by Eugène Ionesco, 1960.
Marat/Sade by Peter Weiss, 1964.
The Memorandum by Václav Havel, 1966.
Lear by Edward Bond, 1972.
Military Secret by Dušan Jovanović, 1983.
The God of Hell by Sam Shepard, 2005.

Long Fiction

Utopia by Thomas More, 1516.
New Atlantis by Francis Bacon, 1627.
Looking Backward by Edward Bellamy, 1888.
The Iron Heel by Jack London, 1907.
Herland by Charlotte Perkins Gilman, 1915.
It Can't Happen Here by Sinclair Lewis, 1935.
Player Piano by Kurt Vonnegut Jr., 1952.
A Clockwork Orange by Anthony Burgess, 1962.
Stand on Zanzibar by John Brunner, 1968.
The Handmaid's Tale by Margaret Atwood, 1985.
Dryco series (*Ambient, Terraplane, Heathern, Elvissey, Random Acts of Senseless Violence*, and *Going, Going, Gone*) by Jack Womack, 1987–2000.
The Giver by Lois Lowry, 1993.
Jennifer Government by Max Barry, 2003.

Short Fiction

"The Machine Stops" by E. M. Forster, 1909.
"If This Goes On—" by Robert A. Heinlein, 1940.
"Solution Unsatisfactory" by Robert A. Heinlein, 1940.
"The Lottery" by Shirley Jackson, 1948.
"Sam Hall" by Poul Anderson, 1953.
"The Minority Report" by Philip K. Dick, 1956.

"Harrison Bergeron" by Kurt Vonnegut Jr., 1961.

"Billennium" by J. G. Ballard, 1962.

" 'Repent, Harlequin!' Said the Ticktockman" by Harlan Ellison, 1965.

"I Have No Mouth, and I Must Scream" by Harlan Ellison, 1967.

"The Punishment of Luxury" by Michael Carson, 1993.

"Resistance" by Tobias S. Buckell, 2008.

"The Things that Make Me Weak and Strange Get Engineered Away" by Cory Doctorow, 2008.

Brave New Worlds: Dystopian Stories, ed. John Joseph Adams, 2011.

Bibliography

Aldridge, Alexandra. "Origins of Dystopia: *When the Sleeper Wakes* and *We*." Erlich and Dunn 63–84.

Baccolini, Raffaella, and Tom Moylan, eds. *Dark Horizons: Science Fiction and the Dystopian Imagination*. London: Routledge, 2003.

Baker-Smith, Dominic, and C. C. Barfoot, eds. *Between Dream and Nature: Essays on Utopia and Dystopia*. Amsterdam: Rodopi, 1987.

Barr, Marleen, and Nicholas D. Smith, eds. *Women and Utopia: Critical Interpretations*. Lanham, MD: UP of America, 1983.

Beauchamp, Gorman. "Jack London's Utopian Dystopia and Dystopian Utopia." *America as Utopia*. Ed. Kenneth M. Roemer. New York: Franklin, 1981. 91–107.

———. "Technology in the Dystopian Novel." *Modern Fiction Studies* 32.1 (1986): 53–63.

Booker, M. Keith. *The Dystopian Impulse in Modern Literature: Fiction as Social Criticism*. Westport, CT: Greenwood, 1994.

———. *Dystopian Literature: A Theory and Research Guide*. Westport, CT: Greenwood, 1994.

Brown, E. J. Brave New World, 1984, *and* We: *An Essay on Anti-Utopia*. Ann Arbor: Ardis, 1976.

Elkins, Charles. "E. M. Forster's 'The Machine Stops': Liberal-Humanist Hostility to Technology." Erlich and Dunn 47–61.

Elliott, Robert C. *The Shape of Utopia: Studies in a Literary Genre*. Chicago: U of Chicago P, 1970.

Erlich, Richard D., and Thomas P. Dunn, eds. *Clockwork Worlds: Mechanized Environments in SF*. Westport, CT: Greenwood, 1983.

Fitting, Peter. "The Turn from Utopia in Recent Feminist Fiction." Jones and Goodwin 141–58.

Gordin, Michael D., Helen Tilley, and Gyan Prakash. *Utopia/Dystopia: Conditions of Historical Possibility*. Princeton, NJ: Princeton UP, 2010.

Hillegas, Mark. *The Future as Nightmare: H. G. Wells and the Anti-Utopians*. Oxford: Oxford UP, 1967.

Hoffman, Thomas P. "The Theme of Mechanization in *Player Piano*." Erlich and Dunn 125–35.

Huntington, John. "Utopian and Anti-Utopian Logic: H. G. Wells and His Successors." *Science Fiction Studies* 9.2 (1982): 122–46.

Jones, Libby Falk. "Gilman, Bradley, Piercy, and the Evolving Rhetoric of Feminist Utopias." Jones and Goodwin 116–29.

Jones, Libby Falk, and Sarah Webster Goodwin, eds. *Feminism, Utopia, and Narrative*. Knoxville: U of Tennessee P, 1990.

Kateb, George. *Utopia and Its Enemies*. London: Collier, 1963.

Ketterer, David. "Margaret Atwood's *The Handmaid's Tale*: A Contextual Dystopia." *Science Fiction Studies* 16.2 (1989): 209–17.

Khouri, Nadia. "The Clockwork and Eros: Models of Utopia in Edward Bellamy and William Morris." *College Language Association Journal* 24.3 (1981): 376–99.

_____. "The Dialectics of Power: Utopia in the Science Fiction of Le Guin, Jeury, and Piercy." *Science Fiction Studies* 7.1 (1980): 49–61.

Klaić, Dragan. *The Plot of the Future: Utopia and Dystopia in Modern Drama*. Ann Arbor: U of Michigan P, 1991.

Kumar, Krishan. *Utopia and Anti-utopia in Modern Times*. Oxford: Blackwell, 1987.

Malak, Amin. "Margaret Atwood's *The Handmaid's Tale* and the Dystopian Tradition." *Canadian Literature* 112 (1987): 9–16.

Matossian, Lou Ann. "A Woman-Made Language: Charlotte Perkins Gilman and *Herland*." *Women and Language* 10.2 (1987): 16–20.

Morson, Gary Saul. *The Boundaries of Genre: Dostoevsky's* Diary of a Writer *and the Traditions of Literary Utopia*. Austin: U of Texas P, 1981.

Moylan, Tom. *Demand the Impossible: Science Fiction and the Utopian Imagination*. London: Methuen, 1986.

_____. *Scraps of the Untainted Sky: Science Fiction, Utopia, Dystopia*. Boulder, CO: Westview, 2000.

Mumford, Lewis. *The Story of Utopias*. New York: Viking, 1962.

Parrinder, Patrick. "Updating Orwell? Burgess's Future Fictions." *Encounter* 56.1 (1981): 45–53.

_____. "Utopia and Meta-Utopia in H. G. Wells." *Science Fiction Studies* 12.2 (1985): 115–28.

Portelli, Alessandro. "Jack London's Missing Revolution: Notes on *The Iron Heel*." *Science Fiction Studies* 9.2 (1982): 180–94.

Rabkin, Eric S., Martin H. Greenberg, and Joseph D. Olander. *No Place Else: Explorations in Utopian and Dystopian Fiction*. Carbondale: Southern Illinois UP, 1983.

Ruppert, Peter. *Reader in a Strange Land: The Activity of Reading Literary Utopias*. Athens: U of Georgia P, 1986.

Sargent, Lyman Tower. "The Three Faces of Utopianism Revisited." *Utopian Studies* 5.1 (1994): 1–37.

Spencer, Luke. "*Animal Farm* and *Nineteen Eighty-Four*." *George Orwell*. Ed. J. A. Jowitt and Richard K. S. Taylor. Bradford: U of Leeds, 1981. 67–83.

Swirski, Peter. "Dystopia or Dischtopia? The Science-Fiction Paradigms of Thomas M. Disch." *Science Fiction Studies* 18.2 (1991): 161–79.

Tambling, Victor R. S. "Jack London and George Orwell: A Literary Kinship." *George Orwell*. Ed. Courtney T. Wemyss and Alexej Ugrinsky. Westport, CT: Greenwood, 1987. 171–75.

Walsh, Chad. *From Utopia to Nightmare*. Westport, CT: Greenwood, 1972.

Weinberger, Jerry. *Science, Faith, and Politics: Francis Bacon and the Utopian Roots of the Modern Age; A Commentary on Bacon's* Advancement of Learning. Ithaca, NY: Cornell UP, 1985.

Widdicombe, Richard Toby. "Eutopia, Dystopia, Aporia: The Obstruction of Meaning in Fin-de-Siècle Utopian Texts." *Utopian Studies* 1.1 (1990): 93–102.

Williams, Raymond. "Utopia and Science Fiction." *Science Fiction Studies* 5.3 (1978): 203–14.

CRITICAL INSIGHTS

About the Editor

M. Keith Booker is the James E. and Ellen Wadley Roper Professor of English at the University of Arkansas, where he also directs the program in comparative literature and cultural studies. He has taught at the University of Arkansas since 1990, when he received his doctorate in English from the University of Florida. Before moving to Florida to study, he spent fourteen years on the scientific research staff of the Oak Ridge National Laboratory. He is the author or editor of more than forty books on literature, popular culture, and literary and cultural theory; these include two books on dystopian fiction, *The Dystopian Impulse in Modern Literature: Fiction as Social Criticism* (1994) and *Dystopian Literature: A Theory and Research Guide* (1994). He has also worked extensively in the related field of science fiction, where his book-length publications include *Monsters, Mushroom Clouds, and the Cold War: American Science Fiction and the Roots of Postmodernism, 1946–1964* (2001), *Science Fiction Television: A History* (2004), *Alternate Americas: Science Fiction Film and American Culture* (2006), *The Science Fiction Handbook* (2009, co-authored with Anne-Marie Thomas), and the *Historical Dictionary of Science Fiction Cinema* (2010). His other publications include *Joyce, Bakhtin, and the Literary Tradition: Toward a Comparative Cultural Poetics* (1995), *The African Novel in English: An Introduction* (1998), *Strange TV: Innovative Television Series from* The Twilight Zone *to* The X-Files (2002), *Postmodern Hollywood: What's New in Film and Why It Makes Us Feel So Strange* (2007), and *May Contain Graphic Material: Comic Books, Graphic Novels, and Film* (2007).

Contributors _____

M. Keith Booker is the James E. and Ellen Wadley Roper Professor of English at the University of Arkansas, where he also directs the program in comparative literature and cultural studies. He is the author or editor of more than forty books on literature, popular culture, and literary and cultural theory, including two books on dystopian fiction, *The Dystopian Impulse in Modern Literature: Fiction as Social Criticism* (1994) and *Dystopian Literature: A Theory and Research Guide* (1994).

Derek Thiess currently teaches rhetoric and science fiction at the University of Illinois. He has published articles on several aspects of science fiction, including utopian and dystopian fiction.

Raffaella Baccolini is professor of English and gender studies at the University of Bologna. She has published articles on women's writing, dystopia, science fiction, poetry, and modernism and has coedited *Dark Horizons: Science Fiction and the Dystopian Imagination* (2003) and *Utopia Method Vision: The Use Value of Social Dreaming* (2007) with Tom Moylan. She is also one of the editors of publisher Peter Lang's Ralahine Utopian Studies series.

Thomas Horan is an assistant professor in the Department of English at The Citadel–The Military College of South Carolina, specializing in twentieth-century British literature and modern drama.

Tony Burns is an associate professor in the School of Politics and International Relations at the University of Nottingham. He is also codirector of the Centre for the Study of Social and Global Justice (CSSGJ) there. He is author of the book *Political Theory, Science Fiction, and Utopian Literature: Ursula K. Le Guin and* The Dispossessed (2008), the essay "Science and Politics in *The Dispossessed:* Le Guin and the 'Science Wars'" (2005), and the journal articles "Zamyatin's *We* and Postmodernism" (2000) and "Marxism and Science Fiction: A Celebration of the Work of Ursula K. Le Guin" (2004).

Andrew Milner is a professor at the Centre for Comparative Literature and Cultural Studies in the School of English, Communications and Performance Studies at Monash University, Melbourne, Australia. One of Australia's leading practitioners of cultural studies, he has worked extensively in utopian and dystopian fiction.

Rafeeq O. McGiveron has published about twenty articles of literary criticism on such authors as Ray Bradbury, Robert Heinlein, Aldous Huxley, Yevgeny Zamyatin, Willa Cather, Amy Lowell, Robert Silverberg, Sharon Olds, and Robert Yellen. He also dabbles occasionally in fiction, poetry, and mobile art. He has taught literature for many years at a number of schools, including Michigan State University, Western

Michigan University, and Lansing Community College and works as an academic adviser at the latter, where he has served since 1992.

Brian Ireland teaches in the history division of the University of Glamorgan in Pontypridd, Wales.

Peter G. Stillman is professor of political science at Vassar College, where his primary teaching interests lie in modern political thought from the Renaissance through the present. He has also taught in the environmental studies program. In addition to the political thought of Georg Hegel and Karl Marx, his research interests include post-Katrina New Orleans (with Adelaide H. Villmoare), ecological political thought, and utopian thought. He has published more than forty articles and book chapters on these topics and has coedited a translation of Jean-Jacques Rousseau's *Confessions* (1995), the essay collection *The New Utopian Politics of Ursula K. Le Guin's* The Dispossessed (2005), and the *Utopian Studies* special issue on Henry Neville's *Isle of Pines* (2006).

Aaron Weinacht is a visiting assistant professor of history at the University of Montana Western in Dillon, Montana.

Enrica Picarelli is an independent researcher whose work concentrates on American literature and popular culture. Her published work focuses on science fiction and 1950s culture. She is a postdoctoral fellow at Leuphana University in Hamburg, Germany.

Alexander Charles Oliver Hall is an active member of the Society for Utopian Studies and the editor of the society's newsletter, *Utopus Discovered*. His interests lie primarily in utopian and dystopian cultural production of the twentieth and twenty-first centuries, on which he has published several essays. He is studying the utopian dimensions of literary film adaptation at Kent State University in Kent, Ohio.

Sandy Rankin is a lecturer in the Department of English at the University of Arkansas in Fayetteville, where she also completed her doctoral dissertation on the fiction of China Miéville. She is the coeditor of *The Galaxy Is Rated G: Essays on Children's Science Fiction Film and Television* (2011).

Susan Louise Stewart is an associate professor in the Department of Literature and Languages at Texas A&M University–Commerce. She has published extensively on young-adult fiction, with a special interest in dystopian fiction.

Sean Redmond is an associate professor of media and communication in the School of Communication and Creative Arts at Deakin University, Melbourne Burwood campus, Melbourne, Australia. He is the author or editor of numerous books, including *Liquid Metal: The Science Fiction Film Reader* (2004) and *Studying* Blade Runner (2008).

Index

narrative structure, 38, 44, 59, 120–22, 215–16, 230–32
Never Let Me Go (film), 1
New Atlantis (Bacon), 4, 92
Nietzsche, Friedrich, 3, 27–28
Nineteen Eighty-Four (film), 261
Nineteen Eighty-Four (Orwell), 8, 54–55, 66–68, 91–105, 115–16, 119–22, 125–31, 209–10, 215, 228, 237, 241–42
nuclear war, 74, 143–44. *See also* atomic age

"Ones Who Walk Away from Omelas, The" (Le Guin), 44
Oryx and Crake (Atwood), 70–71
overpopulation, 142–56
    and birth control, 149, 152
    and racism, 147, 155

panopticon, 211, 248
Perdido Street Station (Miéville), 228
Philosophische Fragmente (Adorno and Horkheimer). See *Dialectic of Enlightenment*
Plato, 22–23
Player Piano (Vonnegut), 10
postapocalyptic fiction, 5, 12, 37, 269
postmodernism, 34
Principles of Scientific Management, The (Taylor). *See* Taylor, Frederick Winslow

racism. *See under* overpopulation
Reflections on the Revolution in France (Burke), 25
reproduction. *See also* sex and sexuality
    as optimistic resolution, 114, 217–18
    without love or intimacy, 127, 264–65
Republic, The (Plato), 22, 91

Road, The (film), 270–71
robots. *See under* artificial intelligence
Rollerball (film), 258
R.U.R. (Čapek), 112–14, 121–22
Russian Revolution (1905), 176
Russian Revolution (1917), 176–77

Sargent, Lyman Tower. *See* classification system (Sargent)
Scar, The (Miéville), 234
science, role of, 56–71, 91–105, 131
scientific relativism and totalitarianism, 103–104
scientific utopia, 56, 91–96, 100–103
scientism. *See* scientific utopia
scientists, role of
    in dystopian film, 264–65
    in society, 56–57, 92
September 11 terrorist attacks, 2, 37, 211, 221, 242, 245, 255–56
sex and sexuality. *See also* reproduction
    androgyny as gender critique, 42
    as bodily function, 164
    commodification of, 164
    as metaphor for conquest, 201
    as political rebellion, 40, 115
    repression of, 29, 127, 265
Shockwave Rider, The (Brunner), 10
Silent Spring (Carson), 144. *See also* environmental concerns
Snow Crash (Stephenson), 12
socialism, 59–62, 66
socialism as dystopian
    Nineteen Eighty-Four (Orwell), 8, 130
    We (Zamyatin), 8
Socrates, 22–23
Soviet show trials (1930s), 188
Soviet Union, 7, 176–83
Soylent Green (film), 263. See also *Make Room! Make Room!* (Harrison)